Blacks
in College

A Comparative Study
of Students' Success
in Black
and in White Institutions

Jacqueline Fleming

:◆:

Blacks
in College

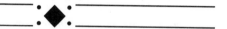

Jossey-Bass Publishers
San Francisco   •   London   •   1985

BLACKS IN COLLEGE
*A Comparative Study of Students' Success
in Black and in White Institutions*
by Jacqueline Fleming

Copyright © 1984 by: Jossey-Bass Inc., Publishers
433 California Street
San Francisco, California 94104
&
Jossey-Bass Limited
28 Banner Street
London EC1Y 8QE

Library of Congress Cataloging in Publication Data

Fleming, Jacqueline (date)
        Blacks in college.

        (The Jossey-Bass higher education series) (The
Jossey-Bass social and behavioral science series)
        Bibliography: p. 253
        Includes index.
        1. Afro-Americans—Education (Higher)—United States.
2. Universities and colleges—United States. 3. Afro-
American universities and colleges—United States.
4. Comparative education. I. Title. II. Series.
III. Series: Jossey-Bass social and behavioral science
series.
LC2781.F55   1984   378'.1982   84-47984
ISBN 0-87589-616-2

Manufactured in the United States of America

The paper in this book meets the guidelines for
permanence and durability of the Committee on
Production Guidelines for Book Longevity of the
Council on Library Resources.

JACKET DESIGN BY WILLI BAUM

FIRST EDITION
        First printing: November 1984
        Second printing: July 1985

Code 8437

A joint publication in
The Jossey-Bass Higher Education Series
and
The Jossey-Bass
Social and Behavioral Science Series

———————— :◆: ————————

Preface

Administrators and educators at black colleges and universities
have felt unfairly criticized in recent years. Historically, black
colleges have been the primary educators of black Americans.
Now, even though most black students choose to go to predominantly white institutions, those who speak for black colleges believe these schools continue to perform a service, chiefly
in motivating students. The colleges have not been successful,
however, in convincing the wider society of their merit, largely
because of the need to document the somewhat intangible service they do or do not render. Until now, major studies of black
colleges have been concerned with objective institutional characteristics, such as endowment, instructional facilities (classrooms, laboratories), library facilities, faculty salaries, research
publication by faculty, and student services. On these grounds,
most black colleges cannot win any comparison with predominantly white institutions. As a psychologist specializing in the
study of individual differences, my concern is more with student outcomes than with institutional characteristics. The central issue seems to me to be what kinds of contributions do
schools—black or white—make to black students. Is it true that
white colleges can make a better intellectual contribution to

black education because of their better resources? Is it true that the value of black colleges lies in a supportive social climate that makes for happier students? Are there other unique conferments that each kind of college environment makes, and if so, how do we go about discovering them?

At the time the study that led to this book was conceived, there was some feeling that the impact of college environments, especially black college environments, could not be studied with the usual empirical methods available to social scientists. This belief, which proved to be in error, stemmed from the feeling that the strengths of black colleges were too subjective or too subtle to be captured by statistics. A prevailing opinion was that the topic could only be researched through the use of anecdotes. I was in favor of putting the effects of college environments on black students to the most rigorous test possible and letting the statistical chips fall where they might. What was needed, it seemed to me, was a very comprehensive study that included a wide variety of measurements of both intellectual performance and psychosocial adaptation—the two areas in which each kind of college, white and black, respectively, was expected to have an advantage over the other.

In trying to discern whether black colleges did anything that white colleges did not do, I formulated a comparative study of the effects on black students of both black and white institutions. Thus, the study became one of black students rather than black colleges in isolation. Although experimental evidence, including studies of my own, has indicated for some time that at least some black students might function better in all-black environments, previous studies have been small and limited. As my work took shape, I realized that no comparative studies existed of sufficient size and scope to answer the questions my data began to imply. As a consequence, I expanded my investigation to include approximately three thousand freshman and senior students in fifteen colleges (eight predominantly white and seven predominantly black) in four states with different social mores and attitudes toward black education: Georgia, Texas, Mississippi, and Ohio. Each of the students underwent from four to eight hours of intensive testing, not only filling out

questionnaires but also taking tests of cognitive growth, working competitively under controlled experimental conditions,
participating in in-depth personal interviews, and submitting
their official transcripts for examination.

The data obtained from that study are contained in a
technical report more than eight hundred pages in length, in
which hundreds of analyses compare students in black and
white colleges on virtually every conceivable point. Although
these analyses provide the foundation for the discussion and
conclusions presented in this book, they are not reproduced
here because of their large numbers and extremely detailed con-
tents. The study also resulted in a large set of detailed tables
that could not be reproduced in this volume. Appendix B at the
end of this book, however, contains summary tables that specify
the results of the investigations at each college. In addition, interested readers may obtain a copy of the original technical report from me, at cost.

Blacks in College is written in as nontechnical a language
as possible. While the simplified language and the emphasis on
results are intended to make the data accessible to a wide range
of readers, the research method I used should be kept in mind.
Readers should note that students were not followed over time,
as in a longitudinal study. This investigation was constructed as
a cross-sectional study that compares freshmen and seniors in
fifteen institutions in order to obtain data that will support
reasonable inferences as to the progress that black students
make in black and white colleges. While the cross-sectional
method is an old and often-used technique in social science,
longitudinal verification of the findings is highly desirable. This
study lays the groundwork for such a verification. I hope that
other behavioral scientists working on isolating the conditions
for optimal intellectual development will follow up the efforts
reported here.

This book will be of interest to anyone who is concerned
about how students achieve optimal intellectual development in
educational settings. The research reported here confirms the already widely acknowledged premise that positive interpersonal
supports constitute a precondition for cognitive growth. Specifi-

cally, the presence of friends and mentors contributes to a positive atmosphere in which intellectual activity can germinate successfully. Educators and student advisers as well as college presidents and policy makers in higher education will find this book a foundation and guide for changing the way education is imparted. For example, my research indicates that participation in campus life, especially in leadership roles, challenges students' intellects and stimulates their interest in classroom affairs. Educators, including student affairs professionals, are in a position not only to encourage more of this kind of activity but also to help black students recognize and cope with social and psychological forces that stifle their confidence and growth in and out of the classroom.

Educators and advisers can make the fruits of this research available to students, both black and white, who need to know how to ensure their own success in college by taking advantage of every opportunity to learn to deal with people and to get things done. Experience in managing things and people in the college arena is one important key to success in the larger world. Male and female students need to learn different ways of maximizing their chances for success in college settings. They will develop best where the environment supports their attempts at intellectual (curricular) activities and extracurricular involvements. Men need to become more aware that allowing themselves to be excluded from active involvement in campus life may result in their feeling frustrated and depressed. Women need to consider the costs of passive dependence on males and the loss of energy that seems to go hand in hand with letting men take over.

Counselors may well want to bring this book to the attention of parents with college-bound children. In addition to learning how important both stimulation and support are to intellectual development in college, parents can apply the same principles at home to give their children an extra edge by being friends to them, by being or providing encouraging mentors, and by encouraging significant participation in family affairs.

In addition to its significance for specific audiences, *Blacks in College* has an important message for the larger society that is concerned with excellence in education. We as Americans are being pressed to find ways of developing our latent intellectual energy. My research suggests that this energy is fired by the warmth of interpersonal connections and further developed by expertise and competition. Only by understanding both aspects of intelligence can we hope to excel in the future.

Overview of Contents

Part One describes the higher education dilemma facing blacks in America. Black students have always been hard pressed to obtain a quality education in any institutional setting. The need for the study reported in this book and its outcomes are clearly an outgrowth of the historical situation. Chapter One reveals that black colleges evolved under pressures, both financial and social, to be nonintellectual, non-liberal-arts schools. Nonetheless, liberal education survived at enough black colleges to impart the tools necessary to create a black middle class. Today, however, most black students are enrolled in predominantly white schools, and the challenge is for them to survive well there. Chapter Two describes the current research on the peculiar situation of black students who have inherited two sets of schools to choose from. Many authorities feel that the inadequate resources of black institutions result in an intellectual disservice to black students. On the other hand, research on black students in white schools indicates that students face an unaccepting environment that provides inadequate support. As a consequence, identity problems frequently surface that tie up intellectual energies.

Part Two reports the results of a four-year research project that challenges many of our assumptions about how intellectual development is achieved. Even with few resources, the evidence is that black students in black schools show more academic progress than their counterparts in white colleges. In white colleges, the problems of an unaccepting environment act to thwart intellectual growth. Chapter Three outlines the comprehensive set of procedures used in the only study of its size and scope that compares freshmen and seniors in a sample of black

and white colleges on a wide range of intellectual and psychosocial instruments. Chapter Four investigates student development at three predominantly black schools in the urban South.
Contrary to all expectations, the effects of these colleges were
largely academic, intellectual, and professional in nature. Even
when positive interpersonal development was found, the advantages seemed largely cognitive in nature. The effects of four
white colleges in the urban South are reported in Chapter Five.
In spite of far better facilities at these schools, black students
showed evidence of intellectual stagnation in the senior year
and frustrated achievement drives. Chapter Six reports the results of four intensive investigations of black students at two
colleges—one predominantly black and one predominantly
white—in the Southwest. These studies combine evidence about
attitudes, performance, motivation, and physiology. The black
college was distinctive in channeling the achievement conflicts
of its students in a constructive manner. Although black students in the white school came better prepared for academics,
they showed little development of their initial abilities. A study
of two schools—one black, one white—in the Deep South, reported in Chapter Seven, showed something of a reversal of the
pattern so far. It appears that in the Deep South there are special problems at work that prevent the adequate development of
black intellectual capacities in either setting. Student identity
problems are common in both institutions. In Chapter Eight
there is shocking evidence for those who thought conditions for
blacks would be better in the North than in the South. Not only
do the black schools produce greater intellectual progress for
black students, but the ambivalent treatment of blacks in the
North may set the stage for the development of intrapsychic
conflict.

     Part Three compares the impacts of college on black and
white students. The question is, is it different for whites in
white schools than for blacks in white schools? The answer is
yes. Chapter Nine finds that despite many complaints by white
students the college environment acts to support their intellectual and professional development. White students develop in
white colleges the way blacks in black colleges do. Chapter Ten

further shows that sex and race matter. White males do best in white schools, and black males do best in black schools. Women of both races and in both settings are at risk from dependence on males and failure to assert themselves or to take leadership roles.

Part Four summarizes the findings and implications from *Blacks in College*. The policy implications are presented in Chapter Eleven. Black schools and white schools obviously need to find ways of providing what they lack: sufficient resources and constructive interpersonal contact, respectively. Black students, however, need to understand that their education is their responsibility and that they must seek friends, mentors, and leadership roles in areas that fit their long-range plans in order to maximize their development. Chapter Twelve presents a summary of the study's findings. This chapter also places the present research in the context of several other bodies of research that verify my findings.

Acknowledgments

A project of this size and duration owes much to many people, only a few of whom can be acknowledged here. The idea originated during a late-night conversation with Leslie Thomas and Michelle Patrick, who made me aware of the need for such a study at a time when I was looking for a way to do useful research. The Carnegie Corporation provided a grant sufficient to send a research staff to four different states, recruit students, and analyze an unwieldy mass of data. I am indebted to E. Alden Dunham, program officer, for his efforts on my behalf and his support over the years.

Gaining access to black colleges was a touchy issue because many officials in these institutions have learned to mistrust Harvard-trained researchers. A cooperative working arrangement with these schools was made possible largely through the liaison work of the United Negro College Fund and the firm backing of its president, Christopher F. Edley. He was willing to risk submitting the efforts of black colleges to a test, not knowing what the findings would eventually show. My sincere appreciation goes to the presidents and officials of the fifteen colleges, who allowed their work to be scrutinized. Although officials at all of the schools felt they were making whole-hearted efforts on behalf of their black students, the study results did not always support that confidence. It should be kept in mind, however, that each institution's participation in the study constitutes a major contribution to the field; the *spectrum* of knowledge gained is the key to full understanding of the issues we studied and to eventually rectifying problems on a broad scale. Since not all the college officials agreed to have their institutions identified in this work, I have used fictitious names for some colleges.

Several remarkable students assisted me in the execution of the project. William Gerald and Diane Elebe assumed enormous responsibilities for data collection and met the organizational challenge as well as any seasoned researcher could have done. Anne Hudspeth, Sheila Campbell, Milton Little, Sharon McKinney, and Michael Beck also made notable contributions to phases of the study. My secretary, Lorna Stewart, was an invaluable help not only in typing the technical report but also in keeping my life organized at the same time. I wish to thank my team of expert consultants who helped get the project off the ground and who reviewed my efforts during the early years: David C. McClelland of Harvard University, David G. Winter of Wesleyan University, Abigail J. Stewart of Boston University, Chester A. Pierce and Charles M. Willie, both of Harvard University. Finally, I thank Michelle Patrick and William Wood for their editorial assistance.

My hope is that the findings of this study will help black students to get the most out of their college educations.

New York, New York   Jacqueline Fleming
September 1984

Contents

—————:◆:—————

xvii

The Author

Jacqueline Fleming is an adjunct professor in the Department of Psychology of Barnard College, Columbia University. She is also consulting psychologist to the United Negro College Fund, Inc., in New York City. She received her B.A. degree (1969) from Barnard College in psychology and her Ph.D. degree (1974) from Harvard University in personality and development.

At Barnard College, Fleming lectures on human motivation and the psychology of racism. Her main research activities have been in human motivation, with a focus on fear of success and projective methods. Her interest in educational research began with the Carnegie Corporation-funded project titled "The Impact of Predominantly White and Predominantly Black College Environments on the Functioning of Black Students," which led to the present volume. Since then she has been engaged in research on motivation and standardized testing. Fleming also writes on the psychology of black women. Her recent articles address such topics as projective and psychometric approaches to measurement, black male and female graduate students' fear of success, and black women in black and white college environments.

Fleming served as research affiliate at the Child Develop-

ment Research Unit, University of Nairobi, where she studied
the role of women in Kenyan national development from 1971
to 1972. From 1974 to 1976 she was a fellow of the Radcliffe
Institute (now Bunting Institute, Radcliffe College), studying
the correlates of achievement-related motives in black adolescents.

Blacks
in College

A Comparative Study
of Students' Success
in Black
and in White Institutions

1

$$\text{---}:\blacklozenge:\text{---}$$

Role of Black and of White Colleges in Educating Black Students

"To be or not to be" is, in a nutshell, the question facing the future of some 120 predominantly black colleges and universities in operation today. This number includes some unaccredited, non-degree-granting institutions, two-year junior colleges, and private four-year colleges, 42 of which are member colleges of the United Negro College Fund. Despite the historical role that these colleges have played in helping black people move into the mainstream of American life, the schools are increasingly being asked to justify their continued existence. Their past successes in educating underprepared youth on a shoestring notwithstanding, they are being evaluated on the same grounds as other institutions of higher learning. Also, the fact of separate black and white institutions challenges our ideals of integration and coexistence. To state the initial question in terms of the immediate, do black colleges serve a worthwhile purpose in the context of modern life? And if they do, what kind of research project could best define this purpose?

The existence of black colleges has been questioned on two basic grounds. First, in the considered opinion of many, the poorer resources of black colleges intellectually undermine the students attending them. Second, segregated institutions are anachronisms in contemporary American society and have outlived their usefulness. The proponents of black colleges, however, point out that these colleges are places where black students can learn without the constant strain of minority status or the tension engendered by the hostile undercurrents in black-white interactions.

Confronting this dilemma, the logical researcher is inclined to marshal relevant evidence on both sides and propose solutions based on the weight of that evidence. But, as with any perplexing dilemma, it is difficult to get to the bottom of the issue or to gain an understanding sufficiently rational to satisfy all parties. Indeed, in trying to ferret out the "truth" of the matter, it quickly becomes clear that the truth depends on whom one talks to and what his or her point of view is. It also becomes clear that there are few tenets held in common between those who defend black colleges and those who think them less than useful.

Although each side of the issue has legitimate arguments, reconciliation rarely seems possible. In the view of those concerned with the future policies of educational institutions as *institutions,* it seems clear that black schools will be increasingly pressured to provide self-justification, especially since separate institutions are maintained at public expense. While some black colleges are facing more immediate financial and legal pressures, the sharp criticism leveled at them threatens their collective reason for being. As stated earlier, it is strongly implied in the criticisms of black schools that they cannot make a substantial intellectual contribution to black youth. Some concede that, despite inferior resources, many incompetent teachers, and a semiliterate student culture, some black students will continue to prefer predominantly black schools for reasons of social and psychological comfort. Yet predominantly white institutions are seen as fully capable of assuming the intellectual responsibility of educating those black students admitted; and proponents of total integration minimize the nature of adjustment problems that black students may undergo.

From the standpoint of researchers and administrators concerned with black students as *individuals,* the intellectual and social issues are weighed differently. The stress of racial tension and inadequate social lives borne by black students in white schools generates feelings of alienation that often lead to serious adjustment problems. These stresses lead to a psychological withdrawal that impairs academic functioning. The factors that provide a positive climate at predominantly black colleges are largely absent or unavailable to black students in white schools. Consequently, black students perform below their ability levels.

It may be that the confusion surrounding this issue results from our faulty attempts to separate the intellectual and interpersonal components of an educational issue, components that are basically inseparable. By looking at one side or another of the problem, we only succeed in avoiding the issue as a whole—by definition greater than the sum of its parts. Thus, we hope for a solution that will integrate the opposing points of view.

Although there is a continual debate in political, economic, and emotional terms over where black students should receive higher education, there are few hard data that might inform the issues. There is little comparative research that demonstrates how black students develop in black versus white educational environments or what the relative intellectual consequences are for matriculation in one college environment as opposed to another. Is it the case that black institutions contribute something unique to black education that is unlikely to be duplicated by white institutions now or in the near future? Or, alternatively, is there evidence that the superior resources available to white institutions produce intellectual gains that outweigh whatever benefits may be derived from the predominantly black educational experience? These are the questions that inspired the Carnegie Corporation to fund an intensive comparative psychological investigation of the issues. Our research strategy is best understood in the context of the historical events and earlier research findings in black education.

Historical Perspective

The current debate over the existence of black colleges is not new but is the product of an old and continuing controversy that dates at least to the close of the Civil War. Since then, each landmark in the history of black colleges has occasioned renewed discussions of the role of those colleges, with implications for the role of blacks in society.

The Post-Civil War Era. The first real landmark in the history of black colleges came in 1865—at the close of the Civil War (following the Emancipation Proclamation)—when large-scale efforts were first marshaled to organize educational facilities that would enable freed slaves to participate fully in society (see Browning and Williams, 1978). Of course, the very first black colleges were actually established in the North before the Civil War (Cheyney in 1830; Lincoln in 1856; Wilberforce in 1856), under the auspices of Christian missionaries who were moved by the conspicuous lack of educational opportunities for blacks at the time (Branson, 1978). Similar efforts were discouraged in the antebellum South, where it was illegal for slaves to receive education. But with the fall of the Confederacy, activities by Northern missionaries swelled to Crusade proportions as school after school was established for newly freed men, until more than 200 existed (Pifer, 1973; Jencks and Riesman, 1968). Founded with haste and limited financial backing, many of these schools had ceased to operate by 1900.

As was customary, blacks themselves played a very minor role in establishing, financing, and administering what were to be their schools (Jencks and Riesman, 1968). Despite their freed status, new black students were treated as inferiors, insofar as educators felt it incumbent upon them to shape students' behavior and morals. Furthermore, the educability expectations for freedmen were low, and white Southerners remained hostile to the idea of educational development among blacks. In the beginning, students in predominantly black schools were different from students in other American colleges: they were the uneducated products of slavery, who had not attained the usual qualifications for college attendance. Most of the colleges were begun in order to train black clergymen, but because of the small pool of qualified clerical students, most became de facto teacher's colleges. For the most part, these schools were colleges in name only, consisting of elementary and secondary school departments. A small number of them developed advanced curricula and began granting bachelor of arts degrees after 1865. Liberal arts curricula were offered in these schools to help blacks become fully participating citizens (Browning and Williams, 1978). In sum, Christian missionaries eagerly took the financial and leadership role in the private education of blacks but remained ambivalent about the intellectual heights to which they should be encouraged to rise.

The 1890 Mandate and Black Public Colleges. The withdrawal of federal troops in 1877 ushered in a wave of repressiveness that ended the benevolent period of Reconstruction. Laws mandating the disfranchisement of blacks took effect, along with a policy to limit the growth of black education to vocational training (Browning and Williams, 1978). In 1890, a federal mandate (the Morrill Act) ruled that states must either provide separate educational facilities for blacks or admit them to existing colleges. In response, all Southern and border states chose to establish schools for blacks. While separate, these public facilities never approached equity, having been hastily conceived and denied anywhere near equal resources. As a consequence, public black colleges have never provided the same number or caliber of educational services to the black community as have their white counterparts. Jencks and Riesman (1968) tell us that these institutions were largely teacher-training schools for black women. In being white-controlled, they were similar to the private black colleges. The majority of black public colleges, then, evolved out of state desires to avoid admitting blacks to existing white institutions, and the facilities provided were accordingly inferior.

The Doctrine of Separate but Equal. The *Plessy* v. *Ferguson* (1896) doctrine of separate but equal highlighted the new emphasis on industrial training for blacks as opposed to liberal arts education. This new emphasis was justified by a campaign to instill belief in black intellectual inferiority. The period from

1900 to 1954 was characterized by a continuing debate of vocational versus liberal arts education for blacks—a debate personified in the characters of Booker T. Washington and W. E. B. DuBois, respectively. Washington believed in educating blacks for the agricultural conditions surrounding them at the time; he felt that this effort provided a firm basis for cooperation between blacks and whites. DuBois believed that a liberal arts education was the vehicle for total equality and opposed the assumption of black inferiority (Browning and Williams, 1978). While both forms of education managed to coexist, disproportionate amounts of public funds were channeled into vocational institutions. Thus, a financial strategy successfully forced most colleges into the role of nonintellectual institutions.

Surveys of Black Colleges. The historical discussions of black colleges proceeded in the absence of appropriate facts about what the colleges were really doing (Browning and Williams, 1978). So scant was real information that it occurred to certain interested groups to survey the colleges for data on the content (that is, industrial or liberal arts) and quality of the education offered. Seven major surveys were conducted between 1910 and 1942. Two were conducted by W. E. B. DuBois, one by the Phelps-Stokes Foundation, and four by the federal government. These studies succeeded in bringing national recognition to black schools. Naturally, the government and foundation surveys endorsed industrial education and white control of it, while DuBois, true to character, maintained that a liberal arts curriculum best fit the needs of black Americans. It was clear that both types of education existed, and, despite the movement to bury liberal arts, such programs were alive wherever black educators exercised sufficient control to maintain them. All of these surveys judged the liberal arts schools and those under private state control superior by the usual national standards and thus brought all black schools into the public eye. During this period, the "Black Ivy League," composed of schools such as Fisk, Morehouse, and Spelman, was born. In sum, the first series of attempts to document the quality of education in black colleges found many of them, and especially the private liberal arts colleges, worthy of accreditation alongside mainstream American colleges. This remarkable emergence of black colleges as an intellectual force in the face of industrial and financial counterstrategies would, however, occasion a renewed debate over racial equality in education.

The Civil Rights Era. A new era began in 1954 with the Supreme Court decision in *Brown* v. *Board of Education,* which declared racial segregation in public education illegal. In the wake of this landmark decision emerged a new goal of racial integration. The net outcome of this decision for black colleges was a re-examination of imbalances in federal aid to these institutions, followed by an attempt to correct them. Now in the habit of commissioning surveys, the government and foundations funded a new series of studies by Jaffe (1968), LeMelle and LeMelle (1969), and Thompson (1973), which gave recommendations for strengthening the colleges. The civil rights atmosphere helped sustain the federal commitment to black colleges and built black and white confidence in the legitimacy of these schools. At the same time, black students earned the right to enter predominantly white schools, paving the way for the most serious threat to the continued existence of black colleges. Browning and Williams (1978) report that, even then, there was concern for the dangers of integration, and there were warnings that services designed for black students would disappear, permitting existing patterns of discrimination to be perpetuated under the guise of equality.

The Modern Era of Black Students in White Colleges. The mass entrance of black students into predominantly white colleges in the 1960s marked a turning point for historically black schools. Hitherto, segregation barriers had made it impossible for blacks to attend white schools in the South. Few Northern institutions were willing to enroll black students, partly because of stereotypical belief in the black inability to benefit from higher education and partly because of the social stigma attached to the black presence in white society (Gurin and Epps, 1975). Less than thirty years ago, over 90 percent of black students (approximately 100,000 in 1950) were educated in traditionally black schools. According to current estimates, however, about two thirds to three fourths of the black students in college are now in predominantly white educational settings (Boyd, 1974; Gurin and Epps, 1975). As of 1967, there were estimated to be 133,000 black students in white colleges; nearly 95,000 of these students attended colleges outside the South (Bowles and DeCosta, 1971). Gurin and Epps report that 278,000 black students were in nonblack institutions in 1968, representing a 144 percent increase from the 114,000 enrolled in 1964. In 1970, the Census Bureau reported that 378,000 black students were attending predominantly white colleges and universities. With so many black students exercising their right to attend predominantly white institutions, the debate over the role of black colleges has renewed itself once more, this time with the query, "Do black colleges serve a worthwhile purpose in a society that strives for integration in educational settings?" Ambivalence over the role of black colleges has been constant in terms of resources made available to these schools and the intellectual heights allowed them. Despite the financial and intellectual limits under which such schools have functioned, a number held their own even by national standards, and many of their students distinguished themselves at the graduate level. Thus, black students earned a foothold among mainstream American colleges, where they continue to cope with the problem of making a place for themselves. Black colleges are now left to tackle the question of whether there is anything left for them to do.

The Role of Black Colleges

With the majority of black students in this country now attending predominantly white colleges, is there a role for black colleges? It has not been forgotten that black colleges assumed responsibility for educating the black population and thus were largely responsible for the creation of a black middle class (Gurin and Epps, 1975; Jones, 1971). Indeed, by 1947, nearly 90 percent of the college degrees held by blacks were earned therein. By 1967, 80 percent of the B.A.s were still earned in black schools, and as recently as 1964, over one half of black college graduates were from black institutions. Black colleges have given us, according to one estimate, 75 percent of all blacks holding Ph.D. degrees, 75 percent of all black army officers, 80 percent of all black federal judges, and 85 percent of all black doctors (Jordan, 1975). No one would question that most of the black teachers—through whom education has passed from generation to generation—have been trained at black colleges (Meyers, 1978). It is obvious that virtually all of the leaders instrumental in solving the problems of race relations in America trace their roots to black institutions (Mays, 1978). The proud attainments of the past notwithstanding, what allurements will now capture the attention of prospective black students?

Although the majority of black students in this country are now attending white colleges, a number of authors and researchers nevertheless express the conviction that a substantial minority of black students will continue to prefer predominantly black colleges for more "personal" reasons. Since black institutions are closer to the problems of blacks, they have already established patterns for dealing with them (Goldman, 1963). In addition to finance and geography, McGrath (1965) suggests that strong psychological and social factors will cause many black students to gravitate toward black schools. Pifer (1973) observes that some black people simply seem happier in black institutions. Similarly, Gurin and Epps (1975) maintain that many black students will still prefer to attend colleges where the campus ambience supports their personal development without the level of conflict and isolation experienced on many predominantly white campuses.

In addition to the social acceptance and support that are important aspects of adolescent development, black colleges still provide an atmosphere in which the concerns of social consciousness are active. Evidence indicates that, even today, black students in black colleges are distinguished by their heightened sense of black consciousness. Gurin and Epps (1975) found the extent of political activism among black college students to be underestimated by researchers who have focused attention on the activities of white students during the civil rights era. Also, they report that the nature of black activism has been misinterpreted as an expression of alienation and powerlessness rather than an expression of a collectivist ideology that places the responsibility for inequality on the social and economic order.

Despite the drop in enrollments, black colleges still grant

a disproportionate share of the degrees conferred upon blacks. According to Pifer (1973), eighty-five black schools enroll about 42 percent of the black students, but they grant 70 percent of the degrees earned among blacks because of the attrition rates at white colleges. Black colleges have also accumulated a unique experience in providing higher education to students from inadequate secondary schools. While predominantly white colleges have historically been able to ignore the problem of remedial education, it has been necessary for black schools to specialize in it—an experience that they are now being called upon to share. Within their walls, black schools have developed tailor-made modes of interacting with students in remedial training, as well as curricula specifically designed to cope with educational deficits (see Thompson, 1978; Monro, 1978).

The Role of White Colleges

Between 60 and 75 percent of black students are currently enrolled in predominantly white institutions. Yet blacks are still underrepresented in college, particularly in private and four-year public institutions, since one half of all black students are enrolled in two-year colleges (Institute for the Study of Educational Policy, 1976). By 1970, only about 25,000 black students were enrolled at more selective white colleges (Levitan, Johnston, and Taggart, 1975). In the last ten years, the percentage of black students has increased from less than 1 percent to 5 percent on many major college campuses (Gibbs, 1974), but on individual campuses, the numbers of black students are actually quite small. In a study of four New York State institutions, Willie and McCord (1972) point out that the 384 black students on the combined campuses represented less than 2 percent of the combined student bodies of 26,750. In many private schools and in most Southern schools, the proportions are even lower (Winkler, 1974; Davis and Borders-Patterson, 1973).

Until recently, major American colleges had very little contact or experience in attending to or meeting the needs of black students (Bowles and DeCosta, 1971). Many black students in these institutions are there by virtue of recruitment efforts that began on a large scale in the 1960s. During this same decade, the formerly segregated institutions of the South were opened to black students. The students were said to be motivated, and scholarships were available for the well qualified. More important, students were taking advantage of opportunities denied blacks until this time, and the numbers of black students suggested that isolation experienced by their counterparts just a decade before would be alleviated. Indeed, Davis and Borders-Patterson (1973) report that incoming black students (in North Carolina colleges) seemed to be "reasonably confident and unapprehensive, to be excited about their eventual opportunity to get a job, and to be open-minded to the prospect of a pleasant new experience" (p. 8). Boyd's (1974) survey of black students on white campuses does indeed bespeak an overall pattern of successful integration. In his study, the majority reaction to the experience was not negative, and black separatist sentiment constituted only a minority view.

However, other authors point to notable academic failure, demonstrations, and revolts as indications of considerable dissatisfaction (Sowell, 1972). Furthermore, the ability of institutions to retain blacks, especially in the advanced years of higher education, and to graduate them on time is in need of improvement (Davis and Borders-Patterson, 1973). As an NAACP *Tract for the Times* (Gallagher, 1971) puts it: "Prior to 1960, most black students on white campuses had been content to be seen, not heard (except within their own peer group). They were rarely involved deeply in campus social life, were generally excluded from membership in social fraternities and sororities and from many of the honor societies, often discriminated against in off-campus housing" (p. 13). But during the 1960s, black college students, being products of their times and increasing numbers, were inspired participants in civil rights activities, only to be disillusioned by the slow progress and the subsequent martyrdom of black leaders. On white campuses, general political turning away from the white establishment was accompanied by a proliferation of black student organizations that expressed a need for black political and cultural identity.

These organizations were instrumental in mobilizing the recruit-ment efforts that dramatically increased both the numbers and diversity of black students on all-white campuses in that decade.

The response to the unprecedented rise in black student ranks was, unfortunately, guided by a set of explicit and im-plicit assumptions about black students that now seem unwork-able. Gibbs (1975) found that administrators and faculty mem-bers expected black students to be assimilated into the univer-sity community without substantial alteration of academic structure or programs. They also expected black students to compete academically with white students, despite the fact that many were admitted with known deficiencies in their high school preparation. In addition, they expected blacks to blend into the sociocultural life of the campus and to be grateful for having been given the opportunity to obtain an integrated edu-cation.

An extensive study by Peterson and others (1979) con-firms the assumptions outlined by Gibbs and further points out that, while administrators expected some change to follow from the new black admissions, they expected the changes to take place smoothly and without conflicts. The inappropriateness of these assumptions became apparent only after racial tensions, interpersonal problems, and lack of remedial help or support services led to widespread protest. In the aftermath of campus unrest, it has become clear, to researchers at least, that black students came to white colleges expecting a degree of flexibility in responding to their needs that would match the flexibility with which many were admitted in the first place.

Despite the increasing acceptance of the legitimacy of black students' expectations, a survey study by McDaniel and McKee (1971) demonstrates that most predominantly white in-stitutions have been unable or unwilling to respond. From a sample of 1,168 predominantly white institutions, these authors report an unencouraging list of findings. For example, while over 82 percent of the reporting institutions had either adopted open admission policies or made special adjustments for blacks in admission requirements, only 50 percent had also adopted academic support programs, and most had made no effort to update their curricula. Only 44 percent were engaged in active efforts to recruit minority faculty as a way of meeting the needs of black students. Furthermore, as few as 8 percent of the colleges were found to be making efforts to provide residential patterns that promoted good race relations, and only one fourth were providing financial programs for blacks, despite the overwhelming economic barriers facing them. While the general mood was one of indifference toward minority problems, public (especially local) institutions and the Western states were the most responsive.

Thus, the enrollment of black students in white colleges constituted the beginnings of fundamental adjustment problems that have yet to be worked through to the mutual satisfaction of both black students and predominantly white educational institutions. The large percentage of black students enrolled in white colleges obscures the fact that blacks are underrepresented in four-year schools and particularly in elite institutions, the colleges most capable of providing black students with what they lacked on black campuses. Numbers obscure the adjustment problems generated by the black presence in white schools, in terms of the well-being of both students and institutions.

Despite the problems, black students are on white campuses to stay. The fact of better facilities and greater prestige will surely not be lost on students who are just as eager to compete for graduate and professional school slots as their white counterparts. There can be no question that predominantly white colleges represent the new challenge for today's black students. Historically, the task of black students has been to achieve distinguished intellectual attainment in the face of inadequate, segregated colleges and low standards. The current task for these students is not only to enter white colleges but to perform and adjust well. The hope is that when blacks master the integrated educational experience, they will gain the ability to cope in an increasingly cosmopolitan world.

2

Issues
in the Education
of Black Students

This chapter reviews three prominent issues in black education: the intellectual crisis facing black colleges, the crisis in social adjustment facing black students in white colleges, and the developmental crisis facing each late adolescent during the college years. The poor facilities at black colleges are the most attention-getting issues. However, studies by social scientists suggest that social adjustment may be just as critical an issue for the intellectual development of black students on white campuses. Developmental theories remind us that individual students need both intellectual and social inputs during the college years in order to gain a sense of direction and to put college learning to good use. A discussion of all of the issues relevant to college education foreshadows the findings of this study by telling us that educational facilities are not the only source of intellectual growth during the college years. It appears that meeting a student's basic needs during a critical stage of the life cycle is far more important than providing the best facilities.

The Intellectual Crisis in Black Colleges

In view of the historical efforts to block their becoming centers of intellectual activity, it comes as no surprise that most black schools do not meet our expectations for intellectual quality. The best black liberal arts colleges are as good as they are only because they defied the industrial educational directive, and did so at the high price of being denied a reliable source of income. Because of a historical reluctance to accept the potential intellectual parity of black institutions, today's black institutions are not the intellectual equals of white institutions. Our sympathies for the plight of black colleges cannot alter the fact that many critics challenge the existence of black colleges in terms of their poorer objective quality.

It is widely acknowledged that most black schools suffer from serious shortages of funds and employ underpaid faculties that devote disproportionate amounts of their time to teaching relative to the faculties of predominantly white schools. Black private schools have never been able to rely on high tuitions as have independent colleges, because of black parents' inability to pay. The struggle to keep tuition competitive has drained funds available for instruction and faculty (Bowles and DeCosta, 1971; Jones and Weathersby, 1978). McGrath (1965) states that each of the 123 black schools he studied could be matched in terms of quality with another American college (for example, Piney Woods Country Life School in Mississippi with Slippery Rock State College in Pennsylvania), but he also points out that more of the black institutions would rank in the lower 50 percent of American colleges. With the exception of a few of the wealthier schools that make up the "Black Ivy League" (Fisk, Morehouse, Spelman, Dillard, Howard, Hampton, Tuskegee), Jencks and Riesman (1968, p. 473) describe both private and public black colleges as "fourth-rank institutions at the tail end of the academic procession." According to Sowell (1972), "none of them (that is, black colleges) rank with a decent state university, and it is a farce to talk of them in the same breath with any of the schools we normally think of as among the leading academic institutions." Sowell further quotes the following statistics from the American Council on Education, *A Rating of Graduate Programs* (1970, p. 256):

(1) There is not one black college in which the students' college board scores average within 100

points of the average at Lehigh, Harpur, Hobart, Manhattanville, or Drew—deliberately picking schools that are not in the Harvard-Yale-MIT category, where scores would average at least *200* points above those at any black college; (2) there is not a black college or university in the country whose library contains *one-third* as many volumes as the library at Wisconsin, NYU, or Texas, or *one-tenth* as many as at Harvard; (3) there is not a black economics department whose *entire staff* publishes as many scholarly articles in a year as outstanding *individuals* publish each year in a number of good departments; (4) there is not *one* black department anywhere in the country which is ranked among the top twenty in anthropology, biology, chemistry, economics, engineering, English, history, mathematics, physics, political science, psychology, sociology, or zoology.

Even the presumably supportive learning atmosphere at many black colleges has been called into question. Both Jones (1971) and Sowell (1972) have suggested that many black schools have vested interests in mediocrity, that it becomes difficult for good faculty to remain or for bright students to flourish in an intellectual atmosphere characterized by rote learning and textbook memorization. Incompetent faculty are alleged to have become the dominant force at some of these schools, perpetuating a system of overconformity to white American ideals at the expense of black literature, culture, and heritage. Jencks and Riesman (1968) claim that the favoritism and sexual blackmail surrounding grades at black colleges are of a different and presumably worse variety than those at white colleges. Some of the schools are said to be presided over by tyrannical presidents who treat them as their personal feudal property (Sowell, 1972; Jencks and Riesman, 1968).

From one point of view, it is considered a matter of simple inefficiency to support the continued existence of two sets of colleges, one black and one white, existing side by side and duplicating services (McGrath, 1965). McGrath makes the further point that "many enroll an economically wasteful and educationally debilitating small number of students" (p. 157). His recommendation is for black and white schools to cooperate in the effort to strengthen different aspects of their curriculum to avoid redundancy. Some authors have suggested that it might be better for black students to learn to function in a predominantly white environment (Meyers, 1978). It is, after all, an integrated society in which we live, and black colleges continue to serve the anachronistic purpose of sheltering black students from the realities of the modern world.

The historical educational feats of black schools are now weighed against assaults on their quality and the presumed capability of white institutions to provide a higher quality of education. The assets of a primarily teaching faculty versed in remedial education are being judged according to standards set by research faculties that laud mainstream credentials and scholarly publications. An atmosphere of social acceptance is compromised by alleged intellectual authoritarianism.

For many students, parents, and educators, the intellectual slur on black colleges is sufficient to turn their attention quickly toward mainstream colleges that receive the most prestige and national blessing. Wanting, as we do, the best that we can get in the way of education—the best as defined by endowment, facilities, library books, publishing faculty, and the like—it would not occur to most of us to question whether the essence of a college education lies in objective facilities and resources. It is only natural to assume that an education from Harvard is better than one from Morehouse. Yet, out of nothing more than academic curiosity, a thorough research investigation must ask whether black colleges contribute something unique to black education that outweighs the resources of mainstream colleges.

The Social Adjustment Crisis in White Colleges

Indications are that life for minority students in white schools, despite their better resources, is no bed of roses. Although black students entered the 1960s with great expectations, the open hostilities of some years later were a clue that something was amiss and a signal for social scientists to investigate. Their efforts leave us with good documentation that a crisis in social adjustment awaits black students who enter white colleges. The results of Boyd's (1974) nationwide study of 785 black students bespeak an overall pattern of success and suggest that attempts to move beyond token desegregation appear to be succeeding. Nonetheless, the results are far from overwhelming. Reactions became more negative over time, with criticisms of low black enrollment, social isolation, the small number of blacks on the faculty and staff, and racial discrimination from faculty members and others.

Willie and McCord's (1972) study of 384 black students in four predominantly white colleges highlights a major theme in this body of literature. Because black students came to college expecting less prejudice and more social integration than they found, their consequent anger and despair contribute to a desire for separation and withdrawal from whites. The lack of trust in whites led many to turn to other black students for social life and mutual validation. Where the absolute numbers of blacks are small, students suffer from social isolation, from a limited range of accessible personalities, from inadequate dating opportunities, and from the confining and oppressive nature of relationships that develop in such intense social situations. To make matters worse, the academic lives of black students are affected by the racial mistrust and the feeling that they (as well as the black experience) are ignored. However, the presence of a black adviser may act as a buffer against feelings of despair. It goes without saying that the serious financial worries of black students interfere with their ability to function well.

Gibbs (1974) has provided the best available data on coping patterns of black students seeking counseling at Stanford University. She describes four modes of adaptation—withdrawal, separation, assimilation, and affirmation—all of which appear to be responses that black students employ in coping with the identity conflicts aroused in a white educational setting. The mode of *affirmation* constitutes the most positive coping pattern but is, unfortunately, utilized by a small minority of black students. Students in this category exhibited self-

acceptance, positive ethnic identity, hyperactivity, high achievement motivation, and autonomous self-actualizing behavior.
Their conflicts were expressed in terms of their inability to live
up to their own ideal expectations, because of conflicting sets
of pressures from blacks and whites and a desire to merge those
elements of black and white cultural patterns that were compatible with their goals and personalities. Gibbs argues that, while
it is impossible to predict how an individual black student will
fare on an integrated campus, it does appear that previous exposure to integration, academic competence, self-esteem, a
wide range of supportive student services, and an encouragement of factors that lead to a mutual give and take with white
classmates would help minimize the risk of failure.

Withdrawal was the predominant mode found by Gibbs
for 51 percent of the sample, characterized by "apathy, depression, feelings of hopelessness, alienation, and depersonalization,
culminating in the student's wish to avoid contact with the
conflict-producing situation" (p. 732). It was associated with
academic failure, feelings of inadequacy, and background factors (low socioeconomic status and segregated high schools)
that may reduce the tolerance for academic and/or social stress
and create a vulnerability to dropping out altogether.

The mode of *separation* was distinguished by "anger, hostility, conflicts in interpersonal relationships alternatively expressed as rejection of whites, contempt for middle-class white
values and behavior patterns, and active protests against white
institutions and customs" (p. 734). This was the second most
likely pattern among non–middle-class students who did not exhibit the withdrawal syndrome and was also associated with
feelings of inadequacy. The mode of separation as defined
by Gibbs is a typical modus vivendi and is undoubtedly the
most noticeable coping mechanism of black students, partly because of the political activism often associated with it. Several
studies have been devoted to the topic. Martin Kilson (1973a,
1973b) denounced the "separatist movement" as constituting
a crisis for black students at Harvard because it creates tension
within black student ranks and prevents a dispersal of black students into the nooks and crannies of the university—where in-

formal learning takes place. Blacks and whites become divided into mutually exclusive communities. As a result, antiwhite militancy and powerful peer group pressures for conformity to black solidarity behavior plague black student communities. Because separatism effectively limits the participation of blacks in extracurricular activities of the university that might contribute to broader development, Kilson links separatism to the "academic disarray" of blacks at Harvard and other Ivy League schools. As evidence, he cites figures showing that bright students (those with high SAT scores) are performing below capacity, that larger proportions of black versus white students were listed as unsatisfactory, and that fewer of the black graduating seniors take honors.

The isolating effects of black separatism are confirmed in Sylvester Monroe's (1973) personal account of his undergraduate years at Harvard. He writes of his almost totally black existence, during which he and compatriots made every effort to avoid any unnecessary contact with whites, immersing themselves in black courses and black ideology. In retrospect, Monroe regrets that he and other blacks essentially hid behind a shield of black solidarity to buffer themselves against contact and participation in the university. However, it seems clear from his account that the withdrawal into the black experience was the result not merely of a desire to avoid whites but of a semiconscious need to protect themselves from insults, ignorance, and prejudice. Only after a three-year period of psychological insulation does Monroe seem able to acknowledge the intellectual price that blacks may pay for the psychological comfort of exclusive togetherness.

Davis and Borders-Patterson (1973), in their study of black students in predominantly white colleges of North Carolina, also conclude that the perception of racial prejudice appears to result not only in a growing dislike and mistrust of whites but also in feelings of alienation that arouse a need to take refuge among the separatist black elements. Black-white tensions and the social isolation, especially the limited range of heterosexual social opportunities, create a far greater concern for their interpersonal problems than for their academic performance. This occurs in spite of allegedly lower grades among black students and a higher attrition rate for them. These authors stress their major finding that "the experience in the white senior college or university in most cases seems to lead the student toward an increasing consciousness of his blackness, toward an identity not with all people, but with black people" (p. 8). The negative experiences of black students seem to be intensified in four-year residential colleges. These authors further point out that the smallness of their numbers on these campuses, together with their experiences, serves to sharpen previous perceptions of themselves as identifiable minorities and also helps them to identify unique aspects of their own cultural heritage that may not crystallize as clearly in an all-black institution.

In a review of the literature on black students in white colleges, Ramseur (1975) also observes that attendance at predominantly white schools leads to changes in black students' racial attitudes and orientation toward whites on two levels. The personal saliency of "blackness" and issues associated with it seems to increase, while broader ideological changes occur involving their cultural, interpersonal, and political orientation toward other blacks and Afro-American culture. Ramseur's own research, using a newly developed black ideology scale, showed that most of the change in black ideology occurred during the freshman year, where there is a decreasing concern for integration (that is a movement away from whites) and an increase in concern for black group unity. By way of example, Monroe (1975), a student at Harvard at the same time Ramseur's research was being conducted, states that "everything I have done since then (that is, Harvard) has been guided by a conscious black perspective" (p. 274).

Much of the literature on black students in white schools is concerned with the problems of interpersonal relationships, identity, and black consciousness. According to Gibbs (1973) and Davis and Swartz (1972), establishing a meaningful personal identity is a major problem for black students in white colleges, and one that affects a large majority of them (perhaps as much as three quarters). The various symptoms of role confusion, anxiety, and depression suggest to these authors the arousal of a classic Eriksonian identity crisis. To the extent that difficulties in establishing satisfactory social and/or intellectual adjustments are experienced by black students on white campuses, they exacerbate the predictable life crisis of this age. The pitfall is that those who fail to resolve the conflicts aroused may have to relive them at a later, less flexible stage in life.

The Developmental Crisis

Typically, then, discussions of the college options available to black students can focus on the poor resources of black institutions *or* on the adjustment problems that black students encounter on white campuses. Furthermore, one's choice of an optimal educational setting for black students may depend on whether intellectual or social adjustment is considered to be the more important aspect of a college education. This section emphasizes that both are important aspects of the college experience; both are necessary to development during the critical four years of late adolescent development. While we intuitively weigh social inputs as less important than intellectual ones, we really do not know how the two work together. Development may equal or exceed the sum of these two parts. This fact may be obscured by looking only at *either* intellectual or social adjustment.

A developmental view of college is the major contribution of a volume by Chickering and others (1981), which reveals that the college experience has the potential to facilitate and stimulate the development of a student. On the other hand, in ignoring some key aspect of individual development, a college may fail to influence student development. In fact, the institution may even inhibit growth. There is a critical interaction between the factors that the individual brings to the educational setting and the opportunities for change offered within that setting. The final outcome depends on both sets of contingencies.

For example, the process of learning, as Weathersby (1981) points out, is accompanied by anxiety and change in the self-system. Such change is capable of stimulating a developmental crisis. The individual can emerge from this crisis with new personality strengths. However, too much inner stress and disequilibrium could place some students "at risk" in the face of life changes. According to Perry (1981), a cognitive style conducive to open-minded thinking can develop gradually throughout the educational process as an adaptation to learning. Yet students may come to college with highly fixed cognitive styles that are unresponsive to the intellectual tasks at hand. White (1981) is concerned with the competitive atmosphere in educational environments, among both faculty and students. While this atmosphere can motivate optimal performance, he says, it also constitutes a block to the development of empathy. While the college experience has the potential for broadening students' social worlds by exposing them to a wide range of people, membership in exclusive peer groups (such as fraternities and sororities) can insulate them from social diversity (Douvan, 1981). Despite the fact that college offers the promise of facilitating intellectual and personal growth, a number of pitfalls exist for any student.

If college students in general face such developmental challenges, what outcomes can be expected for those who come to college with a special set of characteristics to be reconciled with existing educational environments? To the extent that racial prejudice and the psychology of minority status affect development, important issues are raised for black students. What are these issues?

Students are not just people going to college but individuals faced with the resolution of a major stage of development. In Eriksonian (Erikson, 1965, 1968) theory, adolescence is a traumatic period extended artificially in technological society. It is marked by more consciousness than other stages. During this period, a general uncertainty of adult roles may appear to be a way of life, instead of a phase. This is, however, the time during which one must arrive at a definition of one's identity. The "identity" has never been easy to define or describe. For Erikson, identity is born at the fusion point of two critical elements. The first is the idiosyncratic development of adolescence, during which sexually mature individuals seek partners for sensual play and eventual parenthood. The second is the fully developed mind that can envision a career. At the critical fusion point, outcomes for the better result in what Erikson calls a "confluence of the constructive energies of individual and society, which contribute to physical grace, sexual spontaneity, mental alertness, emotional directness, and social actualness" (1965, p. 242). From the dynamic and active tension of this fusion can come the surprise recognition of individual identity.

Identity resolution is the personal goal that coexists with the public attainment of a B.A. degree. How do the inputs of college contribute to or detract from the task of identity resolution? The choice of an occupational goal assumes primary significance in college. Developing the capacity for intimacy is the second central task in establishing a personal identity. But interpersonal relationships and career orientation are *intertwined*. Uncertainty of adult roles can direct students' attention and energy *toward* the interpersonal.

Many pitfalls await the unsuspecting adolescent. Sexuality may not merge into mature loving through intimate connection. Constructive aggression may not blossom into forceful but constructive action. As a result, the student may experience prolonged identity confusion. The inability to settle on an occupational identity disturbs many youths. Doubts about one's ethnic or sexual identity can also lead to serious identity confusion. While attempting to establish secure psychosocial identities, adolescents may engage in behaviors to protect themselves against identity loss. Immersion in adolescent subcultures, clan building, and the testing of others' loyalties constitute protective behavior. Although minority group membership could certainly serve to facilitate identity resolution (Gurin and Epps, 1975), Kysar (1966) suggests that minority students are prone to identity disorders and that the social atmosphere, whether one of acceptance or rejection, plays an important part in the developmental process during this period. The attainment of identity integration is a quest that may require passages beyond adolescence. Nevertheless, accomplishments during this period may help foster identity integration or return to haunt the individual during later life crises.

Conclusion

If there is indeed a developmental process at issue during the college years, how might it help us evaluate the experience for black students in black and in white colleges? Developmental theories say that there is such a thing as an identity that must be "found" or "resolved" in the best of all worlds, but they do not spell out how to isolate it or study it within the context of the practical college experience. They tell us that the intellectual (occupation) and interpersonal (intimacy/solidarity) issues are critical in identity formation and that they do work together. But they do not tell us precisely how these factors combine in systematic terms applicable to college life. So, while theory leaves us in the dark as far as directives for a research project are concerned, it nonetheless gives us a new focus. It confirms that the intellectual and social issues are both worth studying and that there is indeed a connection between the two. Far more important is the message that it is the individual student who warrants considered research attention, not the educational institution per se. If we are primarily concerned with the development of individual identity, we must study the college experience as it affects the individual.

3

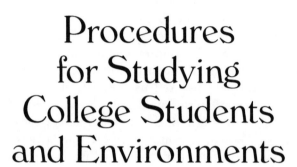

Procedures
for Studying
College Students
and Environments

Given the questions that have been raised concerning where black students should receive a higher education, and the consequent fate of black colleges, which clearly hangs in the balance, what kind of social-psychological study best informs the issues?

If the issues are seen as matters of relative institutional merits, then a research project would focus its attention on concrete aspects of the educational environment, such as building facilities, libraries, and numbers of competent faculty. This has been the case in previous evaluations of predominantly black colleges. In the case of predominantly white colleges, there would be continued attention to numbers of minority faculty, numbers of minority-relevant course offerings, and the presence of counseling programs and support programs, such as remedial academic instruction or extracurricular activities. However, a number of these approaches are already available. Even with their input, there is the lingering feeling that more must be understood before enlightened policy decisions can be made.

The essential problem is how to set up, and then execute,

a research project powerful enough to help inform the policy issues facing black colleges and black students. In order to consider the most critical policy issues, at the very least the strategy is required to (1) attend to the issue of student outcomes without ignoring institutional issues; (2) provide a comparative picture of the progress that individuals make in black and white colleges; (3) be large-scale enough to approximate a survey but intensive enough to approximate a case study; (4) address the issue of general student development but give specific readings of the importance of sex, race, and individual differences in the college experience; (5) be accomplished in such a way that allows reasonable inferences about development during the late adolescent years in college.

Design

A Comparative Approach. First and foremost, we want to know what happens to black students in black colleges compared to what happens to black students who attend white colleges. This means that we want the same information gathered on students in each kind of college setting. Obvious as this sounds, the comparative data on black students in predominantly black and white colleges are alarmingly sparse. Different questions are asked in black colleges from those considered about black students in white colleges. Noncomparable information on noncomparable crises in education is the result. As it is, the information we have is compartmentalized and peculiar to an institutional setting and thus exists in a kind of isolation, whereas comparisons, especially among many populations, place knowledge in a perspective that allows uniqueness to emerge.

However, the broad perspective gained from comparative research carries a certain cost in that comparative approaches emphasize the differences between students in black and white schools, rather than the similarities along the dimensions of interest. Given its approach, the project must seek out the ways in which the experiences of students of the same race, from the same region of the country, matriculating in four-year institutions differ; however, they are certainly more similar than different. Indeed, we know that they all face a similar developmental task of resolving an identity issue as best they can. Nonetheless, it is assumed that the differences observed will yield information about the differential nature of college experiences that should enable the observation of experience unique to black and white institutions.

To complicate the goals of a comparative study, we know that black students differ from those in white colleges in having lower scholastic aptitude scores and in coming from less privileged social backgrounds. A truly comparative study utilizes populations that are similar in important respects, so that the findings are attributable to the treatment of independent variables (in this case, race of college environment), rather than pre-existing population parameters (such as SES or aptitude differences). So in this study, any differences found could well be due to background factors, rather than school attended. Research findings would be more convincing if individuals could just as easily be found in a white or black school. Since matched samples on the basis of aptitude and social class were not practical, even in this large study, without tremendous loss in numbers of subjects, statistical solutions were employed to "correct" the findings so that when direct comparisons are reported between freshmen and seniors and across institutions, the statements made are true of the general population and hold even after relevant statistical controls are instituted.

The sampling strategy was to recruit sufficient numbers of freshman and senior students at each college at the same point in time to determine differences between those at the beginning and those at the end of the college experience. (See Table 1 at the end of this chapter for a breakdown of the subject population finally studied.) Such samples present several options for comparative analysis: (1) analysis of overall differences between students in black and white colleges that would provide an impression of general functioning; (2) analysis of differences between freshmen in black and white colleges assessing differential functioning at that point in time apart from anchoring those differences in experiences specific to the college environments; (3) differences between seniors in the two sets of schools; and (4) differences between freshmen and seniors within each set of schools that give indications of development that can be specifically related to the impact of the college experience, quite apart from how the students stand relative to counterparts in other educational settings. All these analyses were performed for every set of comparative options for all the variables available in the original technical report (Fleming, 1980). Each provides a somewhat different kind of information that completes a picture of differential college adjustment. Yet, because of space limitations, this report concentrates on freshman-senior comparisons that yield inferences as to differences, change, and growth from freshman to senior year in a given college environment. Other comparisons will be alluded to when they augment understanding of the freshman-senior differences.

Cross-Sectional Versus Longitudinal Design. The comparison of freshman-senior differences from which to infer change due to impact of college represents a cross-sectional study approach—automatically raising the longitudinal versus cross-sectional design questions. Researchers have pondered endlessly over which design to use, because each has its own set of merits and shortcomings (see Feldman and Newcomb, 1969; Liebert, Poulos, and Marmor, 1974; Babbie, 1979; Bloom, 1964; Good and Scates, 1954; Anastasi, 1958).

A longitudinal design is theoretically preferred, because the same individuals are followed over time, allowing the most valid *causal* inferences about the stability of various characteristics under study, or lack thereof. In this design, a cohort of students (for example, freshmen) is studied over time, and so it is the preferred method for inferring change. The drawbacks of longitudinal designs are due largely to the problems generated by following subjects over long periods of time and the necessity of retesting with the same instruments. Most serious is the possibility of historical events occurring between test administrations that affect the experiences or character of the sample in a way that obscures the processes under consideration. The eruption of campus riots during the 1960s is a vivid example, as well as change in the basic character of a school (for example, from liberal arts to vocational). Even as the data were being collected in this project, profound historical changes were taking place in some of the schools involved. One school, for example, was in the process of evaluating its academic mission in an attempt to become more selective. If admission policies change in this direction, the black population in particular would become smaller than and radically different from the present one, rendering future comparisons difficult, if not meaningless. Still another college eliminated its premedical program, in which substantial numbers of black students were enrolled. This change will also alter the numbers and characteristics of the minority population in the future, even more than that of the general student body. While longitudinal designs might, in theory, require fewer subjects than other designs, the greater actual experimental mortality requires careful selection of subjects for stability of residence and continued cooperation. The need to retest subjects introduces problems in that it is sometimes difficult to separate practice effects in test taking and effects due to real change. Furthermore, some instruments, most notably the Thematic Apperception Test, do not easily lend themselves to retest without introducing a new series of problems in interpretation (see Winter and Stewart, 1977). Among the other practical problems associated with longitudinal designs are the necessity of using the same instruments at both time periods even if better ones emerge, the need to maintain satisfactory relationships with subjects in order to motivate them to keep on cooperating, staff turnover that creates problems in continuity in terms of relationships with subjects, and coding procedures (Good and Scates, 1954).

In a cross-sectional design, measurements of student characteristics at different cohort levels (for example, freshmen versus seniors in college) are taken at one point in time, and, if significant differences are found, change is inferred. The advantage of a cross-sectional design is the infinitely greater practicality of being quicker and cheaper. The many problems of longitudinal designs are effectively handled by this method, since all data are collected at one point in time. Cross-sectional designs are easier to cross-validate and replicate, so that possibilities for detecting and testing the correctness of inferential errors do exist. Problematical, however, are the spurious effects due to factors other than the college experience. There may, for example, be undetected generational differences or differences due to changing admission procedures between freshmen and seniors that would lead the two groups to score differently. Greater selectivity in the senior year owing to attrition is the classic problem in assessing impact of college. Fortunately, statistical solutions (described later) lessen the problem of attrition, but the issue of what is normal maturation versus what is change due to the college environment is trickier, and problems of selection by maturation interaction can never be adequately solved (see Campbell and Stanley, 1963; Winter, McClelland, and Stewart, 1981).

As if trying to choose between designs were not hard enough, the recent consensus among developmentalists is that a combination of both designs is necessary for a full understanding of any developmental issue. Most notably, combinations of both designs allow one to separate the effect of cohort; that is, different groups may change differently regardless of exposure to the same experience (Baltes, Reese, and Lipsitt, 1980). It does seem to be the case, as Feldman and Newcomb (1969) and others observe, that changes inferred from cross-sectional differences are often about the same as those shown in longitudinal designs and that, in any given change area, the consistency or inconsistency of directional trends in longitudinal studies is generally paralleled in the cross-sectional studies. Though the direction of results is largely the same with both methods, each design produces different estimates of the magnitude of changes (for example, Pace, 1979b).

The choice of a cross-sectional study was made for this project for practical reasons. Even so, data collection took the better part of three years and drove more than one research assistant out of social science into law or business school. The project stretched over five years, and to ask the already generous Carnegie Corporation for money to repeat it all was inconceivable. If combinations of both designs are desirable, the first step is clearly the cross-sectional one. Yet, with cross-sectional data from an enormous population, the groundwork is laid for later longitudinal verifications. Even though we must be content with cross-sectional findings for this volume, the size of the project, with its large number of fifteen cross-sectional comparisons for black students alone, amounts to a long series of internal cross-validations. We are not dependent on a picture of development from one college, or a pair of comparisons, or a pair of states, for that matter. So, with the number of cross-sectional comparisons made here, there are sufficient possibilities for detecting the correctness of inferential errors.

Execution of the Study

The Exploratory Year

The task of executing the research strategy in four states spanned three academic years, from the spring of 1977 to the spring of 1979. Unfortunately, it was far from an armchair exercise. It required an equivalent of four field expeditions led by the principal investigator and two faithful research assistants (Anne Hudspeth and William Gerald), who had already relocated from Cambridge to New York City to begin the project. Armed with boxes of test protocols and a minimum of their earthly possessions, the team descended upon the unsuspecting state of Georgia to see what they could see in its black and white colleges.

Rationale. The idea of the exploratory year was to take a modest sampling of freshman and senior students from a relatively large variety of colleges that would amount to a series of "pilot" efforts. This initial exploration would presumably provide a broad idea of the many possible patterns of adjustment, indicate the major dimensions distinguishing the experience of students in these colleges so that more sophisticated confirmation could be planned for later years, and demonstrate the usefulness of the instruments in the hope of eliminating some from the thirty-two-page questionnaire. In short, the guiding principle was to come away with enough of a feel for variations in black student life to inform the work of succeeding years.

A metropolitan area in the state of Georgia lent itself to

these objectives. The city in question is a center of cosmopolitan influence in the South and attracts many black students from all over the state as well as from other areas of the country. In this respect, it might well provide data with less region-bound generality than many others. From this old area of the South with a number of historically black colleges, the traditions of black schools were expected to emerge in the data. The three black schools participating in this state include members of the "Black Ivy League." The state also possesses an encouraging number of predominantly white schools from which to choose. However, the choice was dictated by the numbers of black students enrolled. Only a few of them have been enrolling black students long enough to have populations large enough from which to attempt sampling. Four colleges were chosen, but the small numbers of students at two of them did pose sampling problems.

The matching of student background characteristics was the principal concern of the exploratory research effort. Since students in black and white colleges differ most in socioeconomic background and aptitude (Bayer and Boruch, 1969), the closest matching of these background characteristics was expected from this state because of the presence of "Black Ivy League" colleges, which pull the best and most privileged black students. This concern took precedence over attempts to match institutional characteristics, but, even so, students in black schools were significantly lower on both factors.

Since no effort was made to match institutions, all seven are unique schools, with little overlap among them. Two of the black colleges are single-sex institutions. This was true of none of the white colleges, all of them being coed. All the black colleges are private, whereas only one of the white colleges is, the remaining being public institutions. All of the black colleges are small, smaller than the smallest of the white institutions, several of which are giants by any standard. All of the colleges are liberal arts colleges, with the exception of the predominantly white school of engineering. Of course, all the white colleges have vastly superior institutional resources. Thus, in terms of institutional characteristics, this sample of seven colleges amounts to a potpourri of educational experiences, short on institutional comparability but long on variety.

Recruiting the Students. Encouraging black students to participate in psychological research is difficult. Even with all the incentives that our generous grant permitted, black students in particular respond only to the influence of positive personal contact. (This recruiting fact undoubtedly is a generalization of the findings that they also learn the most under similar interpersonal conditions.)

Liaison persons, appointed by the administrator of each participating college, made the task much easier by providing lists of students and assisting the project staff in publicizing the study through campus newspaper bulletins and announcements at major extracurricular functions. Those liaisons who took on the major interpersonal burden of contacting students (such as Herman Reese and Jane Smith-Browning) remain close to our hearts.

The first step was to send a letter to each student, not describing the explicit comparative purposes of the study but offering them the chance to explain why they had chosen their colleges and how satisfied or dissatisfied they now were with the choice. The letter was followed by a personal phone call from a staff member well coached in the art of friendly persuasion to impress upon the student the value of his or her participation. The phone calls were valuable in giving a reading of how much additional effort would be necessary. The $5 monetary incentive (generous by social science standards) was little compensation for what proved to be a lengthy (three- to four-hour) ordeal. A refreshment break midway through the testing seemed the least we could do to show appreciation for their enduring so much psychological probing.

The group testing sessions themselves were always conducted by a male and female member of the project staff. Along with the usual consent forms, students worked on a Thematic Apperception Test (TAT) consisting of six pictures of black people in everyday life and on the thirty-two-page questionnaire that constituted the basic study instrument. In retrospect, Georgia students were the most cooperative and the field experience relatively free of frustrations. Sufficient data were obtained in two (at most black schools) to four (at the white schools) group sessions. At the time, however, the burden of collecting data from about 1,000 students at seven colleges (and three high schools, which are omitted from this report) in the space of five months seemed quite a job. Furthermore, the data had to be analyzed in time to use the results to inform the second year's work. Yet, in comparison to the difficulties encountered in the second year, it was a picnic. At the time, we were also not prepared for the results indicating stronger growth in the cognitive domain of experience, which became the methodological guiding light thereafter.

The Second Year: Confirmation

Rationale. With the early return of the exploratory data from the summer analysis performed in New York, the research team was then ready for a year of intensive work to confirm (or disprove) conclusions from the first year. There seemed to be no basis on which to eliminate any of the instruments in the basic battery, since all the measures yielded significant freshman-senior differences in at least one of the seven colleges. Thus, the plan was to readminister the entire battery but to augment it with three additional series of measures to test the importance of cognitive development. First, measures of cognitive growth from a nontraditional study of liberal arts education by Winter, McClelland, and Stewart (1981) were given. Second, an ambitious experimental study of achievement-related performance on math and verbal tasks in black and white work environments was carried out. The addition of measures of motivation and pulse and blood pressure make it the pinnacle of the entire project. Third, personal interviews on the sources of stress and satisfaction in the college years were given to see whether the bulk of happy and sad experiences fell in academic or in interpersonal experiences.

This research plan required four separate testing sessions (as opposed to only one in the first year) and, thus, a very large black student pool from which to recruit enough students willing to return for all four phases of the project. Clearly, the choice of schools for this year would be dictated by which colleges had exceptionally large black enrollments. Even the enrollments in black schools such as those in Georgia would have been too small for the job. Furthermore, matching institutional characteristics was now a priority, so that two large, reasonably similar black and white schools had to be found. Since size of the student bodies was of the essence, it is no wonder that we found our way to Texas, where two large urban universities held the promise of fulfilling our ambitious goals. Texas Southern, with an undergraduate enrollment of about 7,000, is one of the largest black schools in the country. Located only a few blocks away, predominantly white University of Houston enrolled 21,665 undergraduates, including an encouraging 2,321 black students.

With so many bodies available for the recruiting and the entire 1977–78 academic year within which to conduct the study, success seemed sure. Successful we were indeed, but not without difficulties of a magnitude that threatened the life of the project. Lulled into a false sense of security by the numbers of available students, we hoped to get away with recruiting students only by sending recruitment letters. When the first series of letters did not do the job, we were certain that personal phone calls would turn the tide. No such luck. Furthermore, the promise of money (up to $20) and refreshments and the usual publicity routines left us after two months of work without sufficient students to satisfy even the first (of four) project phases.

True, a harder job would be expected on urban campuses with large commuter populations, who often work full time and who might have families of their own. The essential problem, however, was that Texans (perhaps more than most) did not respond to strangers, especially for psychological guinea-pigging, which has generally a bad name among blacks. What then followed was an all-out campaign to make the project a household word in the community as well as a prominent fact of campus life. Social gatherings following test sessions and additional monetary incentives were offered to students willing to recruit among their friends and to fraternities and sororities willing to sponsor test sessions for their membership. Special efforts were made by the University of Houston Deltas, who organized a telethon, and Kappas, who staged a week-long effort on our behalf. We gave impassioned speeches to twenty-seven sections of freshman English at TSU and a sample of advanced classes that promised enough ears for the talking and to all Afro-American studies classes at the University of Houston that would permit the intrusion. We gave announcements of test sessions at every campus organization and social function that it was humanly possible for the staff to attend and organized dances of our own, with extravagant door prizes. There were television and radio interviews and gratis public-service announcements made by KCOH, the local black radio station. This incomplete list of necessary maneuvers was capped by a campus newspaper endorsement of the study by then Congresswoman Barbara Jordan, arranged through the United Negro College Fund. By this time, the second semester was under way, and the final recruiting efforts pulled just enough students to make the experimental study and interviews worth attempting. Personal contact, then, saved the day.

Oddly enough, our active participation in the life of the campus community and hard-won feelings of success seemed to catalyze a love of Texas that can be described only as feelings of social connectedness. We still like to recall the good old days of the Texas campaign. Psychological theory, therefore, makes living sense to us that feelings of success and participation are ingredients for growth (see Chapter 11).

Determining Generality of the Study. The summer of 1978 was again spent on a quick analysis of the Texas data (largely coded by a cadre of helpers in the field), in time to meet the annual funding deadline and embark on yet another year of recruiting. Fortunately for the principal investigator, the talents of Diane Elebe, who began as a summer coder, became apparent. This Barnard College graduate in psychology possessed more than enough innate organizational genius to handle the nightmare of fieldwork. Aided by Sheila Campbell, from Texas, this new team managed the remaining fieldwork with only a little coaching. Replaced by new talent, the unnecessary principal investigator was retired to home base for the duration.

A quick reading of the Texas projects told us that the

Georgia impressions were not a fluke and that, especially relative to what a white urban university can do, a black college can be more promising. Convinced that the emerging patterns of development were real, at least on the average, for students in our samples in two states, the question was whether this counterintuitive outcome could be possible anywhere else in the world. After all, the cities in which the previous target colleges were located were unusual in being cosmopolitan centers of the South and Southwest, where commerce and cross-pollination contribute to rapid change in values. What, for example, might the differences be in a more rural area of the Deep South, where values are older in origin and change is slower? With the matching of institutions still a priority, the lure of two small liberal arts colleges with a cooperative relationship—white "Magnolia College" and black "Freedmen College"—took the study to Mississippi.* For this, the questionnaire alone supplied the data, since the days of intensive experiments and interviews were finally over.

Actually, the value of this comparison had been anticipated in early discussions with the five consultants, and the groundwork had been substantially laid by the third year. In the early stages of spotting institutions with good comparative promise, these two schools were highly attractive choices. The problem was that "Magnolia" enrolls only about 50 black students, making the subselection of freshmen and seniors less than encouraging. On the verge of scrapping the whole Mississippi idea, David Winter suggested sampling freshmen and seniors three years in a row—a procedure that, according to his calculations, would yield over 90 students over the course of data collection, provided that we were able to recruit every single available student. It required a trip to Mississippi each spring in the middle of ongoing data collection and imposing on liaison and fellow psychologist Russell Levanway a dangerous number of times. The "Freedmen" testing was left for the third year for

---

*Officials at several of the institutions included in the study requested that their colleges not be identified. Quotation marks around a college's name indicate that the name is fictitious.

practical logistical reasons. There was always the possibility that events would change our minds about the value of the comparison by the time the third year actually came, and the preceding effort would be for naught. Also, a 90-person subject data pool was small by the project standards (as was a 50-person college population), but we knew that very small numbers of black students were the rule in Southern white colleges and that this usual experience should be tapped. The effort seemed worth the solution, and we decided to go ahead. We continued the strategy even after the first year, when "Magnolia" discontinued the premedical program that enrolled 50 percent of the black student population. The first- and second-year field trips were conducted by Donald Cunnigen, a graduate student at Harvard who hailed from Mississippi and "Freedmen." Only his familiarity with Mississippi students and where to find them made it possible to recruit virtually all freshman and senior students in a short amount of time. The resulting student pool of 51 was smaller than we wanted and did not do justice to David Winter's ingenuity. But the comparison produced valuable results that departed from the general pattern observed so far. The understanding of black student strategies for success that came from this data adds a theoretical richness that is the sole purpose of the comparative search for behavioral differences.

When the idea for the project was first proposed to the Carnegie Corporation, it was a modest two-year study that even then seemed an ambitious undertaking. But as enthusiasm for the project grew, so did concerns for the practical application of the findings for policy—which meant ruling out the possibility that the benefits to black college students and the plight of their white college counterparts was a Southern phenomenon that probably did not extend to the North, where most black students are in school. If the pattern was a product of mores that were not operative outside the South, the policy implications would be limited considerably. There was no alternative but a good test of the findings in the state of Ohio. Like all previous choices, that of Ohio was made for us because of the presence of two predominantly black colleges, one private and one public, each with reasonable comparisons. Again, the questionnaire was analyzed for this group of students. As in the entire project, the testing sessions were conducted by a male and female experimenter (either imported or trained on site), while those assistants who knew the hypotheses and early return findings attempted to direct recruitment from the background to the extent possible. The Ohio fieldwork was a lesson not only in the vast differences in the Northern and Southern personalities that are reflected in the findings but also in the constrictedness of the black sense of community that is unmistakable by Southern comparison.

White Students. Aspiring to the widest generality possible in a study of this nature, we had to include the college experience of white students. If there were doubts about the need for their inclusion (and there were), the experience of Winter, McClelland, and Stewart (1981) in conducting their own studies of college impact convinced us that some aspects of the black students' experience would remain latent or lack salience until brought into view by the comparison.

Overburdened as the staff was by the problem of recruiting black students, efforts of similar magnitude were not possible for white students. Thus, black-white comparisons could not be made in each predominantly white college, and the range of methods was not as broad. The choice of schools was not always ideal but was dictated by logistical convenience for the on-location white staff members upon whom we relied to do the job. Because so little time or money was left to be invested in the recruiting of white students, the initiative and responsibility taken by such people as Nancy Stahl, Sharon McKinney, and Michael Beck were greatly appreciated.

A total sample of 388 white students is included in the study. In Georgia, 134 white students came from Georgia Tech. The choice of a school with an engineering curriculum and few female students was far from ideal, but it was the only feasible comparison located in the same city as were our experimenters. In Texas, 109 students participated in two test sessions, where the standard battery and measures of cognitive growth were given. Sixty of these also returned for a version of our experimental study. Unlike the case with black students, who worked in either black or white environments, only all-white experimental settings could be arranged for them, owing to time constraints and the small student pool. For the same reasons, no personal interviews were scheduled. In Ohio, 145 students from "Northern University" gathered to take the standard battery.

The same procedures were followed as described for black students, with white male and female experimenters presiding and similar methods of communication (by letter followed by some phone calling). The measures were initially designed without reference to race to avoid loading the racial issues and to allow them to surface spontaneously. Thus, almost all instruments could be administered unaltered to white students. The exceptions were the black TAT pictures, for which a parallel white set was developed, and the Ramseur Black Ideology Scale, simply omitted for white students.

If the level of effort required to enlist black students had also been necessary for white students, there would be none included in the project. In most cases, only a few sessions (two or three) could be organized because of the shortage of staff. But white Texans, like their black counterparts, were the most reluctant to be studied.

Measures

Just as a variety of comparative and methodological strategies were used, a broad range of measures seemed desirable. Given that the project aspired to nothing short of a general systematic understanding of black student development in the college years, anything less than the assessment of a full range of behavior was clearly inadequate. The goal was to assess as many aspects of college functioning as students and time would permit. Indeed, this volume does not begin to do justice to the wealth of data waiting to be understood and incorporated into our theories of student development. It took students four to eight hours of testing to complete the necessary instruments.

With so comprehensive an objective as assessing a broad range of behavior, almost any measure could have been considered. To limit the search in some way, care was taken to include questions or instruments that had been used in or suggested by previous research on black students or general college impact. Only in a very few instances were new approaches attempted because existing measures were not satisfactory for our express purposes (such as sex-role conflict and self-concept). It seemed wise, given the currents in developmental theory, to include measures that covered the areas of functioning that push for integration at this age: sexual (interpersonal, social, intimate) and aggressive (forceful action in occupational, academic, intellectual areas). With these two broad ranges of behavior tapped, it was possible to examine developments within each sphere as well as their interaction.

In keeping with the broad-range view of things, the measures run the gamut from the softer subjective to the harder objective. In the measurement of academic intellectual skills and experiences, softer measures are those that ask and rely on the individual's opinion or subjective assessment with no external verification. Harder measures are less subject to distortion; they require objective verification of behavior by performance standards such as grades (having good intra-institutional validity) or achievement performance on tests standardized across institutions. Interestingly, within the socioemotional domain of experience, there are no hard measures like those available in the intellectual domain. Projective measures are the most revealing but also the most problematical from a methodological point of view.

With the availability of many measures, the real problem is what to do with them. Many measures create their own problems of teasing out interdependence (that is, how much they overlap and which are the most important), and the possibility of statistical error (the number of false-positive findings) increases with the number of measures. Solutions to these problems have to be found in analysis, but the greatest problem is, in Davis's (1971) words, the "formidable intellectual task in handling large numbers" (p. 169) when the aim is to generate conclusions, not just churn out numbers. The analytical tools to be described pave the way for synthesis of the data into an interpretable package.

Analysis

A number of analytical tools are needed to cope with a combination of design, methodological, and measurement strategies. The heavy reliance on cross-sectional comparisons of freshman and senior differences requires the analysis of mean differences. While several methods are available, analysis of variance (ANOVA) is the most versatile, because it can do many things at once. It not only can determine significant freshman-senior differences but can also determine whether the interaction of sex makes a difference. Throughout most of the report, sex and class interactions are downplayed in favor of differences for students in general. In Chapter Ten, specific attention is devoted to these interactions. The ANOVA technique can also provide a simultaneous control for the two most salient background factors that are expected to interact with college impact measures. For each dependent variable, correlations with SES (Hamburger, 1971) and aptitude (math and verbal SAT) were determined. When findings were significant (at the .05 probability level), a separate analysis of covariance was performed. Thus, each dependent variable was submitted to up to three different analyses of variance: uncorrected analysis, a control for social class, and a control for aptitude. Only findings significant across all required analyses were considered for interpretation. In the exploratory year and in the experimental study, all dependent variables were submitted to all three tests, regardless of whether they were called for by correlational tests. These requirements for significance call for a robustness of effects rarely found in social science. The statistical controls have several other desirable effects. First, the major problem in cross-sectional studies is the possibility of greater selectivity among seniors because of attrition. But since social class and aptitude are the two variables most associated with attrition (for example, Astin, 1977), our analyses of covariance provide some reasonable assurance of controlling the attrition problem. Second, social class and aptitude are also the two major dimensions along which black students in black and white colleges differ and along which black and white students differ (for example,

Bayer and Boruch, 1969). Thus, our controls make it possible
to say that the differences reported are true of the general
populations being compared and hold even beyond differences
attributable to social class and aptitude.

Determining which freshman-senior or other differences
are statistically significant does not constitute interpretation.
The same results, especially if the list is long, can lend themselves to a number of interpretations. The tack taken here was
to work toward interpretation of a picture or pattern of development at each school. Since conclusions that depend on the
strength of a single result are more likely to be in error than
those depending on a consistent pattern, the search was for the
degree of support for an interpretation. Similarly, the emergence of similar patterns across more than one set of school
comparisons strengthens our faith in the pattern's validity.
Examining patterns within cognitive and socioemotional domains to determine the greatest area of impact may provide
clues to the interaction between domains of experience. Finally, the statistical tool of factor analysis, a means of sorting variables into clusters with a common underlying dimension, can
serve as a way of testing the legitimacy of interpretations. In
this case, factor analysis cannot be used to unearth stable gener-
alizable factors, because the N in a given college sample is too
small for this purpose, but it can clarify the important dimensions (factors) and their relationship to one another. As it happened, there were few factors observed across measurement
dimensions, so that self-concept variables clustered among themselves, and so on. Yet the graphic quadrant analysis provided
by the computer program allows an assessment of the degree of
association between two factors. The interdependence of
measures is not completely solved by factor analysis, but if
their results are not due to differences in coding, they suggest
that the measures used tap relatively nonredundant aspects of
functioning that make independent contributions to an understanding of the college experience. The problem of increasing
error rate (false positives, in particular) with many variables is
lessened when a pattern of development is the interpretative
goal, for a significant difference that is not truly significant,

such as perceived cognitive growth, is far less likely to throw the interpretation if it must depend on consistent evidence of cognitive development from more than one finding (for example, greater career involvement, academic performance, achievement motivation, and causal thinking, in addition to perceived cognitive growth).

Conclusions generated by this basic interpretative approach to cross-sectional survey data could then be compared with conclusions from other methods. Thus, in Georgia, within-school difference analysis was supplemented by analysis of sex differences and a correlational approach to individual differences. In Texas, the survey data were supplemented by a more thorough examination of cognitive development, by experimental verification, and by personal interview. To the extent that the conclusions from all modes of method and analysis converge, our faith in the conclusions is strengthened.

Table 1. Subject Population.

Category	State	School	Freshmen		Seniors		Total
			Males	Females	Males	Females	
Black students at predominantly black colleges	Georgia	Morehouse College	92	0	54	0	146
		Spelman College	0	102	0	83	185
		Clark College	39	102	22	46	209
	Texas	Texas Southern University	126	203	55	71	455
	Mississippi	"Freedmen College"a	15	35	11	19	80
	Ohio	Wilberforce University	74	55	55	38	222
		Central State University	61	63	57	51	232
Black students at predominantly white colleges	Georgia	"Southern University"	10	9	1	18	38
		"Traditional University"	25	57	18	25	125
		"County College"	7	41	8	22	78
		Georgia Institute of Technology	41	27	21	0	89
	Texas	University of Houston	65	130	53	76	324
	Mississippi	"Magnolia College"	11	18	13	9	51
		"Northern University"	32	48	34	39	153
	Ohio	Ohio State University	57	86	20	41	204
White students at predominantly white colleges	Georgia	Georgia Institute of Technology	74	23	29	8	134
	Texas	University of Houston	30	53	7	19	109
	Ohio	"Northern University"	40	35	41	29	145

aQuotation marks indicate fictitious names.

4

:◆:

Black Colleges in the Urban South: Settings for Growth

Do black colleges contribute anything unique to black education? To find out, this chapter examines the impact of three private black colleges in Georgia on 500 students. The schools were Morehouse College, Spelman College, and Clark College. Each of the colleges explicitly sets out to do something special, and each produces a special kind of product. As we look for the unique contributions of these colleges, we must remember that each exists in a certain environment. These students matriculate in the modern, cosmopolitan world of the Old South, an area with a plantation history of charm and grace. Through the various methods used, something of the Old South does indeed emerge in the data.

The methods vary throughout the exploratory examination in ways that are meant to provide different views of what is happening to our sample of students. The cross-sectional comparisons of freshmen and seniors in each of the colleges, with statistical controls for generational differences in social class and aptitude, provide inferences as to the developmental impact of the four-year experience. Because two of these schools (Morehouse and Spelman) are single-sex institutions, their consideration allows us a feel for the sex differences in develop-

47

ment and a sense of who gets the most out of the black college experience. Then, an internal look at functioning in coeducational Clark College is provided by correlational analyses of three achievement types: the achieving personality, the fear-of-success personality, and the fear-of-failure personality.

The conclusion drawn from these analyses is that predominantly black colleges promote good intellectual growth from freshman to senior year. This conclusion is surprising, because intellectual development is the one area in which, guided by previous writings, one would expect black colleges to fail.

Development at Morehouse College

The Morehouse sample was composed of 92 freshman and 54 senior males. We know from reputation and the college catalogue that Morehouse sets out to "make men." Indeed, we find from the data provided by these 146 students that the school succeeds in producing an entrepreneurial kind of man, concerned largely with career development. But we also find that there are costs associated with masculinity in terms of the ability to relate well to other individuals.

The image of the Morehouse man is a familiar one to those who know the products of black colleges (see Bowles and DeCosta, 1971). For most of its history, which began in 1866, Morehouse has insisted on an intellectual climate and has maintained a tradition of educating leaders. The school stresses values and self-awareness over isolated skills and knowledge. In order to maintain its commitment to excellence in developing men who will be the teachers of tomorrow, the Morehouse education is designed to serve three basic aspects of a well-rounded man: the personal, the social, and the professional. If the making of well-rounded men is the goal of a Morehouse education, there is much in the data to suggest the successful accomplishment of this purpose. This profile shows that Morehouse students grow personally (in becoming more confident and energetic), professionally (in becoming more career oriented), and socially (in becoming more assertive).

In terms of intellectual development, there was no evidence that Morehouse men improve from freshman to senior year in their academic functioning. However, if students do not show evidence of intellectual gain on objective measures of performance, they do show such evidence on more subjective measures. When asked to describe how college had influenced them, senior men were more likely than freshman counterparts to say that they had grown intellectually. Furthermore, on measures of self-concept, senior males were less likely to describe themselves as intellectually incompetent. While intellectual self-confidence is an important part of education, there is always the possibility that these men think that they have learned more than they actually have. Senior males were less likely than freshmen to feel that grades are important, and this may partly explain the lack of improvement in academic efficiency.

If getting good grades becomes less important to these men over time, more of their energies seem to be directed into extracurricular activities by the senior year. Seniors participated in more such activities and were more likely to hold offices in them—a good source of leadership training. Indeed, seniors more often said that extracurricular activities were the very best part of the college experience. The worst part of the college experience for them, however, seems to be the experience of unfairness and favoritism in the classroom. Seniors more often complained of this kind of classroom abuse, a factor that may help explain the lack of improvement in grades. But even if some instructors fail to do their jobs in the classroom, these men still have the opportunity to establish informal relationships with faculty outside the classroom setting. Senior males more often reported this kind of informal faculty-student liaison.

There are several indications that Morehouse men become career oriented in a positive way. The career plans are more specific and definite in the senior year, and seniors are more likely to have enterprising vocational interests. These latter interests are compatible with business enterprise and organizational gain and are certainly ones for which there are societal rewards. Furthermore, the energy suggested by such ambitions is confirmed by self-concept evidence that senior men describe themselves as enterprising and more energetic. The career ambitions of these men seem to be compatible with family interests, inasmuch as senior men were more likely to think that marriage would have a positive effect on their careers and less likely to foresee difficulty in combining the two. At the same time, these men seem more family oriented in the senior year.

Morehouse College also seems to have a positive effect on the assertive tendencies of its men, since seniors are less likely to describe themselves as passive. Seniors also scored lower on the shyness factor of the social assertiveness scale. Seniors were also higher on the Black Ideology Scale, indicating that the college experience has heightened their appreciation of black culture.

Despite a lack of improvement in grades, Morehouse seems to have an impact on its students that is positive and well rounded. However, there are some sore spots in the developmental profile. First, senior males were found to have stronger conventional vocational interests, compatible with conforming personalities. It is interesting that this kind of personality conformity can develop alongside enterprising ambitions, but this concurrence might suggest that some of these men become leaders while others become followers. Secondly, although seniors express stronger feelings of black ideological conviction, seniors were also more defensive about their black identities, as indicated by the defensiveness factor of the Black Ideology Scale. Third, seniors scored lower on the genital stage of maturity. The genital stage is the highest stage of development and represents personality integration and concern for others. Therefore, lower scores among seniors are a cause for concern.

In short, the nature of the freshman-senior differences suggests the development of personal, career, and social attributes compatible with the Morehouse image. The Morehouse catalogue's emphasis on making men who will lead clearly has its empirical analogue. However, there also seem to be certain costs associated with the effort.

Development at Spelman College

The Spelman sample was composed of 185 women (102 freshmen and 83 seniors). The data provided by these students indicate that Spelman produces excellent academic development among women who are very pleased with institutional life. However, just as Morehouse is good at making men, Spelman may unintentionally make "good" women who know when to be intelligent and when to lapse into feminine passivity.

Spelman College was established in 1881 and has the distinction of being a college for black women situated within a larger university environment. It developed beyond its initial role as a teachers' college to become a liberal arts school, with quality as the official goal. Its quality has been recognized a number of times during its history by such bodies as the American Association of Colleges and the American Association of Universities. Spelman subscribes to the philosophy that free and unrestricted communication among all members of society is a sure approach to achieving democracy in personal and social relations. The college strives to provide the kind of opportunities calculated to prepare students for significant participation in society.

If we rely on the reports of our sample of Spelman women, there is no reason to question the quality of the institution. Seniors are more positive than freshmen on all the issues pertaining to the institution itself. Seniors were more satisfied with their courses. They were pleased with their academic performance, and although grades and studying were not as important to seniors as to freshmen, their grade averages increased on four of the six indices. Seniors were less test anxious and felt that they worked well under pressure. Seniors had a higher estimation of their general ability than freshmen, and they less often thought of themselves as incompetent. Informal associations with faculty members also appear to increase over the four years. The Spelman environment is also conducive to participation, if not in society, then in extracurricular activities, in which seniors take more positions of leadership.

If the college's goals of quality and participation are clearly upheld, there are still some sore spots apparent in the development of career orientation and social assertiveness among Spelman women. The women of this college are certainly involved in seeking career guidance and jobs that would further their careers. Yet their career goals become more traditional over time. Ambitions toward male-dominated professions are less frequent among seniors. This suggests that a significant number of women have given up plans to cross traditional sex-role boundaries and enter the competitive world of male-dominated occupations. We wonder whether these women find that their originally high aspirations are unrealistic. Has something happened to thwart aspirations that might have been attainable and satisfying?

The answer lies in the development of social assertiveness or, rather, the lack thereof. Spelman women show much evidence of increasing social passivity. It is true that seniors are less given to emotional suppression than freshmen. They are more willing to express annoyance, even to the point of hurting the feelings of others. But this kind of expression does not carry over into other assertive behaviors. From significant trends on three factors of the social assertiveness scale, seniors show increases in shyness, submissiveness, and fears of confrontation with others. Seniors also show more acceptance of external authority (on a factor of the Black Ideology Scale) and describe themselves as less argumentative by the senior year.

Why Spelman women seem to become more passive by the senior year is a question still open to debate. Several attempts to answer this question (see Fleming, 1982b, 1983a, 1983b) have suggested that informal interactions with male peers who are enjoying a social ascendance may help condition women to passive roles. But it also seems likely that these women must be susceptible to passive role playing because of their early conditioning as women. Whatever the causes, it does seem that a passive social orientation suppresses energy that is necessary to support high-level career ambitions (such as those in male-dominated occupations), where the free use of aggressive energies is critical for success.

Further evidence from the factor analysis of these findings shows that the losses in assertiveness are directly related to the gains in academic performance. In other words, the effort not used to master social situations is channeled into academics. No wonder, then, that seniors report expending less time studying and not caring about grades! It is as though they can tap a reservoir of assertive energy that is ready and waiting to be put to good use. The ability to redirect aggressive energies in this academic way has probably been learned much earlier in life and has been a useful ability up to this point. Indeed, the grades they earn in college will undoubtedly take them to graduate school. Yet their academic accomplishments do not seem to prevent losses of high ambitions. Thus, there is reason to suspect that they may have trouble over the long haul in sustaining the dreams they now hold.

There is one more cost associated with the trends in socioemotional development. There are declines in their reported ability to enjoy social gatherings—a logical by-product of passivity as opposed to active social participation and maneuvering. Finally, there may be fewer traumatic changes going on in their lives as seniors, but there are more psychosomatic symptoms.

It is worth noting that a longitudinal study conducted by the college itself (personal communication) confirms the declines in career aspirations. But also note that studies by sociologist Elizabeth Tidball (personal communication) find that Spelman is exceptional for a school of its kind in placing large numbers of women in medical school. It all seems to mean that Spelman women have great potential and that the institution encourages excellence—as it sets out to do. However, other strategies will be necessary to help female students break the bonds of sex-role conditioning so that their education can be put to maximum use. Spelman women already have a reputation for participation in society as far as social and community service is concerned. With more help on the social-assertiveness front, their level and breadth of social participation might expand greatly.

Sex Differences in Development:
A "Black Ivy League" Marriage

We do not leave Spelman and Morehouse without presenting a view of the sex differences in development. In the Ivy League, we know the tradition of educating men in all-male schools and leaving the education of women to the "Seven Sisters" colleges. The idea behind separate education was that men and women were prepared not to be the same but to fulfill complementary roles of a social and economic unit—that of traditional marriage. Women would, of course, have their usual traditional functions to perform. An education would assist in these functions, but a guiding principle of "Seven Sisterhood" was to develop intelligent women who could understand and converse with the enterprising men being groomed to lead. The social mixing of those years was romantically calculated to match men and women who brought the parts that make up a whole marriage unit.

In the "Black Ivy League," evidence of the same phenomenon can be found in our Spelman and Morehouse data. While the vast majority of black colleges are coed, there do remain single-sex institutions that seem to serve traditional purposes. If we were to try to fit the idea of complementary attributes to the Spelman and Morehouse data, how well would it work? There is no question that the major aspects of Morehouse development contribute to the emergence of an enterprising male. The college shapes entrepreneurial men with high ambitions who gravitate to business careers. They develop intellectual self-confidence and energizing social assertiveness. They maneuver through the institution just as they will maneuver around the male world. Their major failing seems to be a loss of real concern for others.

Spelman women develop in a way that does not compete with their male counterparts, and their profile presents a perfect picture of traditional femininity. Their stellar academic development promises that they will be intelligent and understanding companions for any ambitious male. Yet they begin to retract their own ambitions in male occupations, just as their male counterparts prepare to take over that arena. They become less assertive and embrace their institution, much as they would embrace the home front, while their complements go further afield. Since passivity in women is so often perceived as sweet and considerate by others, this feature of development nicely complements the decreasing ability in this area shown by Morehouse men. A notable flaw among women is a decreased capacity to enjoy others in social situations—which may well be linked to having their identities molded (perhaps out of shape) to fit an image that does not express their identities. Such is the price of traditional roles, despite the charm, romance, and economic utility associated with them.

Black colleges, then, do not seem guilty of perpetuating a black matriarchy. Quite the opposite. These two colleges, at least, groom men and women to assume complementary roles with traditional overtones.

Development at Clark College

Two hundred and nine students (39 male and 102 female freshmen and 22 male and 46 female seniors) composed the Clark College sample. It is clear from the Clark catalogue that this school sets out to encourage friendliness as well as scholarship. While the data do indicate a preoccupation with interpersonal development, Clark College students also get their share of academic development.

Established in 1869 with a curriculum limited to vocational subjects and only basic academic courses, Clark had developed an emphasis on the training of teachers and preachers within ten years of its founding. Interest in vocational education was gradually replaced by an academic orientation, and by 1920, Clark offered the standard curriculum of the period. The catalogue indicates that the essence of Clark College is the special quality of its people. Clark subscribes to the idea that the right people can make a college alive and exciting, and Clark is composed of many different kinds: the bright and friendly students; a faculty concerned about the education of its students; a progressive administration; thousands of alumni who return regularly and financially support the college; large numbers of staff people who keep the college running smoothly; and prominent men and women who serve on the board of trustees and help guide the policies and future plans of the college.

Clark students and faculty share a tradition of friendliness. In deference to the variety of people in the college, Clark aims not to impose a cultural mold upon students but to offer a variety of campus activities intended to satisfy a range of interests. Through the college's organizational structure, students affiliated with campus organizations can make their opinions and desires known—the objective being to contribute to the continual improvement of the college.

Consistent with Clark's catalogue-affirmed emphasis on people, the empirical findings reflect a certain student preoccupation with interpersonal development. Seniors complain less about social isolation or problems arising from interpersonal tensions. Males in particular see female students as one of the better aspects of college and feel that they have gained in their ability to deal with people. The sense of these findings is that positive and negative interactions with others are part of the college experience, contributing to feelings of effectiveness in coping with people. Positive and negative interactions with faculty are also apparent, as they have been throughout the exploration of these black colleges, but are additions to the list of interpersonal involvements in the Clark community. There is an increasing feeling among seniors that the worst aspect of college is the instructors, who exhibit unfairness and favoritism in the classroom. Yet students still develop more informal contacts and positive relationships with faculty.

At Clark, the stated purpose of campus activities is to promote self-expression. The evidence is that students become more involved in these extracurricular activities, hold more positions of responsibility, and take a more positive view of them over time. There is further reason to think that progress has been made toward a goal of self-expression. Seniors more often described themselves as outspoken, as well as aggressive and independent—suggesting enhanced verbal assertiveness and a willingness to articulate their own points of view. Evidence from the Social Assertiveness Scale confirms that senior students are generally assertive in social situations.

In academic development, Clark students do not lag behind the other black colleges. Although students experience more academic problems over time, their grades are better in the senior year on two of the six indices. In self-concept, students show increased evidence of intellectual self-worth in describing themselves by the senior year as more intelligent and less often describing themselves as intellectually incompetent.

Thus, Clark College seems particularly suited to helping students develop their interpersonal skills. At the same time, there is solid evidence of intellectual development and reports by students that the college environment has broadened their cultural horizons.

Individual Differences in Functioning at Clark College

The previous analyses of students in black colleges have focused on the mean differences between freshmen and seniors. This approach to analysis provides only a sense of the average differences in the sample discussed; it obscures the individual variation that undoubtedly exists within a college population. There should be important differences in the way individual black students approach learning situations. Some individuals may benefit more than others from black (or white) environments. This section, then, attempts to look not between groups but within groups, to examine the range of possibilities in adjustment to college life of three achievement-related personalities. Such an approach conveys a more informal feeling for some of the personality types that can be found on different college campuses. In this way, we are talking more about college functioning than college development. Individual differences in three of the best-known motivations were chosen for study: need for achievement, fear of success, and fear of failure.

Students chosen for this analysis were the 61 males in the Clark sample (30 percent of whom were seniors). Clark was chosen for this investigation because it provides the best match for a similar analysis performed in one of the white colleges. Furthermore, it provides a closer look at male functioning in a school where only general student development has been considered so far. Although only male students are considered, much of the achievement-motivation literature is concerned with males.

A correlational approach was used with two criteria for

statistical significance. Each correlation must, of course, reach
the usual .05 level of statistical significance. Secondly, since an
effect-size estimate can be directly applied to the correlation
coefficient, only correlations of .30 or better are reported, that
is, those being of "moderate" effect size and observable to the
naked eye (Cohen, 1969). Motive scores were also corrected for
social class, aptitude, and verbal fluency (that is, story length)
where necessary.

The Achieving Personality. The need for achievement,
measured from the Thematic Apperception Test (TAT), was
first isolated in fantasy by references to intelligence and leadership ability and is traditionally associated (in white males) with
a desire to do things well and to compete well against available
standards of excellence (McClelland and others, 1953; McClelland, 1961). This psychological orientation predisposes an individual to the restless activity compatible with the entrepreneurial spirit. Less success has been achieved in using this measure to predict achievement-related behaviors in women (Veroff, Wilcox, and Atkinson, 1953; Horner, 1974) or in blacks
(Veroff and Peele, 1969; Baughman and Dahlstrom, 1968).

The need for achievement does not measure achievement
per se. It identifies habituated thought patterns, the behavioral
consequences of which vary with the early conditioning history
and concurrent environment of subjects (making them appropriate measures of differences in the present subjective college
environment). Thus, different people learn to express achievement thoughts in different ways. Despite previous difficulties in
using this measure successfully among blacks, the achieving personality at Clark College is almost indistinguishable from the
classic profile of white males. Males high in achievement motivation more often feel that racial tensions are the worst aspect
of college life but also feel that college has influenced their personal development. They are happier with the decision to come
to Clark and are satisfied with their own academic performance,
achieved without cramming during exams. Their satisfaction
with their academic performance is certainly justified, since
they make a better showing on four of the six measures of academic performance: average grade-point average (GPA) for the

most recent semester, grades in the major for the most recent semester, honors status, and cumulative average GPA. With better academic records, these men are more likely to major in political science and plan for graduate school and careers in law. Educational aspirations are only marginally significant, but achievement-oriented men more often plan advanced educational degrees and have higher vocational aspirations. True to the traditional picture of achievement motivation, Clark men so characterized exhibit better academic adjustment, better academic performance, and higher educational and occupational ambitions in law (rather than the expected business). However, they are sensitive to racial tensions. It is interesting that the vast majority of the findings are in the intellectual domain, while none were psychosocial or interpersonal in nature—a substantial departure from the larger developmental picture.

The Success-Fearing Personality. The TAT measure of fear of success involves an unconscious expectation of negative consequences of success and more specifically involves an inhibition of instrumental competence, or redirection of it into what are perceived to be role-appropriate behaviors (Horner, 1974; Fleming, Beldner, and Esposito, 1979). The fear-of-success phenomenon was originally known to psychoanalysts as a problem for both sexes but has re-emerged in the empirical literature as a motivation central to the female personality. In women, it often predicts the inhibition of achievement behaviors such as competitive performance in the presence of males. It also predicts avoidance of career ambitions, particularly in male-dominated professions. The empirical correlates of fear of success have been little studied in males, but fear of success seems to predict a weak positive approach to achievement.

Very few significant results were found for fear of success at Clark, suggesting that the fear-of-success conflict is largely inactive in this environment. The motive did predict stronger career ambitions in male-dominated fields and an avoidance of careers with fewer men, particularly those in neutral fields with equal numbers of both sexes. Fear-of-success men more often felt that marriage would help their careers and scored lower on the black defensiveness factor of the Black Ideology Scale.

Thus, while fear-of-success men show evidence of less defensiveness about blackness at Clark, there is a hint of sex-role defensiveness (in their avoidance of sex-role-ambiguous careers) and some sense that marriage would serve a validating purpose.

The Fear-of-Failure Personality. Fear of failure is measured from a fifteen-item test-anxiety questionnaire rather than the TAT but is nonetheless the method of measurement commonly used in motivation research (Mandler and Sarason, 1952; Atkinson and Litwin, 1960). The anxiousness expressed over test evaluation reveals a conflict over the shame of failure, which subjects traditionally handle by avoiding the competitive arena in order to avoid realistic feedback on their performance. Thus, these individuals behave antithetically to achievement-oriented individuals. They avoid tasks of intermediate difficulty, receive poor grades, spend less time on exams, and exhibit less perseverance and more task-irrelevant behavior (French and Thomas, 1958; Smith, 1969).

Clark males strongly characterized by a fear of failure exhibit profiles remarkably similar to those of achievement-oriented men. They, too, more often feel that the worst aspect of college is racial tensions and also perform better on four measures of academic performance (including three of those excelled in by achievement-oriented males): average GPAs for the last semester and for the cumulative record, cumulative grades in the major, and honors status. They were less likely to plan the B.A. as the terminal degree and desired careers in education. There were several self-concept findings, showing that the fear-of-failure men described themselves as nice but also as leaders. They scored higher on the ambition self-concept factor. In many respects, then, fear-of-failure men at Clark resemble their high-need-for-achievement peers in that they perform better academically and express similar problems with racial tensions. They are different from achieving males in describing themselves in ways that leave some sense of inconsistency (nice versus leader), opt for less competitive careers in education, and express less satisfaction with their successful profiles.

This internal look at the correlates of three achievement-related personality types has allowed us to tap a particular dimension of college experience not apparent hitherto, and we can attempt to say who among the achievement personalities benefit most from the Clark College environment. The most striking fact from this view of college life is that all the male achievement personalities gain from the environment. In the psychological literature, the achievement motive seldom produces a positive picture of success among blacks. But in this black college setting, the achievement motive correlated with a full-fledged blossoming of the achieving personality, complete with a hard-to-find capacity for joy in academic mastery. Those men characterized by the approach-avoidance conflict motives inherent in the success-fearing personality appear to enjoy a period of rest, with this conflict in a virtual state of dormancy. We might venture to say that fear-of-failure personalities benefit most from this college environment, since their most nonproductive achievement tendencies seem literally to be turned into their opposite. The fear-of-failure conflict has somehow been channeled so constructively that these men are able to function as if they had been blessed with achieving personalities. The only clue to their real identities is that they fail to express happiness with their successful attainments.

We do, indeed, obtain a different view of Clark College from that provided by the developmental picture. The higher educational and vocational ambitions of achievement-oriented males and their greater sense of personal development are aspects of functioning that run counter to overall development. In a sense, this suggests that the environment allows achievement-oriented men a style of functioning that is independent in defying the average influences. The sex-role defensiveness of success-fearing men was a new feature that affected men and women of Morehouse and Spelman but was not a general influence at Clark. The profile of fear-of-failure men made us aware for the first time that this college setting has the capacity to turn achievement conflicts into academic success. Finally, the impact on interpersonal development so prominent in the developmental profile was nowhere to be seen in connection with achievement-related motives. Perhaps this major influence of Clark has a heavier impact on the affiliative (interpersonal-relatedness) or power (interpersonal-mastery) dimensions of activity. In the realm of achievement, the general influence of the college was to enhance academic functioning.

Conclusions

In our discussion of the complexities of life in three black colleges, one point has surely not been lost—that black colleges promote development in the academic and intellectual domain of experience. This kind of growth stands as a prominent feature of black college impact precisely because it is the one area in which black colleges were expected to fail. Most researchers would expect black colleges to show evidence of gross intellectual disservice to their students. On the contrary, some improvement on the six measures of academic functioning was found in most analyses, and the extent of the improvement ranged from two to four of the indices used. Strong gains in intellectual confidence (evident from a number of measures) were apparent in all the developmental (that is, freshman-senior) comparisons, and perceived gains in cognitive growth were particularly evident among men. Positive achievement motivations were maximized among individual personality types, and the conversion of the most severe conflicts about achievement into academic success was undoubtedly the most dramatic testament to the power of the black college environment. Greater feelings of success and satisfaction with academic life were also prominent at black colleges.

In view of the complaints among students about the poor quality of instruction and instructors, how have black colleges managed to accomplish so much? Complaints about teachers were numerous, but they seemed to coexist with the development of positive relationships with particular instructors, including the very valuable informal relationships. If classroom atmosphere was often unfair, with favoritism a particular sore spot, concentration on the development of career interests (with faculty help) could be observed. While some students (especially women) were satisfied with both their academic lives and extracurricular lives, others (often males) might channel their disenchantment with the classroom practices into their extra-curricular lives and still show intellectual development. Even when interpersonal tensions with peers were prominent, their occurrence in the context of other positive interactions seemed to catalyze growth.

At these black colleges, the problems in development were likely to occur in the socioemotional domain of experience. When developments in this area were positive (as they were for men and at Clark College) and supported the intellectual development taking place, gains in energy, enterprise, and assertiveness were the result. But in the case of women, where socioemotional development did not support the academic gains, the loss of energy in one sphere seemed capable of restricting the long-term potential of cognitive gains.

5

:◆:

White Colleges in the Urban South: Obstacles to Adjustment

We have seen that development in three predominantly black colleges is largely a story of good adjustment to college and good intellectual growth. We now turn to what life is like for the 330 black students in our sample who chose nearby predominantly white schools in Georgia. Four colleges participated in the study: "Southern University," Georgia Institute of Technology, "Traditional University," and "County College" (quotation marks indicate fictitious names). These institutions are different from the black colleges in several ways. All the white schools are coed, as opposed to only one of the black colleges. All the white schools have larger student bodies than the black colleges, and three are vastly bigger institutions. All the white schools have considerably greater resources to work with, and the black students entering these schools have higher SAT scores and come from more privileged social backgrounds. Thus, our task is to find out what better equipped white colleges do with better equipped black students.

The methods employed in this chapter are the same as those used to study the three black colleges. Inferences as to the developmental impact of college were made by comparing samples of freshmen and seniors on a host of measures. The significant differences reported are those that could not have occurred by chance, according to standard statistical procedures, and those that remain significant after the influence of generational differences in social class and aptitude scores were also statistically controlled. The interpretive task is to determine the patterns of adjustment that can be observed in college functioning. The analysis of individual differences proceeds a bit differently. Correlational techniques are employed to provide an internal look at college functioning, rather than at development from freshman to senior year.

The results of these analyses show that black students show poor intellectual development in predominantly white colleges. In fact, black students in these schools are more likely to show evidence of thwarted intellectual development and even intellectual deterioration. Although many writers on the subject feel that white colleges should take over the responsibility of educating black youth, these findings show that the poor adjustment that these students make on white campuses is sufficient to thwart good development.

Development at "Southern University"

Black students do not seem able to share in the best that prestigious "Southern University" has to offer. Indeed, the big problem for these students is a growing feeling of alienation, that is, the inability to feel part of a whole. These feelings of alienation seem to be associated with the absence of intellectual gain and a drop in the level of career aspirations. As a big-league university in the South, "Southern" is concerned with developing attitudes and intellectual habits that guarantee a continuing growth toward maturity. It thus admits only students who have demonstrated by their level of academic achievement that they can profit from its intellectual environment. In an undergraduate enrollment of 2,600, there were about 50 black students, 38 of whom became study participants. Because of the small numbers, participants came from all classes. Thus, there were 12 freshmen, 7 sophomores, 9 juniors, and 10 seniors, treated in the analysis as under- or upperclassmen. The sample includes 11 males and 27 females.

With such a small representation of undergraduate blacks in a vast university, a relative sense of isolation would seem inevitable. And, indeed, seniors scored lower than freshmen on identity affirmation, a factor of the Black Ideology Scale. This finding reflects a drop in feelings of being successfully integrated into a larger whole—which is highly suggestive of alienation. From a theoretical point of view, feelings of disconnectedness indicated by this finding are most discouraging. The process of alienation that can be observed among these students appears to be a dual one, involving disengagement from academic involvement and futile (from an academic point of view) attempts to find ways of asserting themselves.

No significant gains were found for any of the six measures of academic performance. The absence of effects for academic functioning suggests academic inertia rather than growth, especially in the context of lower estimations of instructional quality among seniors. The experience appears to devastate both the educational and vocational aspirations of males, which decline significantly from freshman to senior year. There is no sign of the enhanced faculty involvement that might awaken the intellectual energies that these students must have possessed to have been admitted at all. And, even more strangely, there is no evidence of more involvement among seniors in extracurricular activities that could serve as tension release. As such, the indications of increasing assertiveness among seniors appear to serve no useful purpose and result in no apparent developmental gain. Although seniors describe themselves as less passive and more emotionally expressive than freshmen, this evidence of growing assertiveness may be only a reaction to a hostile climate. Seniors do, however, experience more severe illnesses than freshmen.

It is interesting that the brevity of information given in the college catalogue, with its absence of emphasis on student life or extracurricular activities, indicates a sense of coldness that is reflected in the black student experience. The thrust of "Southern"'s message is geared toward intellectual competition, arousing academic curiosity, and career preparation—goals clearly not realized among its black students. The isolation and alienation experienced in the "Southern University" environment may have special consequences for black students but are problems for the general student body—so much so that a task force was appointed to find ways of improving the quality of campus life for all students. With university recognition of a campus environment problem, there are hopes for a solution.

Development at Georgia Institute of Technology

In a student body of 9,000, there were about 450 black students at Georgia Tech, and 89 of them (41 male and 27 female freshmen and 21 male seniors) constitute the sample. Georgia Tech is distinguished in this study in being a college of engineering. Yet this school is also distinguished in producing the worst academic deterioration found among black students in the white colleges studied.

From the subjective assessments given, it is clear that the worst problem in the eyes of these black students is racial conflict. Furthermore, this college environment has an effect on student motivational dispositions that is relatively unusual in the study and suggests a strong institutional impact. The nature of that effect is not encouraging. Black seniors show more fear of power motivation than freshmen—that is, more anxieties about their desires for interpersonal importance, recognition, and impact. It is little wonder that would-be engineers with a penchant for manipulating things might retain some residual desire for interpersonal maneuvering. Indeed, the manipulative and power-laden undertones in the larger environment were empirically demonstrated in the parallel study of white students at Tech (see Chapter Nine). Unfortunately for black students, desires for a sense of mastery of the larger interpersonal environment are fraught with frustration. In an academic environment so characterized, there are two major consequences: intellectual deterioration and defensive extracurricular involvement.

Two of the six measures of academic performance show indications of marked academic deterioration, with losses on both indices measuring major subject performance. This alarming evidence of intellectual decline is, not surprisingly, accompanied by more academic problems among seniors and less time spent studying. It is notable that deterioration is so evident in the major subject, where the strongest ego involvement and effort would be expected. The findings, then, bespeak a decathexis of academic energy.

In this case, there does seem to be an outlet for the energy apparently withdrawn from academics. Seniors more often take leadership roles in extracurricular activities; they find the involvement of fellow students in cultural and political activities to be the best aspect of college. Seniors more often feel that college has helped them gain coping and survival skills, and many of these skills were undoubtedly learned in pursuit of extracurricular interests. The research project staff can testify to the time, energy, and enthusiasm displayed by these students as they held numerous meetings of black student groups and busied themselves organizing a successful career conference.

Unfortunately, the arousal of a defensive, oppositional style is also evident and may be part of the reason why the display of assertiveness and organizational ability is incompatible with intellectual development. Black consciousness is higher among seniors. There is less evidence of emotional suppression among seniors, and this would be a more encouraging sign if not accompanied by aroused opposition to authority (that is, an increase in the phallic stage of adaptation). Furthermore, the areas in which they have chosen to redirect frustrated energies are associated with greater stress among seniors in the three domains of life experience investigated: personal, academic, and legal. Seniors exhibit higher scores than freshmen on the conventional vocational orientation. This could suggest that the observed patterns of behavior are the result of strong expectations latent in the college environment, because this scale measures conforming elements in the personality. In short, these students seem to be developing skills that enable them to act out a defensive assertiveness, a waste of valuable black talent.

Once again, the absence of findings indicating involvement with faculty members may help explain why so much activity is not directed into the classroom experience.

Development at "Traditional University"

At "Traditional University," there is little evidence of intellectual growth from freshman to senior year—much like the situation at the other predominantly white institutions. While the aspirations of men at this particular college do become more ambitious by the senior year, the aspirations of women become less ambitious.

"Traditional University" has the distinction of being the oldest chartered state institution of higher education. It is therefore appropriate that tradition, tempered by innovation, figures prominently in its philosophy. It is the idea of tradition tempered by innovation that allows the university to see itself as up to date and in step with the times. Its academic goals are consistent with the development of strong intellectual goals and well-rounded people capable of holding responsible positions. So far, the goals of white institutions have been found to shape the nature of black student development in some way, even if the effect is not that expressly desired. Thus, we can expect up-to-date tradition to reveal itself in the profile of the 125 students (25 male and 57 female freshmen and 18 male and 25 female seniors) in the sample, who were recruited from a pool of 367 in a larger liberal arts population of 20,000.

The developmental profile for "Traditional University" suggests that blacks here are functioning in a deprived environment. Senior scores on the general academic adjustment factor are lower than those of freshmen, indicating less positive feelings about the administration, faculty, and even fellow students. Seniors have more complaints about the teaching methods and do not feel that teachers use fair grading methods or that teachers are interested in them. Getting good grades seems less important to seniors, and in the context of such apparent academic discontent, there was no evidence of improving academic performance. Students' social adjustment also seems to suffer, with seniors scoring lower on this scale. There is evidence of widespread academic and personal sources of stress among seniors. The harsh environment seems to have motivated students to learn to cope and survive under less than optimal conditions, and seniors do participate more in their extracurricular activities.

There is also evidence that black students at this college may suffer from a conflict over orientation to authority. On the one hand, there is evidence of opposition to authority, but on the other hand, submission to authority is indicated. Seniors score lower than freshmen on acceptance of white authority, a factor of the Black Ideology Scale that taps stronger desires to defend and control black territory among seniors. In addition, total scores on the Black Ideology Scale are higher among seniors, confirming that their consciousness about blackness has been heightened. Taken together, these two findings suggest opposition to white authority. But seniors also have lower scores on the anal stage of adaptation to the environment. The anal stage is an indication of an autonomous approach to the environment, so that lower scores on this dimension among seniors seem to mean acquiescence to authority and perhaps a surrendering of autonomy. This set of results could mean that black students at "Traditional University" develop ambivalent feelings about authority or that some students respond to the inhospitable climate by becoming rebellious, while others acquiesce.

There do indeed seem to be cross-pressures facing these students. The drama is further played out in the arena of career development. Seniors are more likely to have ambivalent plans for graduate school, which may explain why more seniors have higher educational aspirations but also fewer plans to attend graduate school so that they can work right after college. Women in particular seem to become less ambitious, since the level of vocational aspirations is lower for senior women. Senior women are also more traditional in their sex-role orientation. The specific effect on vocational aspirations is that the interests of men are less investigative in nature by the senior year. In short, the development for black students at "Traditional University" presents another unencouraging list of findings.

Development at "County College"

In many ways, "County College" seems to offer the most sympathetic institutional auspices for black students. However, evidence of intellectual stress makes us suspect the same difficulties for black students that are seen in the other white colleges. The "County College" campus is located outside the metropolitan area in the former capital city of the state. It was a women's college until 1967. With an enrollment of 2,500, it is the smallest of the white colleges and close to the size of the three predominantly black colleges. The similarities with black colleges do not end there. Its educational mission is also much the same. As a small rural college that cannot compete for the state's best students, it must attempt to work with the students who require special assistance if they are to raise the level of their academic achievement. The college's efforts are thus geared to meet students' needs. About 400 black students are enrolled in "County College," 78 (7 male and 41 female freshmen and 8 male and 22 female seniors) of whom provided the data to follow.

"County College" is the one predominantly white college where there is a measurable improvement in grade averages. Senior overall grade-point averages are higher than those of freshmen. Thus, there is evidence of gain on one of the six measures. The rarity of any improvement at all at white colleges makes this institution almost cause for celebration. Why is "County College" unique in this regard? We do not find evidence of improving faculty-student relationships, which would suggest encouragement of student abilities. But neither is there evidence of vociferous dissatisfaction with instructors or with the administration. There are simply no effects in areas where black student complaints are routinely found in previous white college profiles. Instead, the results show that "County College" students, for some reason, seem more able to put effort into academics. More seniors than freshmen report that they work well under pressure, and senior males were the most likely to report working hard and cramming during exams. Directing this kind of energy in the classroom is associated with higher senior grades and more evidence of enterprising career interest among seniors. Seniors place less importance on getting good grades than freshmen, so that seniors are trying harder for other reasons. Encouraging development was also in evidence on the psychosocial front.

Seniors describe themselves as more extroverted, and their outgoingness extends to stronger interest in white culture (a factor of the Black Ideology Scale). Greater involvement in extracurricular activities among seniors undoubtedly contributes to the positive aspects of this college experience. While the "County College" findings provide us with the best display of constructive academic energy among black students at white colleges, there are still problems in sight. More seniors report conventional vocational aspirations—compatible with conforming personalities—and the level of vocational aspirations is lower among seniors. Finally, seniors suffer from longer illnesses. So, while this college does more for black student development than the others investigated so far, there are still problematical aspects to development.

Sex Differences in the Impact of White Colleges

Male Development. In the effort to find out what factors are responsible for the grim developmental prospects at white colleges, we first consider freshman-senior differences among the 131 males (83 freshmen and 48 seniors) in the total sample of black students at these four predominantly white colleges. It is worth noting at the outset that, when differences among freshmen in black and white schools are considered by sex, black males in white schools appear to be the most competitive and career oriented (see Fleming, 1980). Given this feature of their initial profiles, what follows is all the more distressing, since males seem to reflect more of the dark side of black student development in white schools. As seniors, males in white schools report less positive evaluations than freshmen of the administration, faculty, and peers. Their specific complaint about teachers is that they do not grade fairly. Seniors score lower on the social adjustment scale, which seems to reflect a general disenchantment with interpersonal sources of satisfaction. Seniors also score higher on indicators of academic stress, personal life stress, and feelings of personal threat, signaling stresses on all major life fronts.

We now see that it is the males who show the strongest signs of academic demotivation. There is no evidence of improved academic functioning, only of lower grades in the major subject among seniors. Grades are also less important to seniors. With the loss of interest in grades and worsening academic performance, seniors complain less about academic failure, perhaps because they have become accustomed to it. The heightened aspirations for graduate school and master's degrees found among seniors can only appear defensive in the context of relative failure.

One of the more discouraging aspects of male development is that senior males report being less energetic than freshmen. The academic demotivation that is apparent among these males certainly suggests that energy is withdrawn from academics. But if these students are suffering from loss of academic energy, there is some evidence that the energy left over is channeled into certain extracurricular pursuits. Senior males seem to take the most pleasure in participation in activities of a cultural and political nature. Such outlets may help black males channel their energy in a positive way. Indeed, senior males score higher on the Social Assertiveness Scale and the Black Ideology Scale, and it may be that involvement in extracurricular activities is responsible for some of the few positive developments seen among this group of men. Such activities may well serve tension-releasing purposes, but they evidently do not help failing academic motivation. Thus, the little energy that seems available to these men is directed away from the classroom into nonacademic activities. This profile is a far cry from the energy and enterprise of male development in black colleges. Clearly, something very different is happening to males in these white schools.

It saps the academic drive of initially competitive men and precludes intellectual growth of any observable kind.

Female Development. The developmental profile for the 199 black females (134 freshman and 65 seniors) in white schools is at least a bit brighter than that of their male counterparts. The list of grievances more apparent among women by freshman-senior comparisons is similar to that of their male counterparts in many respects. Senior women are more disillusioned with the administration and unhappier with the college choice. Senior women are also more disenchanted with faculty who, in their estimation, do not grade fairly. They are more dissatisfied with teaching methods, and getting good grades becomes less important by the senior year. Seniors think less of their abilities and report having less energy. Among seniors, social adjustment scores are lower, and the opposite sex is a particular source of disappointment. (Our data do, indeed, indicate far fewer black males than females in white colleges, especially among seniors.)

But, from there, the similarities to the male picture end, as the female profiles begin to show some sign of reward for the apparent trouble. It seems safe to say that black women are able to get more out of the white college experience than black men. Despite general disillusionment with faculty, more senior women can point to someone on the faculty or staff that they admire. Their grades show improvement on one of the available measures, that is, overall grade averages. Seniors are less emotionally suppressed (according to the emotional suppression factor of the Social Assertiveness Scale), and seniors describe themselves as more outspoken and articulate. Senior women participate more in campus activities (though not in positions of responsibility) but do not appear to use them as a means of tension release. Although seniors are less likely than freshmen to feel that college has aided their personal development, more senior women feel that they have gained in their cultural awareness and abilities to cope and deal with people.

In short, black women seem to suffer from many of the same problems (with faculty, staff, and peers) as do black males. Yet they manage to gain something more from the academic experience. What females display that males do not is growing involvement with faculty members. Perhaps this means that if faculty role modeling takes place, academic interest can be sustained, so that intellectual energies are not entirely withdrawn from academics. Thus, women seem able to direct tension from frustrated social lives into academics, as long as they find encouragement in this direction.

Individual Differences at "Traditional University"

For a look at the college life profiles of the three achievement-related personality types—those exhibiting need for achievement, fear of success, and fear of failure—in a predominantly white environment, "Traditional University" was chosen. As a coed liberal arts institution with a reasonable sample of 43 males (42 percent of whom were seniors), "Traditional University" provides the best comparative match for a similar analysis done with Clark College men (see Chapter Four). The methodological procedures described for Clark are also utilized here.

A similar investigation at Clark College showed that all three achievement types flourished in a supportive black college environment. The academic orientation of these men was maximized, and achievement conflicts were largely dormant in this environment. However, this is not the case at "Traditional University." In fact, the opposite is closer to the truth. All three achievement personalities appear to be suffering academically, and each personality shows signs of an unresolved conflict over authority.

The Achieving Personality. The correlates of need for achievement are ideally expected to reflect relative skill in tasks having achievement significance. They can also be expected to exhibit a capacity for satisfaction in the knowledge gained through testing individual abilities. But not all studies find this evidence. Studies of blacks almost never fit the classic entrepreneurial mold. Researchers continue to ask why some people with high achievement motives sometimes look good and others do not. At Clark College, the black achieving personality is at its best. But at "Traditional University," we are again faced with a reversal of the expected behavior profile.

At "Traditional University," achievement-oriented men

display none of the characteristics of their counterparts at
Clark. Very little can be said of them other than that they seem
to suffer from exhaustion and withdrawal. Specifically, more of
them describe themselves as tired and shy and score higher on
the fatigue self-concept factor. The only vestige of their sup-
posed achievement spirit is the feeling that instructors are the
best part of college life. Somehow, their college experience acts
to block almost all evidence of achievement need and drive.
Said another way, the independence of thought and action said
to characterize such individuals appears to have no appropriate
behavioral outlet. The few results tell us that the achievement
motive has virtually disappeared. It has gone underground, as it
were.

The Success-Fearing Personality. The fear-of-success personality is built around a conflict: a desire for competence in
achievement activities, coupled with a fear of punishing disap-
proval from significant others for the effort. In recent studies of
this motive in black men, this conflict is often associated with
displays of anger, hostility, or rebellion (Fleming, 1982a). At
Clark, this motive is largely dormant. At "Traditional University," this conflict is a highly active motivational disposition.
However, the activity produces little achievement gain.

Success-avoidant men, unlike their achievement-oriented
counterparts, were the least likely to think that their instructors
were the best thing about college. Among these men, there is a
significant departure from some of the general patterns linked
to valued but stressful involvements with instructors. Although
they do not feel that courses are particularly demanding, there
is no evidence of any intellectual or emotional gain from academics. The motive is unrelated to any of the measures of
academic performance. The two remaining results in the achievement area show success-fearing men planning for graduate
school in government. They seem to avoid graduate school or
career plans in law—the favorite choice of achievement-oriented
men at Clark! Little is happening for fear-of-success men on the
academic front.

Their academic inactivity is not due to lack of energy or
involvement in campus life. More success-fearing men display in-

volvement in extracurricular activities and hold positions of responsibility in them. Social gatherings are also on their list of enjoyed activities. What they do not like is other students' lack of involvement in cultural and political activities. Perhaps because of their many active involvements, they are generally more assertive. In particular, fear of success is negatively related to the Social Assertiveness Scale but positively related to emotional openness. Fear-of-success men also describe themselves as less shy and more aggressive and outspoken than other students. They also score higher on the extroversion self-concept factor.

In their interpersonal relationships, dissatisfaction with the opposite sex is the only finding. Finally, they show more signs of stress in reporting the onset of more psychosomatic complaints and seeking more medical assistance for them. Here, the rebellious potential of the fear-of-success motive is displayed, as these male students resist distasteful interactions with instructors. As if angered by their forced retreat from academics, they redirect this frustrated energy into social, cultural, and political involvements and into developing their assertive skills. Unfortunately, the assertive skills have no apparent intellectual value.

The Fear-of-Failure Personality. As the one with the most serious achievement conflict, this personality type typically withdraws from achievement activities where the pain of failure might be too great. While Clark males of this type are encouraged to transform themselves into achieving types with behavioral profiles like achievement motive (nAch) counterparts, no such transformation occurs at "Traditional University." By any standard, their academic adjustment would be judged poor. They are less likely to think that class and learning activities are the best part of college. Indeed, they feel unprepared for college, spend less time studying and even less during exams, and do not work well under pressure. All that can be said of their academic performance is that they are not likely to attain academic honors. Despite this dismal academic experience, they plan for graduate school in science and desire master's level degrees. Their ambitions strike us as out of sync with their actual academic behavior. Even they think of themselves as lacking in ambition and more obedient than other students. Obedience is certainly not a useful quality in scientific inquiry, in which they profess interest.

They do not channel academic frustrations into campus involvements, as do success-fearing men. Instead, their personal lives appear to become an arena for coping with the feelings of intellectual insecurity. More of these men feel that marriage is very important and that having a family is even more important. They feel that marriage will help their careers, and they show a stronger family (versus career) orientation. Although marriage is expected to help their own careers, their wives may not derive the same benefit from the union. In fact, they desire a woman with relatively weak career orientation, one who works in the service of the family rather than toward career goals. Thus, as far as career orientation goes, failure-fearing men clearly want the dominant role. A family situation that allows them the sense of dominance that they do not feel in academics is obviously calculated to assuage insecurity.

What these individual differences in achievement types may tell us is that the overall male development at "Traditional University" may actually be a composite of at least three types. It looks as if, though nAch individuals are the ones who become involved with faculty, they show severe emotional strain as a result. It is success-fearing men who rebel against relationships with instructors and act out a cultural, political, and social protest in campus involvement. Fear-of-failure men, who withdraw from academic life, are the ones who seek importance through taking the dominant role in a relatively traditional household. The profiles also confirm that there is something critical about relationships with faculty and/or the experience in the classroom. Those who become involved with instructors suffer a loss of psychological independence. While various coping strategies are used by these men, none of them has much academic value.

Conclusions

What cannot be overlooked in this report of black students in four white colleges is the impoverished nature of intellectual development. Contrary to much public opinion, these white colleges are not able to encourage growth in the cognitive domain to any substantial degree. In terms of academic performance, these colleges produce either no effects at all, gross academic deterioration, or a gain on one measure that is compromised by losses on others. Gains on more subjective measures of intellectual development are just as infrequent.

The relative absence of cognitive growth is hypothesized to be related to an absence of positive relationships with faculty. These students are relatively unable to develop strong relationships with faculty, and there was rarely evidence of informal contacts with instructors. The isolated effects for faculty involvements suggest lack of positive involvements with role models on these campuses. To a lesser extent, serious absorption in the major subject (or in finding a career) seems to substitute for an interpersonal connection. But the minimal observed involvements of either kind result in only minimal intellectual gain. Rather than complementing intellectual growth, socioemotional development becomes a defense against the feelings of inadequacy engendered by thwarted cognitive development.

This initial investigation has isolated cognitive development as the important dimension in which students in black and white colleges differ. Students in black colleges show consistent evidence of intellectual development, but the intellectual development of black students in white colleges is more often thwarted than encouraged. The following chapters are devoted to determining how widespread this phenomenon is outside the traditional South.

6

:◆:

Colleges
in the Southwest:
Findings
from In-Depth Studies
of Student Growth

The exploratory study of three black and four white colleges seems to indicate that predominantly black schools promote more positive growth in academic functioning and intellectual self-concept. In short, black colleges seem likely to promote growth in the cognitive domain of experience. They have the ability to produce admirable gains, even with so little to offer in objective resources. At the same time, black students in white colleges gain little in the midst of intellectual plenty. Nevertheless, one would be remiss not to consider the possibility that the exploratory findings were a fluke. Could a similar pattern be found in different kinds of colleges in different parts of the country? This chapter attempts to verify the exploratory findings in the Southwest.

The black colleges chosen for the exploratory study are hardly representative of all predominantly black institutions. They are three of the best black colleges, of which two have exceptional reputations. Could, for example, the initial findings be verified in larger public institutions? Also, might not the pattern of results be different in the Southwest, where black-white relations have a different character? To answer these questions, patterns of college development were considered in two large urban universities in Texas: predominantly black Texas Southern University and predominantly white University of Houston.

The measures used in Georgia to assess intellectual development are "soft" in several respects and may not provide the best test of cognitive growth. Some variables, such as those assessing academic adjustment, tap inner thoughts and feelings of students (that is, perceptions), measuring subjective rather than objective reality. Other measures, such as vocational orientation and postgraduate plans, assess interests and aspirations that may not always bear a one-to-one correspondence to future behavior. Finally, while grades have good objective validity within institutions, the varying standards on which they may be based make them less useful in cross-institutional comparisons. What might happen, then, if "harder" measures were utilized, that is, those that assess objective behavior and are standardized to the extent that they have meaning beyond a particular subjective environment? The inclusion of a series of more objective measures seemed warranted, given the central importance of cognitive issues in education.

The goals of this chapter are fourfold. Development in black and white colleges is considered in two large urban universities in the Southwestern state of Texas. A far more extensive study of intellectual development is employed, one involving two new projects that included more objective measures of cognitive skills. Finally, personal interviews with students are employed to hear student voices more directly. This plan required an effort conducted in four phases: (1) replication of the exploratory study; (2) a study of cognitive growth; (3) an experimental study of competitive performance; and (4) an interview study of sources of stress and satisfaction. The chapter is organized around the discussion of comparative findings from each of the investigations.

The results of the four projects add up to a bold confirmation of the findings in Texas. Again, the predominantly black college promotes the best development. Once more, black students in a predominantly white learning environment seem to be more handicapped than helped. Even with harder, more reliable instruments, the results are plainly in favor of black schools. What is more, this chapter tells why the black college environment is so encouraging of intellectual growth. The answer, we know now, lies not in the quality of available facilities but in the interpersonal environment. The opportunity to make friends among peers, faculty, and professionals helps students to survive the stresses of the college years. But for students on white campuses, the absence of enough people to talk to creates a loneliness that interferes with intellectual functioning.

✗ To help us assess the general impact of college environments in Texas, students filled out the standard 32-page questionnaire used in previous studies and took the Thematic Apperception Test. For this series of analyses, each of the dependent variables was submitted to as many as three separate analyses of variance. That is, if the dependent variables were significantly correlated with the background variables of social class and aptitude test scores, they had to be submitted to additional analyses of covariance to control for each of these factors. Although this replication of the exploratory findings was carried out in a different part of the country in very different kinds of institutions, the pattern of findings is much the same as that in Georgia. Black student development within predominantly black Texas Southern can be described as well rounded, while that within the University of Houston is, at best, conflicted.

Development at Texas Southern University

With an undergraduate enrollment of 8,405, Texas Southern University (TSU) is one of the largest black institutions. It maintains a liberal admission policy in that high school graduation is the only requirement, and standardized tests are used for placement purposes only. Nonetheless, the student-centered philosophy of education emphasizes an individual commitment to a tradition of excellence in achievement. Much of the university's growth can be attributed to its expertise in seeking solutions to urban problems, to its involvement in all aspects of urban life, and to its role as an agency for fostering those who will implement change. There were 455 TSU students in the initial student population (126 male and 203 female freshmen and 55 male and 71 female seniors), 230 of whom filled out the questionnaire. They exhibit significantly lower aptitude (SAT or ACT) scores than their counterparts at the University of Houston but no difference in social-class backgrounds.

As a whole, development at Texas Southern is exceptionally positive. Generally, research suggests increasingly broad student participation in academic and campus life. For example, more seniors report strong involvement with faculty whom they admire, greater involvement in the career selection process, and involvement in extracurricular activities. In addition, more seniors report being happy with their college choice. The only fly in the ointment is that seniors complain more about the attitude of the administration.

The findings for academic matters suggest enhanced efficiency and stronger motivation among seniors. Seniors more often report that they work well under pressure, although women tend to cram for exams. Seniors receive better grades on one of the six indices (cumulative GPA), and senior males perform better on cumulative grades in the major subject. Perhaps as a result of improving academic efficiency, seniors report higher estimates of their general ability and stronger feelings of intellectual competence than freshmen. Finally, seniors score higher than freshmen on the measure of achievement motivation. This is the first evidence of stronger positive motivation seen so far among seniors.

The achieving spirit manifests itself in career development. Fewer seniors plan to stop their educations after graduation, while more have serious plans to go to graduate or professional school. Educational aspirations are generally higher among seniors. While seniors are more likely to choose their occupations because of good job-market opportunities, they are also more likely to choose vocational options that offer the promise of a challenge. These sentiments are more characteristic of senior males.

The findings in career development for women at TSU are more encouraging than for women in many of the other black colleges. Here, senior women are less likely to show stronger conventional vocational interests. Conventional vocational interests are associated with conformng personalities, so that it is especially encouraging that these women seem able to escape from some of the usual conventional imprinting at a black college. Yet this freeing in the vocational arena may have its price, since senior women report being less popular than their freshman counterparts. Thus, intellectual growth among women in Texas seems to have its social costs.

When development goes well, according to theory, the integration of emotional and intellectual aspects of the personality produces a rise in energy level. Such an integration is observable at Texas Southern. Although seniors describe themselves as more polite than freshmen, they also report being more energetic, as well as more competitive and ambitious. Men, if not women, also develop in a way that bodes well for assertiveness. Senior males describe themselves as more outspoken, argumentative, and capable of leading. They also report being less arrogant but more militant. On a factor of the Social Assertiveness Scale, senior males were more emotionally expressive than freshman counterparts. Although seniors of both sexes exhibit greater competitive energy, males still appear to have an edge when it comes to social assertiveness and aggressiveness.

Texas Southern individuals, then, can expect to become increasingly acquainted with academic success and campus life. Their new drive and energy should be an asset as they go on to greater challenges after college.

Development at the University of Houston

The vast central campus of the University of Houston (UH) has an enrollment of 30,000, including 2,321 black undergraduates. It is one of the largest white educators of black students. Unlike TSU, its admission procedures are competitive, based on a combination of class rank and standardized test scores. With so large an enrollment (in so vast a university), UH remains aware of its responsibility to influence the individual student in becoming a fully integrated person. Maintaining its proud reputation as a research institution that discovers and disseminates knowledge in a diversified cultural and ethnic atmosphere is another of its objectives. The number of black faculty on this campus is about 24, making a ratio of 1 to every 100 black students. A number of academic and social student organizations, such as Greek letter organizations, serve the extracurricular needs of black students.

A total subject pool of 324 students (65 male and 130 female freshmen and 53 male and 76 female seniors) was recruited for phase one of the study, in which the TAT was given. Of this number, 228 returned to fill out the questionnaire instrument. In many ways, black student outcomes at UH are the best yet for a predominantly white school. With both TSU and UH showing some of the best in development, we have to wonder about the residual influences of the frontier spirit. Does the Southwestern environment foster greater potential for growth among blacks? The absence of a plantation heritage must be a relevant factor. The regional allegiance to rugged individualism, combined with a freedom from the polite traditions of the Old South, may account for some of the different flavor in these results.

Up till now, stellar academic functioning of black students has been the sole province of predominantly black colleges. UH student performance rivals that of any black school. Seniors perform better on five of the six measures of academic performance. Furthermore, seniors more often report that they work well under pressure, and they are more likely to choose their subjects to increase their knowledge. The fact that students seem to form attachments to faculty members may account for their academic successes. Seniors report more informal contact with their teachers. We have already learned from the studies in Georgia that some attachment to faculty seems to help sustain academic motivation. Thus, it is not surprising that seniors more often intend to go to graduate or professional school and to use their careers to make a contribution of some kind.

Senior black women are most likely to find helpful and admirable role models, to function well under pressure, and to harbor aspirations that include graduate education. While their feelings of competence and personal motivation suffer relative to freshmen, they more often appreciate the cultural experience of a white environment. They also more often report feelings of cognitive development and do indeed score higher in achievement motivation. As seniors, they are motivated more by working at careers that can benefit their race, although competition in the job market is their biggest worry.

In sum, good cognitive development is in evidence at UH, especially in academic functioning. Women are best able to derive internal feelings of cognitive growth and motivation, feelings that lead to graduate and professional school ambitions. This seems to be due to their ability, for whatever reason, to develop the most positive ties with instructors.

The experience in Georgia conditions us to expect a dark side to black student development at white schools. Unfortunately, the University of Houston is no exception. The sad part of the story begins with the poor aspects of black student adjustment to the institution. Seniors evolve from thinking that school has had little impact on them to thinking that the impact of college is negative. Findings from the academic adjustment factor indicate that seniors have less positive attitudes toward every aspect of college life, including the administration, faculty, course offerings, and fellow students. Although there is evidence of positive attachment to teachers, certain types of tensions with faculty become worse. More seniors feel that the teaching methods are not fair and that teachers are not interested or encouraging. More students of both sexes express feelings of incompetence in the senior year, while senior women are the least satisfied with their academic performance. The problem is not one of institutional quality, as senior men more often tell us. It is the pressure of racial tension, which is felt most acutely by the senior students.

Poor adjustment to the institution seems to result in loss of student connectedness to others. Seniors score lower on the social adjustment scale and also score lower on affiliation motivation. Most important, seniors score lower on the identity integration factor of the Black Ideology Scale. This scale assesses feelings of being successfully integrated into the larger community, a necessary ingredient for any healthy identity.

At the same time that students begin to feel less socially integrated into the campus community, they are also becoming more assertive. Seniors describe themselves as less passive. They also score lower on the self-concept items' social decorum factor, which assesses a concern for polite behavior. Findings from another factor of the Black Ideology Scale show that seniors are less accepting of white authority than freshman counterparts. Seniors score lower on the oral stage of adaptation to the environment, which measures a passive incorporative orientation; this trend suggests increasing assertiveness. Seniors, in fact, score higher than freshmen on the Social Assertiveness Scale and also exhibit stronger black consciousness. The previous studies in Georgia indicated that assertiveness is often a defensive response to an inhospitable college setting. The same certainly seems to be true at the University of Houston. This interpretation is confirmed by the fact that seniors score higher on the defensiveness factor of the Black Ideology Scale. The final note is not a happy one. The difficulties suggested in this set of results culminate in seniors describing themselves as less ambitious and less happy by the end of their four-year experience.

In interpreting these Texas data, we must, for the first time, weigh the evidence with care to determine the comparative advantage in cognitive development. At Texas Southern, the findings suggest improvements on two measures of academic performance. These academic improvements are accompanied by subjective feelings of enhanced intellectual competence and motivation for both sexes. Furthermore, the positive developments in the socioemotional domain of experience act in a complementary way to generate energy and ambition. Thus, the improvements in all areas of functioning activate the opening channels of intellectual activity. At the University of Houston, five of the six measures of academic performance register a freshman-senior gain. At first blush, this suggests better cognitive development at the predominantly white institution. But the corroborative evidence, that of enhanced feelings of intellectual growth and gains in achievement motivation, is found only infrequently and largely among black women. Furthermore, developments in the socioemotional sphere suggest increasing feelings of alienation and frustration. These feelings seem to be defensively channeled into assertive behavior. The conflicted nature of development at the University of Houston presents a less than convincing picture of growth.

The fact that the University of Houston is an urban school with a large commuter population may account for the admirable academic performance. For one thing, students who commute may have more opportunity to escape the negative influences of daily campus life, influences that extract their toll quietly beneath awareness. When on campus, student attention may be more squarely focused on academics. In the face of social and racial isolation, UH students still do not direct energy away from academics. Instead, they put more effort into getting good grades. If many students at UH are able to leave campus and return to a family atmosphere supportive of their goals, they may react defensively to racism and isolation but retain the ability to gain something from the classroom.

Cognitive Growth

We have seen that students in black colleges show more positive intellectual development. Also in black colleges, socioemotional development is more likely to reinforce growth in the intellectual domain. At the University of Houston, black students are, to be sure, able to channel feelings of alienation into positive academic accomplishments. But at TSU, there is greater evidence of generalized cognitive development on both cognitive and affective indices. Can we confirm that TSU produces more generalized intellectual development?

Our challenge was to find strategies for locating the necessary evidence. Grades were the most objective measures available in the initial study. Although they provide good evidence of relative freshman-senior functioning, they are less useful for cross-institutional comparisons. Relative change on SAT to Graduate Record Examination (GRE) scores could be examined, much as it was in a study conducted by Centra, Linn, and Parry (1970) at several black and white colleges (which showed no significant differences in cognitive growth between black and white schools). In this sample, however, too few seniors had taken GREs to make such an investigation worthwhile. Furthermore, traditional standardized tests such as the GRE have certain shortcomings in a study of this kind. According to the new study of liberal arts education by Winter, McClelland, and Stewart (1981), traditional aptitude measures have failed as adequate measures of cognitive growth or of the effectiveness of higher education because they were never developed for this specific purpose. They require knowledge of facts that are too quickly forgotten, and they are far better measures of initial intelligence than of intellectual skill imparted by colleges. Also, the forced-choice format required for computer scoring means that students do not have to generate answers of their own; they need not demonstrate any thinking.

These authors have developed special tests to assess the stated goals of higher education: critical thinking, effective communication, and intellectual flexibility. To take these tests, students must demonstrate problem-solving abilities, so that important thought processes can be investigated. The tests are also independent of a student's major subject or of his or her knowledge of specific facts. Unlike traditional tests, these instruments are sensitive to the intended effects of a college education. The authors find that the better the institution, the stronger the effects measured by the tests.

The following tests were administered to students in Texas: (1) *Test of Concept Formation*. The Heidbreder (1948) test of concept formation was used in the exploratory research of Winter, McClelland, and Stewart. It measures the ability to attain and remember concepts that someone else (for example, the tester) has defined in advance. Thus, it is a simple measure of concept formation. (See the Appendix for details of this and other cognitive tests.) (2) *Test of Thematic Analysis*. Developed by Winter and McClelland (1978), Thematic Analysis consti-

tutes a test of critical thinking employed in a "compare and
contrast" essay examination. With no single correct set of facts
to be used, a good answer depends upon organization and interpretation. Liberal education increases the precision, parallel
structure, breadth of coverage, and objective emotional neutral-
ity of comparisons involving complex concepts. (3) *Test of
Analysis of Argument.* Stewart (1977b) developed this measure
of intellectual flexibility, which measures the ability to keep
cool and see the elements of truth in all sides of a heated controversy. Asking students to defend both sides of an emotional
issue puts them under the fire of their own emotions in a way
that a standardized test cannot.

Effects were found for two of the measures, confirming
that positive cognitive development is more generalized at Texas
Southern. Texas Southern seniors score higher than freshmen
on concept formation and thematic analysis. Of course, students come to TSU scoring significantly below UH students on
both measures. They nevertheless make strides in bridging the
gap, so that there are no significant statistical differences among
seniors in thematic analysis—the more complex task. At University of Houston, only concept formation registers a freshman-senior difference. Senior black women gain, but senior
black men show a decline, even in this relatively simple cognitive ability. Analysis of argument is a relatively undeveloped
ability that remains uninfluenced by either college environment.

In sum, special tests designed for assessing the impact of
college on cognitive skill provide further validation that TSU
produces stronger cognitive development in its students. Black
women may gain most from the University of Houston, but
black men show worsening performance even at simple cognitive tasks. Since senior males are no less intelligent than freshmen, according to their SAT scores, the experience of alienation seems to affect their motivation to exercise basic cognitive
skills.

Competitive Performance

How useful are the cognitive abilities gained at black institutions such as Texas Southern? Intellectual development

during the late adolescent college years is allegedly preparatory to the occupational endeavors that students will soon undertake. How well will black students integrate gained intellectual skills for more practical use in the real world? We cannot predict how these students will perform in the future. But we can observe their performance in a simulated work setting that previews aspects of real-world performance. Under controlled laboratory conditions, we can learn more about students' ability to compete against other individuals in work settings. In so doing, we hope to gain a glimpse of how well predominantly black and predominantly white colleges prepare students to work competitively in an integrated world.

Method. The experimental paradigm used in this investigation was inspired by a long series of studies by Irwin Katz and his colleagues (for example, Katz, 1964). In these studies, black (male) students worked on achievement tests in all-black or in integrated work settings. The tests were taken in many situations, ranging from highly interactive to noninteractive, and under highly threatening conditions or highly supportive conditions. In most of the studies, the performance of blacks is seriously impaired in white work environments. This is true for all except those individuals with a history of academic achievement, subjects who are stimulated by the challenge of competition with whites. On the other hand, performance is usually enhanced in black working environments. Black students perform best in the presence of a supportive black experimenter.

Experimental findings such as these almost exactly parallel the unfolding pattern of cognitive development in black and white colleges. But how will each of our Texas schools affect the ability to compete in black and white work settings? Perhaps black college students learn to work well in black situations but suffer in white environments, just as they do in white colleges. The experiment is designed to test just such a question.

Students from each college were randomly assigned to a white environment or a black environment. "Environments" were created by an older-looking male experimenter and a same-sex peer (a confederate). In these environments, students competed on a math and verbal achievement task, labeled "National Scholastic Achievement Tests" in the white environment and

"United Negro College Fund Scholastic Achievement Tests" in the black environment. The experimental conditions were meant to approximate the most usual real-world conditions, in which males work and compete with other males and in which women most often work with other women, but under a male supervisor.

The high degree of experimental control in the laboratory situation made it possible to test the effects of competition on a range of student behaviors. First, students performed on a math and verbal achievement test. Then they evaluated their own performance, their emotional state, and the experimenter's adequacy. A counterbalanced version of the TAT was given between the two achievement tests (that is, during competition) to provide a reading of change in motivational states as a result of competition. Finally, a trained nurse assessed the students' physiological responses to competition from pulse and blood pressure (systolic and diastolic) readings taken before competition, immediately after competition, and following a fifteen-minute recovery. These measurements provide an unusual opportunity to examine two types of functioning: that which reflects highly conscious and controlled activities (performance and subjective judgment), as well as that less subject to the voluntary control of the student (motivation and physiology). The integration of cognitive, psychological, and physiological indices ought to give us a revealing picture of achievement orientation in black and white work settings.

The details of the method and treatment of data are given in the Appendix. Suffice it to say here that the instructions were intended to maximally arouse motivation in this noninteractive work situation. Unfortunately, time constraints did not permit us to design an interactive work situation, in which the effects would certainly have been stronger. Nonetheless, the present paradigm should be sufficient to give us an idea of the differential impact of a black and white college on competitive performance. Controls for social class and aptitude were employed, as they have been throughout the study. In addition, controls for baseline measures of verbal ability, motivation, pulse, and blood pressure were also used. Two hundred and fifty-nine students participated in this experiment, so that near-equal numbers (from 14 to 17) filled the 16 cells created by the experimental design (see Table 1 in Chapter Three).

Impact of Texas Southern University on Competitive Performance. The experimental study of competition supports the previous evidence that Texas Southern has a greater positive impact on cognitive development. The only evidence of gains in ability to compete were found at this college. No freshman-senior effects appear in performance on a two-step math test (given for ten minutes), using the math SAT scores as the control for initial math ability. After taking the TAT, students then competed on a ten-minute anagram task (Clark and McClelland, 1956), for which a baseline measure of ability (the 1952 Lowell Scrambled Words Test) was given earlier in the first testing session. On the anagram test, seniors perform somewhat better than freshmen, whether they are competing in black or white environments. Probably the most amazing fact about Texas Southern's effect on student competitive ability is that performance improves most in white work environments! Thus, seniors in a white work setting perform significantly better than freshmen working in white environments. This black college manages to impart a facility for functioning in integrated settings. Furthermore, according to ratings on the postexperimental questionnaire, seniors enjoy the competition more than freshmen.

In addition to freshman-senior differences, which suggest the impact of college on competitive functioning, the experimental design allows direct comparisons between Texas Southern and University of Houston students. With verbal ability controlled, TSU freshmen performed worse than UH freshmen, mostly because of the poorer showing of TSU freshmen women. But by the senior year, the initial gaps in performance have been closed; no differences were apparent in the competitive performance of TSU and UH students, given a rough parity in their initial aptitude. TSU students also enjoy competition more than UH students and feel that it is more important to do well in competition. TSU males and the students of both sexes who worked in white environments report the strongest motivation to do well. Texas Southern appears not only to help students function better in competition but also to foster positive attitudes toward competition.

So far, so good. TSU students appear to learn to integrate the intellectual skills gained in college for practical use in competition with whites, and in a way that allows them to enjoy it. But this evidence comes from measures of achievement test performance and subjective reports that are largely under the conscious control of the student. As we descend into the student's inner world, by way of motivational and physiological instruments much less subject to voluntary control, another side of the story unfolds.

Despite the encouraging performance of these students, competition arouses stronger achievement anxieties in them. On a counterbalanced version of the TAT, inserted between math and verbal tasks, fear-of-success scores are elevated at TSU. The college experience has little impact on this anxiety reaction to competition, since no freshman-senior differences have been found. If black students come to TSU with fears of success in competitive situations, they leave with this motivational problem intact. The black college environment does little to change the nature of the conflict. TSU does, however, help students channel the conflict in constructive ways that enhance the intellectual and competitive potential of the individual.

Pulse and systolic and diastolic blood pressure readings were taken before, immediately after, and fifteen minutes after competition. These measures established baseline rates, competition-induced changes in these rates, and the persistence of effects. Pulse rates are most affected by the experimental manipulation, while diastolic blood pressure was the least reactive. Accordingly, elevations in blood pressure, particularly diastolic rates, are more serious indications of physiological stress. There are higher postcompetition pulse rates (corrected for initial rates) at TSU, and these rates are highest among TSU males in white work environments. Among females, the pulse rates are higher in black environments. After a fifteen-minute recovery, TSU males in white environments still show elevated pulse rates. There are no freshman-senior differences in these pulse rates. After competition, systolic blood pressure is elevated among males at TSU in both black and white environments. This effect disappears after the recovery period, but seniors of both sexes take longer to recover than freshmen. No effects peculiar to TSU appear in the diastolic rates.

The stress that TSU students experience from competition cannot be detected in intellectual performance. But further probing suggests that fears of successful competition do have physiological consequences. Although intellectual performance does seem to improve over the college years, the fears remain. These fears appear to create a physical vulnerability to the stress of competition that is progressive. This means that the body is under a kind of stress that may show up only years later in strokes or heart attacks. Males working in white environments, if this study is any guide, should be most at risk. Well-known medical facts bear out this pattern. This study substantiates medical researchers' suspicions that black hypertension is rooted in conflicts springing from alienation and repressed hostility (see Cooper, 1975). The findings suggest that achievement-related conflicts are among the deficiencies black students bring to black colleges.

Impact of the University of Houston on Competitive Performance. Considerably fewer effects were found in favor of UH black students. The few appearing indicate no freshman-senior gains on competitive ability, further confirming that these students show limited cognitive development in the college years. The one freshman-senior difference in this entire experiment proves only that UH seniors enjoy competition in white environments less than freshmen. The paradox is that students in a white university lose the capacity to enjoy competitive interracial encounters, while students insulated in a black college show more capacity to enjoy competition with whites.

This study has considered a number of intellectual skills, but competitive skills are the ones on which UH students show no sign of progress. Another part of the paradox is that UH students give higher ratings to the experimenter's capabilities in the white environment. At TSU, the highest ratings were given to black experimenters. So, although UH students become alienated and lose interest in using cognitive abilities around whites, they still overvalue things white. The trap in such thinking is obvious.

Stagnation in this kind of intellectual performance may slow down progressive physiological reactivity to stress. The only motivational effects show that competition arouses stronger fear of power in women, despite the fact that they also report the strongest motivation to do well in competition. The only physiological effects are that UH males have higher resting levels of diastolic blood pressure than their TSU counterparts, but no postcompetition effects were in evidence.

Sex Differences in Competitive Performance. Men and women retain certain differences regardless of the colleges they attend. Men are the achievers and women the underachievers. The men set higher performance goals and do perform better in math. They are more satisfied with their performance and report less anxiety during competition. Yet their admirable competitive effort is associated with stronger fears about succeeding and with elevated systolic and diastolic blood pressure. Undoubtedly, the greater the competitive stress levels of their normal circumstances, the higher their resting levels of systolic blood pressure.

Women, on the other hand, set lower levels of aspiration on the math test and, perhaps for this reason, perform poorly. They are less satisfied with their performance and report more anxiety. But, in spite of these indications of low ambition and lack of confidence, competition inspires them with stronger needs for achievement. Their pulse rates increase with the experience, but they do not suffer from the more serious elevations of blood pressure that afflict males. Women do have higher resting levels of fear of success and pulse rates, which suggests a stable kind of anxiety that acts to depress aspiration and disrupt abstract thought. Thus, it appears that the stress of competition arouses strong motivation and physical stamina, of which these underachieving women may be quite unaware.

Stress and Satisfaction in the College Years

Before we left Texas to explore development in other states, we made one final attempt to understand why TSU and UH affect students in such different ways. To do this, we approached students on a more intimate basis, using the vehicle of personal interviews. Our purpose was to listen to student voices and derive more understanding than emerges from the highly structured examination of grades, test scores, and questionnaire responses. This approach did not ignore statistical considerations, but the focus on student sentiment did not lend itself to the usual corrections for social class and aptitude. From the initial subject pool, 118 students (15 male and 13 female freshmen, and 15 male and 15 female seniors from TSU; 13 male and 15 female freshmen, and 17 male and 15 female seniors from UH) returned a fourth time for a forty-five-minute interview with a same-sex member of the project staff.

The Experience of Stress. We wanted to determine the differential impact of college on the experience of unhappiness. The operative words are *the experience of,* since the college environment may not necessarily determine the occurrence of crisis incidents, such as death, illness, divorce, or heartbreak. However, the current environment may well influence the *perception* of these events as constituting or initiating the most unhappy periods in an individual's life and the response to crisis. Following a procedure for investigating stress developed by Abigail Stewart (1975), students were told: "We are interested in studying stress in people's lives. I would like you to describe the period in your life that you think of as the most *unhappy* or *unsetting* time you've lived through. Any period is all right (not just a time in college), but choose a time when—for an extended period, not just briefly—things really seemed to go badly—about six months or more. It should be a time when you were less happy, when you were frustrated or distressed. The time needn't be catastrophic, just when things were not going well."

In attempting to discover the sources of college student unhappiness or stress, we found how remarkably similar students were at Texas Southern and the University of Houston. Despite the differences between these groups in measurable scholastic aptitude, very similar problems engaged the negative emotions: academics, intrapsychic tensions, traumatic events, and frustrating circumstances.

School-related problems with academics and interactions with faculty, administration, and staff are most likely to initiate serious periods of unhappiness among 30 percent of these students. The academic problems related by students reveal how seriously they take their studies and to what extent the experience of academic uncertainty or failure arouses intense insecurity: "I sat in the class for about two weeks before I really realized what was going on. . . . I'm in a class and I don't know whether I'm going to pass it. . . . I failed every test that I took. . . . Getting upset with myself and my study habits. . . . I had not achieved the success in college that I thought I would. . . . Some instructors don't expect too much out of me. . . . I thought you'd have instructors that would help you and explain things to do."

Seventeen percent of the students complain that intrapsychic problems have ushered in periods of unhappiness, that is, problems with an internalized focus that are associated with feelings of confusion, helplessness, and resignation: "I was growing up then, and I didn't want to grow up at all. . . . Making the change from an all-black to an all-white environment . . . I was feeling less than a man. . . . I had to adapt and was trying to understand myself. . . . On entering school, I started getting sick, like stomach ulcers, a nervous condition. . . . I wasn't motivated. . . . I seemed very confused, didn't have any goals. . . . I was walking around kind of dazed. . . . I was so depressed I really felt like quitting."

Reality problems, that is, traumatic life events beyond one's control, are the source of unhappiness for 15 percent of the sample: "I was only 16, and a man raped me. . . . Every time I go home, one of my kin is dead. . . . My father had a severe stroke." Ten percent of the problems involved difficulties with significant others, people with whom the students had close or intimate relationships. "My father has an alcohol problem. . . . My parents were in the process of separating. . . . My marriage started falling apart. . . . I had two beautiful daughters, and in leaving my home, I had to leave them behind. . . . I fell in love with a girl and then caught her messing around." Closely related were social problems in relating to nonsignificant others and the social environment. Nine percent of the problems were of this variety: "Problems getting along with other people. . . . I had never stayed on campus before, and everyone seemed so rude. . . . I really didn't know how to meet people. . . . I never felt I was given a fair chance. . . . Roommate trouble." Thus, these three categories (together accounting for 34 percent of the worst experiences) speak to the various kinds of interpersonal vulnerabilities, ranging from traumatic loss or injury to the absence of friendship.

Finally, 8 percent of the problems are due to constraint, that is, circumstances that prevent goal attainment: "Injuries prevented me from getting a scholarship. . . . I wanted a job and could never get one. . . . I was frustrated because I didn't have any money. . . . I had to go out and get a job to take care of my child." The problems in this category boil down to those of financial constraint, the one area in which there is a difference between TSU and UH students, with the former experiencing more financial problems (13.5 percent versus 7.8 percent, p = .05).

Another interesting aspect of stress is the manner in which students handle the unhappy periods. Many students, (47 percent of them) handle their problems in directly instrumental ways by taking some positive action. "The first thing was summer school, and another was to study more. . . . I got in there and fought with it. . . . I started making friends. . . . I quit my boyfriend. . . . I got a new roommate." Only 16 percent took a passive approach to stress by doing little or nothing to change their state of affairs: "I just let time take its toll. . . . There was nothing that could be done. . . . I just gave up after I tried. . . . I really have stepped away from it. . . . I regressed, withdrew into a world of my own."

The Experience of Satisfaction. In order to probe what constitutes happy experiences in the lives of college students, we asked them to describe the time in their lives that was the happiest or nicest. They could talk about any period, not just a time in college, as long as things were really going well for an extended period of time.

Academic achievements are most likely to be a source of happiness for both TSU and UH students, with 20 percent of the happiest times revolving around such incidents. "My course loads seemed to get more interesting. . . . This course had the most tremendous impact on me. . . . My major is journalism, and I did very well in it. . . . I was getting straight A's. . . . I made dean's list." Positive interpersonal relationships were second most likely to initiate happy periods. Thirteen percent of the responses were of this nature: "I met a lot of nice people. . . . A whole new set of people. . . . My roommate and I have a very good relationship. . . . When I met her, everything was cool." Extracurricular activities constituted another 11 percent of the responses: "I had just made the team. . . . I was the most valuable player. . . . I was running for black homecoming queen. . . . I've been in the community choir, and I go places singing. . . . I get to organize things and help people." Finally, family-related events were the source of happiness in 10 percent of the cases: "My father came back with us, and we were all back together again. . . . I made my mother happy. . . . I got married, and things just kind of rolled along. . . . I used to stay with my cousin Ruth—she wanted to adopt me."

Several other categories assume minor roles in student responses, such as graduation from high school, maturation, childhood events, nonacademic accomplishments, travel, and religion. A few students even cite the mere absence of any identifiable problems as the happiest time, while 11 percent cited unclear events that usually involved time periods ("last two years of high school," "one of my birthdays") rather than events. In this last category, TSU and UH students did differ such that 17 percent of UH students but only 5 percent of TSU students referred to unclear time periods ($p = .01$).

The Differential Experience of Stress and Satisfaction. At Texas Southern, students are more likely to cope with stressful experiences by talking to people: "I talked to people. . . . I talked to my advisers. . . . I talked to friends. . . . I started asking people who had gone through the same thing. . . . I went to a psychiatrist. . . . I kept talking to them to make them see my point of view." Freshmen and seniors do not differ in their inclination to handle stress by talking it out with someone. It does seem that the greater the opportunity to talk troubles away, the less the likelihood of interpersonal stress.

TSU seniors report fewer instances of stress involving significant others. Eight of the nine instances reported by TSU students come from freshmen. It takes very little imagination to see that the presence of interpersonal supports (that is, people willing to listen) seems to constitute a buffer against feelings of personal disappointment. It is as if a burden that arises from impaired relationships is partially lifted by the comfort of another relationship. In other words, a broken interpersonal connection can be repaired if a new interpersonal connection can be established or an old one invoked. Over time, the cumulative effect of knowing that there are people available to talk one over the interpersonal rough spots is much like developing an immunity to failing relationships. However, other problems, such as academics or frustrating life circumstances, seem less responsive to interpersonal catharsis.

Of course, individuals may find different uses for the immunity to interpersonal disaster conferred by a black college environment. TSU has an impact on the manner in which males interpret happy experiences. Senior males report fewer incidents of interpersonal happiness than freshmen. The differences hold even when subjects consider only happy experiences occurring during college. Men seem to use reduced vulnerability to interpersonal stress to divest themselves of positive emotions in the same area. This tendency smacks of macho behavior that conjures visions of men who have their emotions under control, men who neither cry nor laugh about their relationships with other people. Yet the image of interpersonal detachment is suspect, especially given what we already know about men who are struggling to suppress achievement-related conflicts. Note that the motivation literature clearly attributes the source of achievement conflicts to early relationships with significant others (McClelland, 1961; Sullivan, 1953).

Detachment may well have some immediate costs for our black Western heroes. Rather than citing specific events that initiated happy periods, a few young men insist upon pointing to unclear occurrences delineated by past periods (for example, "last two years of high school," "one of my birthdays"). As a group, TSU students give vague answers much less often than UH students. But, over time, TSU males become more likely to give vague time referents. If this tendency is related to their quest for interpersonal detachment, it may be a stylistic consequence of their avoidance of focusing on specific events. As they struggle to avoid awareness of conflicts that may be interpersonal in nature, their conversation may take on a vague quality in the service of forgetting the past.

TSU also affects women's thinking about critical events, but in a different way. Some students report that their happiest periods revolve around high school graduation—a period in the past. Only among women is the reporting of such past events affected by college. Senior women at TSU report fewer such incidents than freshmen. It is probably natural that seniors should think less about the nostalgia of their happy high school years. As time goes on, new experiences attain more immediacy than past ones, so that one can live in the happiness of the present or look forward to good times in the future. Yet, of these students, TSU women are best able to break nostalgic ties.

In sum, the TSU experience is different from that at UH in that it offers more opportunities to talk to people in times of need. This kind of interpersonal support can confer a kind of immunity to interpersonal stress. During such times, the chance to establish new relationships or call upon old ones has a power to restore the sense of interpersonal belonging. Women seem best able to use this immunity to enjoy happy times in the present, rather than to revel in nostalgia. Men, on the other hand, tend to misuse the social comfort of college and strive for interpersonal detachment from others. Possibly they may also seek to flee the interpersonal conflicts of the past. Ultimately, however, they may lose touch with themselves.

College life at the University of Houston seems to offer an interpersonal experience that is the exact opposite of that at TSU. UH students are less likely to report solving problems by talking to other people. Instead, they make more use of mental distraction to handle unhappiness: "I decided to block off my mind. . . . I tried to forget about it. . . . Hysterical amnesia, I just forgot it." This method may not allow students to discharge the lingering tension. It may therefore give rise to as many problems as it solves. UH students show increasing vulnerability to interpersonal stress from freshman to senior year, with seniors reporting significantly more incidents of interpersonal unhappiness. With fewer opportunities to share sorrow and only the comforts of one's own mental processes, the experience of interpersonal trauma is felt more acutely over time.

The impact of this obviously lonely environment is felt more keenly by black males. As seniors, they dwell more on periods of interpersonal happiness than freshmen, suggesting that the strongest positive and negative emotions are drawn upon to fill the interpersonal void. These men also become more specific in the happy incidents that they mention. This pattern is the reverse of the detached and vague style employed by TSU men. Perhaps, as the stressfulness of the UH environment prompts these men to think more of closeness with significant others, their achievement conflicts, rooted in early relationships, are closer to consciousness. If so, the relative immediacy of interpersonal issues may obviate the need for vagueness in conversation. However, the stress of loneliness and alienation during the college years probably serves little purpose as far as intellectual development is concerned. UH women seem to respond to their situations by becoming more nostalgic about the good old days of high school—another way to avoid coming to terms with the present situation and coping successfully with the source of one's difficulties.

Thus, to the extent that the UH and TSU environments are different, the relative loneliness of college life at UH deprives black students of the opportunity to talk to people in times of stress. Unable to discharge emotional tension through interpersonal catharsis, they become particularly susceptible to disappointments from people they care about. Feelings of disconnectedness make these students sensitive to abandonment by others. However, the stress of abandonment seems to be exacerbated by a lonely college environment. Students' unresolved conflicts seem to prevent mastery of a bad situation.

Summary. After listening to black students in two college environments, we must notice that they share many of the same kinds of stress and the same sources of happiness. College influences their perceptions of stressful and happy times in only one respect. They are not different in their perception of academic and intellectual concerns, as we might expect from the differences in degrees of cognitive development. They differ only in their vulnerability to interpersonal stress and in the degree to which they are absorbed with interpersonal issues. They differ in the number of people they talk to and in the quality of their interactions.

At Texas Southern, more students cope with stress by talking to friends, advisers, teachers, and professional counselors. In other words, they seem able to call upon a wide range of contacts to help them through difficult times. Over time, their ability to use old or new relationships for help confers a relative immunity to the stress of impaired relationships. The presence of supportive people, who listen to their troubles, offers them a protection against the experience of loss, rejection, or abandonment. On the other hand, the relative loneliness of the UH environment leaves black students unprotected from interpersonal trauma. Because they are unable to share interpersonal burdens, these students appear to experience more instances of interpersonal stress. They also tend to dwell more on the joys of interpersonal relationships. One aspect of alienation, so apparent in the development profiles of UH students, appears to be an inadequate number of people (or inadequate use of people) to satisfy normal adolescent needs for sharing.

Clearly, the pattern of interpersonal stress is associated with differential patterns of cognitive development at TSU and UH. The sense of connectedness to others apparent at TSU seems to free students from interpersonal trauma. It may also free their energies for constructive use in cognitive development. At UH, the preoccupation with interpersonal issues may bind energies, making them unavailable to assist the process of intellectual growth. If, as we suspect, black students bring to the college environment conflicts over achievement that are, by definition, rooted in early relationships, these students may be particularly susceptible to the presence or lack of interpersonal supports in their new environments. Perhaps for black students in particular, the presence of sound interpersonal anchors not only may be associated with intellectual development but may well constitute a precondition for growth in the cognitive domain.

Conclusions

The four studies reported in this chapter have been designed to confirm or negate the exploratory findings in Georgia,
where predominantly black colleges promote more positive intellectual growth than predominantly white institutions. In
Georgia, the black and white colleges studied possess very different institutional characteristics; these differences had a potential to confound results. In Texas, on the other hand, subject
institutions exhibit markedly similar characteristics. Both are
large urban universities with larger than usual commuter populations. Each of the four studies performed in Texas provides a
different kind of confirmation that predominantly black Texas
Southern University fosters more positive growth than does
predominantly white University of Houston.

First, a study of the impact of college on the general
functioning of black college students shows that Texas Southern fosters a well-rounded development, in which students show
gains in grade averages, intellectual self-confidence, and achievement motivation. Positive developments in both the intellectual
and psychosocial aspects of functioning seem to produce greater
energy and ambition over the four years. In contrast, at the
University of Houston, student development appears to be conflicted. While students show excellent progress in academic
functioning, they also show signs of identity alienation, unhappiness, and loss of ambition.

The second study employs three nontraditional measures
of cognitive growth and finds that students at Texas Southern
show evidence of gains on two of these new instruments. But at
the University of Houston, black women show a gain on only
one of these measures, while black males show more evidence of
declining cognitive skill.

In the third study, students competed on achievement
tests in either black or white working environments. Although
Texas Southern students show signs of achievement-related conflicts and physiological stress during competition, they nonetheless show evidence of improving ability to compete well, especially in white working environments, and greater capacity to

enjoy competition in the senior year. These results suggest that Texas Southern helps students channel conflicts in a constructive manner that prepares them to compete well in integrated settings. On the other hand, at the University of Houston, there are no signs that students improve in their ability to compete. In fact, they seem to suffer a diminished capacity to enjoy competitive encounters.

Finally, an interview study that probed sources of stress and satisfaction during the college years shows that Texas Southern provides a more supportive interpersonal environment. The presence of more people to talk to appears to help students most during times of stress and confers a relative immunity to interpersonal stress over the four years. These results suggest that the stronger interpersonal supports found more often in predominantly black colleges constitute a necessary precondition for intellectual development. In contrast, the University of Houston is a relatively lonely environment for its black students, who do not have enough people to talk to in times of need. This means that valuable energies are diverted from the growth process to cope with the immediate feelings of loneliness and abandonment.

These studies suggest that, while objective institutional resources may be necessary for maximal growth in the college years, stronger interpersonal supports may be the essential ingredient for solid intellectual development.

7

:◆:

Colleges in the Deep South: Reversing the Patterns of Cosmopolitan Environments

The pattern of stronger intellectual growth in predominantly black colleges has been discovered and confirmed in two cosmopolitan areas of the South. In both major cities, black colleges provide more favorable learning environments, but distinct regional differences flavored the pattern of results. Different as the two metropolitan areas are, they are both major centers of business, education, and cultural activity. In both, the Southern way of life is changing rapidly. If, as we suspect, the regional environment has a definite influence on black and white college environments, what is the impact of colleges on black students in smaller towns in a remote area of the Deep South? Will black schools' pattern of greater cognitive gain hold up where life in general, and the traditional status of blacks in particular, have changed less dramatically than in Georgia and Texas?

The state of Mississippi offers the necessary contrast. A truly rural state with a slow record of economic and educational development, Mississippi also has the reputation of an extreme resister to racial integration. Would this state's extreme posture toward blacks have an effect on the pattern of cognitive growth that has emerged thus far in the cosmopolitan South? To find out, we added predominantly black "Freedmen College" and predominantly white "Magnolia College" to the sample. These two schools also offer a good comparative look at the differential effects of small, private institutions on black students.

The small populations of the Mississippi colleges suited us, since we intended to conduct only a limited replication of the previous studies. With a compelling pattern of stronger cognitive growth in black colleges established in nine colleges and two states, the purpose of the remaining work was to determine only the potential generality of this pattern. The 80 students (15 male and 35 female freshmen and 11 male and 19 female seniors) recruited from "Freedmen" and the 51 students (11 male and 18 female freshmen and 13 male and 9 female seniors) from coed "Magnolia" were sufficient for this purpose. The design problems encountered in recruiting from "Magnolia," a school with very small numbers of blacks enrolled, are discussed in Chapter Three. The basic questionnaire comprised the battery of instruments used to determine the generality of the findings. As usual, these instruments were administered to cross sections of freshmen and seniors, with the significant differences between the two groups used to infer developmental change.

Development at "Freedmen College"

The investigation of "Freedmen" and "Magnolia" colleges dramatically underscores the fact that Mississippi is indeed a very different region from Georgia and Texas. Not only are the results different in this state, but they also present us with something of a mystery. In Mississippi, the results come closest to a reversal of the usual pattern of better cognitive growth in black colleges. In both colleges, net psychological growth is stunted. The results leave us with the problematical and abiding suspicion that too much is hidden from view in Mississippi; too many paradoxes are left unexplained.

If a school's reputation is any guide to its impact on intellectual growth, "Freedmen" should produce admirable student development. "Freedmen College" is one of those black schools known for doing a lot with very little. Despite its small size and resources, it boasts many distinguished alumni and has been described by Jencks and Riesman (1968) as a "pedagogic leader." "Freedmen" was in its 100th year at the time of the study and enrolled about 1,000 students. Its history began in 1869, although the school did not begin granting B.A. degrees until 1901.

Over the years, "Freedmen" has involved itself in a number of notable cooperative and exchange programs with other institutions. The Brown-"Freedmen" relationship has attracted national attention and serves as a model for other institutions with similar interests. The Brown-"Freedmen" program began in 1964 and has become one of the most wide-ranging and pervasive undertakings of its kind. "Freedmen" also cooperates with American University, the University of Denver, and "Magnolia College." It also participated (with "Magnolia") in the effort to establish a free university during the civil rights era. In philosophy, "Freedmen" strives to encourage students to apply critical thought to all areas of life and to bridge the gap between a college education and practical experience. Of course, the college remains dedicated to the belief in the equality of all people.

Despite "Freedmen" 's reputation and philosophy, this study's findings show more evidence of intellectual stagnation and even deterioration than at any other black college. By comparing freshmen and seniors, we glimpse the devastating developmental implication that "Freedmen" students show not only intellectual stagnation but deteriorating ambitions and identity disintegration. There were no gains at all in academic performance. This absence of academic development occurs alongside admiration for faculty members. In general, positive involvement with faculty helps stimulate growth. In Mississippi, it does not—at least not at "Freedmen." Motivation to get good grades drops off. However, students also profess choosing majors because of competence in the area—a finding that suggests intrinsic reasons for performing well academically, reasons that are not reflected in actual performance. Of intellectual development at "Freedmen," the best that can be said is that students develop a desire for competence in an academic area. This competence, however, is not readily displayed.

In intellectual matters, "Freedmen" students show little evidence of improvement, but in career ambition, they display unmistakable evidence of lowered goals. In vocational interest, seniors become less investigative and enterprising. Respectively, these dimensions represent the desire to know that culminates in scientific investigation and the outgoing organizational skills that bespeak business enterprise. Clearly, losses in such skills are losses in areas highly valued in this society. Paradoxically, enterprise is an area in which black colleges often enhance interest. Scores for "Freedmen" students on the career orientation scale drop, indicating losses not only in investigative and enterprising interest but in general career ambitions. Finally, on the self-concept measures, "Freedmen" seniors show lower scores on the ambition cluster of items. Thus, even in their own estimation, there is evidence of waning ambitiousness. Seniors desire earlier ages for marriage than freshmen. This could suggest that curtailed personal career ambitions result in a heightened interest in marriage and family.

Stagnant academic development and losses in ambition are problematical enough for college impact; but, from a psychological point of view, the adjustment problems signaled by losses in identity integration are greater causes for concern. The identity integration scores from the cluster of black ideology items drop from freshman to senior year. There are also difficulties revealed by the adjustment problems factor, which assesses the presence of both academic and personal dilemmas. The psychophysical evidence is that the reported duration of illnesses increases. Furthermore, the personality indications are problematical. Black militance scores from the Black Ideology Scale drop, but blacks in Mississippi would probably do well to curtail their expressions of antiwhite sentiment. Seniors do not consider themselves as dogmatic as freshmen, though dogmatism is another hardheaded quality that blacks in Mississippi might find it expedient to relinquish. However, there is also a drop in scores on the social decorum factor of the self-concept items, a factor that measures a concern with manners and polite behavior. This is one concern that Mississippi blacks may develop to replace militance. Yet polite behavior decreases along with militant attitudes. Perhaps, then, the personality findings indicate a withdrawal of concerns on all fronts, an indication consistent with the other evidence but one suggesting an impoverishment of personality.

Clues as to what is happening to "Freedmen" students are not easy to come by. It is easiest to point to the larger environment of Mississippi and the fact that these students have been raised in a more traditional setting with respect to black development, one very different from any other in this investigation. But if we keep our noses strictly to the data, we find one other possibility. The only student complaint that increases over time is that of unfairness and favoritism in the classroom. This is a complaint not uncommon in black colleges and one that appears to be associated with much bitterness and resentment, especially among male students. However, in other black colleges, students manage to cope with unfairness and simultaneously find ways of growing intellectually through informal instructor relationships and extraschool involvements. At "Freedmen," there is evidence of some positive faculty involvement and extracurricular maneuvering, but these aspects of college do not seem to serve the same function that they do in other black schools. Could the problem of unfairness and favoritism in the classroom be serious enough to thwart intellectual development and douse career ambition?

We can answer this question only with a hypothesis. Suppose that the basic problem for blacks in Mississippi is racial unfairness and favoritism toward whites. And suppose that harsh racism of this kind has a serious effect on developing black motivation and outward display of abilities. This latter point would not be difficult to document. Suppose that black students in college, like Mississippi blacks in general, have a strong adverse reaction to unfairness, to which they respond by withdrawal: withdrawal of motivation, withdrawal of ambition, and withdrawal of the competencies they harbor deep within themselves. This withdrawal mode might be a conditioned response that occurs in the face of unfairness, no matter what the source. It may even be that unfairness on the part of those from whom it is least expected is all the more devastating.

There is a second explanation for the results, which need not contradict the first. Development in the protective environment of "Freedmen" may prepare blacks to function in their traditional roles as blacks in Mississippi. In other words, the pattern of results may amount to a dissimulation strategy, in which an interest in individual competence develops but is safely protected behind a nonambitious demeanor. Such a strategy would explain "Freedmen" 's reputation in the face of these discouraging data, and it would not be the first time that blacks in the Deep South have managed to disguise their intents and purposes. Yet psychological damage to the developing identity is clearly a steep price for the subterfuge.

Development at "Magnolia College"

At predominantly white "Magnolia College," black students run into the now usual problems of adjusting to the social and academic life of the campus, which means that they are faced with a good deal of stress and feelings of personal threat. "Magnolia" black students are unsure of themselves and shy, but they are ambitious enough and have enough family support to try hard. Unfortunately, in the process of trying without making much headway, they lose touch with themselves.

Founded in 1890 as a college for males, later to become a coeducational institution, "Magnolia" enjoys the reputation of an excellent liberal arts college. Students are selected on the basis of their ability to think, their desire to learn, their good moral character, and their intellectual maturity. Students are admitted primarily on the basis of their ability to do college work efficiently. When our research began, almost half of "Magnolia" 's black students were enrolled in a premedical program, which was, unfortunately, discontinued during the three years required to gather the student population (see Chapter Three).

"Magnolia" boasts close personal relationships among students, faculty, and the administration as one of the most vital parts of the college experience. If this congenial atmosphere is realized for other students, black students do not seem to share in the warmth. Yet the college does strive to create a place where persons of all religious faiths can study and work together. As a liberal arts college, "Magnolia" seeks to give students adequate breadth and depth of understanding of civilization and culture in order to broaden their perspective, enrich their personalities, and enable them to think and act intelligently amid the complexities of the modern world. As evidence of its intentions, "Magnolia" has cooperated with "Freedmen College" in a number of educational endeavors over the years. Clearly, "Magnolia" attempts to create the kind of college climate that could benefit any student, but the experiences of black students reveal that they do not reap the benefits expected.

Unlike students at "Freedmen," black students at "Magnolia" manage to salvage something of their cognitive development and to maintain their ambitious career commitments. Also unlike "Freedmen" students, they appear to fight hard to maintain their ambition. But fighting against a poor adjustment to social and academic life creates enough stress to place the identity in serious jeopardy.

"Magnolia" students certainly show more evidence of cognitive development than those at "Freedmen." Overall grade-point averages (for the most recent semester) are the one index where objective evidence of growth can be found. Even if the objective evidence of cognitive growth is not overwhelming, senior students report stronger feelings of intellectual competence. Scores on the intellectual incompetence factor of the self-concept instrument were lower among seniors, and, in particular, seniors reported improvements in their memory. We can be certain, then, that "Magnolia" students experience enhanced feelings of intellectual development over the four years.

While "Magnolia" students maintain their career commitments, their career interests are taking an introspective turn. Commitment to their careers is suggested by their choice of part-time jobs related to the career choice and by family support for their career goals. The family support that these students receive is clearly an important factor, one absent among

"Freedmen" students. Yet, if their commitment to career is firm, the exact nature of their career interests is changing from the artistic to the investigative, especially among males. The move from artistic expressiveness to the investigation of knowledge suggests a turning inward and a development of the introspective side of the personality.

"Magnolia" black students seem stalwart enough to hold their own as far as cognitive development and career commitment are concerned. However, the mounting evidence of an internal focus in feelings of competence and career interests may be a response to the difficulty of adjustment to the social and academic life of the campus. Their academic adjustment can only be described as poor. Scores on the academic adjustment factor are lower among seniors, as are their ratings of the faculty and the course of instruction. Seniors, especially women, are least likely to describe their teachers as encouraging or interested in them. Not surprisingly, the effort put into academics falls off over time. Seniors at "Magnolia" do express positive feelings about extracurricular activities and other students, but these sentiments do not outweigh the fact that seniors have poor scores on the social adjustment scale. In addition, seniors suffer more from severe illnesses and feelings of personal threat. Clearly, this portrait of college life is one of a stressful existence.

As could be anticipated from the growing internal focus among "Magnolia" students, many of the changes influencing them are in the subjective world of the personality. The experiences of the four years seem to have made them feel more aggressive, more conscious of their blackness, less accepting of white authority, less shy, and less fatigued. These trends toward more aggressive personalities are, of course, common at white colleges, where the treatment black students receive inspires them to greater assertiveness. Merely as a defense against poor treatment, this syndrome has rarely had positive consequences for black development. Here, evidence of progressive identity disintegration (from the Black Ideology Scale) confirms that black personalities are suffering, in spite of aggressive displays.

Despite the aggressive trends reported by these students, they still feel more passive as seniors than as freshmen. This inconsistency may be a signal that they are having a difficult time pulling all of the pieces of themselves together in the face of their external environment. The end result, of course, is a psychological sense of identity that has suffered a serious setback in these four years.

Conclusions

We took a cursory look at the state of Mississippi to see whether the regional impact of the Deep South would affect the pattern of greater cognitive growth in predominantly black colleges. The effect of the Deep South is different indeed. It is different not only in the fact that the predominantly black college does not promote better cognitive growth but also in that there is a reversal of the usual pattern. The predominantly white college promotes better intellectual development, while the black institution fosters what can best be described as intellectual stagnation and deteriorating ambition. What accounts for this surprise turnaround in the results, and how much does it have to do with the social climate in Mississippi?

There is a subtle but noticeable sense of a mystery in the data, a feeling that something is being hidden from view. For example, "Freedmen College" has a good reputation and boasts many distinguished alumni, but the data show only that, on the average, students at this school are worse off as seniors than as entering freshmen. Of course, the evidence for "Freedmen" 's poor showing comes from developmental analyses of cross sections of freshmen and seniors. It is, however, unusual that the comparisons of freshman and senior cohorts show nothing of what happens to students in the institution—giving the impression that all is well, when it is not. This last point may seem trivial, but add to it the fact that a concern with competence does grow among "Freedmen" students, despite the fact that this concern is overshadowed by lowered ambition, cognitive stagnation, and impoverished personality.

"Magnolia" development is very different, but there is also the feeling that more is happening to these students internally than externally. The best evidence indicates that their expressive interests become introspective, as if they have begun turning inward to find something that they might have lost. We know for sure that students in both colleges have lost a grip on pieces of their identity. Identity disintegration over the four years of college is what black students in both Mississippi schools have in common. If there is anything to be said for the development of black students in the Deep South, it is that the process of higher education does not appear to be helping in a psychologically important respect. Unless something happens to turn the tide, students in both of these liberal arts schools will have difficulty finding their sense of direction or experiencing feelings of success or belonging. Yet, if we examine the strategies used by students in each school—for even the poorest patterns of development represent coping strategies—we may discover some of the coping mechanisms of Mississippi blacks.

Consider the "Freedmen" pattern of development as a mode of self-protection that has distinct survival value in Mississippi. Furthermore, think of this pattern as a response to or defense against racial (or interpersonal) inequity. These students begin to develop their competencies, but then they stop. Perhaps the first feel of real competence is too threatening, because they have learned somehow that overt displays of competence among blacks do not curry much favor in Mississippi. And so they display no gain in competence in their schoolwork and profess as little ambition as possible. The nonambitious demeanor is, unfortunately, not a ruse; for these students also abdicate the desire to manage their world effectively or to know more than they must about why competence is taboo. The scores on both enterprising and investigative vocational interests support the interpretation that abdication is necessary. Giving up in this way leaves students able to do what they are told, performing easy, conventional tasks that do not tax the bitter adjustment they have made. We have to ask why this mode of coping is observed in the black but not the white college. Perhaps in Mississippi, blacks have invested a great deal in surviving. Self-protection by a nonambitious demeanor is undoubtedly a survival tactic that has worked well and is thus communicated to young blacks in many conscious as well as unconscious ways. The pattern may not do much for intellectual development, but then survival has always been the first priority of blacks in hostile surroundings.

Just to show that there is more than one way to skin a cat, black students at "Magnolia" have adopted a different strategy for surviving college in a predominantly white community. Probably the most important ingredient in their pattern is the family support for their career goals. These students appear to have a different kind of family orientation from that of their counterparts at "Freedmen," one that spurs them on to a more aggressive outlook. They aspire to ambitious heights and hang on to their career commitments during the four years. Indeed, despite the interpersonal tensions they are subject to, they show as much cognitive growth as black students in most predominantly white colleges. Their personalities take on an aggressive side, while they attempt to satisfy their interests in white culture and still hold on to a black consciousness. But the stresses are great and affect them academically, emotionally, and physically. The stresses affect them in a particular way. They do not give up in any of the ways that their "Freedmen" counterparts do, but they exhibit a more introspective turn in their career interests. Thus, they maintain and manage their internal feelings and external tensions by developing a heightened need to know. Perhaps through this mechanism, the personality beckons to the individuals who have lost hold of their identity; perhaps it invites them to discover either themselves or the secrets that humanity needs to know.

The protective and discovery modes of coping with life in Mississippi are extreme insofar as the troubled identity is concerned. They may also seem peculiar to life in the Deep South. But there are some lessons in Mississippi that could benefit our understanding of black development in other states. For instance, it may be that cognitive stagnation or deterioration is a way of self-protection not only in Mississippi but also in other environments. Students at "Freedmen" may resort to this mode readily, but circumstances in many of the predominantly white colleges observed so far may also trigger subliminal mechanisms that lead black students to hide their competence and profess less ambition than they started with. Indeed, the "Freedmen" survival strategy may have value beyond Mississippi.

8

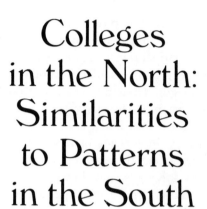

Colleges in the North: Similarities to Patterns in the South

In terms of intellectual development among black students, the South is characterized by poor intellectual development in predominantly white colleges and greater intellectual gains in black colleges. This pattern is strong in progressive cities of the South that act as crossroads, centers of growth and change. But in the Deep South, where the position of blacks is still relatively constricted, blacks, consciously or unconsciously, still direct their energies toward survival rather than development. Yet the reversal of our pattern in the Deep South comes almost as a relief. We are observing, it seems, not a hard and fast rule but patterns of personal adaptation to environments that vary by region. If the Southern phenomenon is not immutable, what does development for black students look like in the North? Are we talking about a pattern that is linked to Southern mores regarding blacks, which does not extend to the more benign North, where most black students attend school? Will the North's traditional

118

sympathy for blacks in the South be reflected in Northern black students' current educational development?

The state of Ohio offers a perfect testing ground, because of the presence of two predominantly black institutions (Wilberforce and Central State) and two predominantly white colleges ("Northern University" and Ohio State). These pairs of institutions provide a reasonable match of private and public institutional characteristics. About 800 students were recruited (see the breakdown for each college in Table 1 at the end of Chapter Three). A limited replication of the study was planned. Only the questionnaire instrument provides data on black students in Northern colleges. The questionnaire data show no significant edge for black students in white schools over their counterparts in predominantly black schools. In fact, the dominant pattern of better cognitive development in black schools in the South emerges to haunt the North. Yet the North possesses an environment all its own. The Southern phenomenon is bolder, while that of the North is quieter and, thus, harder to observe. Like the South, the North produces positive and negative aspects of development in each of the schools investigated, black and white. The subtle effects of the Northern environment are imprinted on all four of the schools studied. Attitudes in the North toward blacks are said to be marked by far more inconsistency than those in the South. The inconsistencies found in our results, then, document the emotional consequences of ambivalent treatment.

Impact of Private Colleges in the North

The first set of comparisons considered are those between the two private colleges, predominantly black Wilberforce (where our study population consisted of 74 male and 55 female freshmen and 55 male and 38 female seniors) and predominantly white "Northern University" (where our population consisted of 32 male and 48 female freshmen and 34 male and 39 female seniors). Just as they were in the Southern findings, the differences in development between black and white schools are more pronounced in private colleges. The differences in cognitive growth in favor of the black private college are more noticeable, as are the consequences of inconsistent developmental pressures at the white college. The consequences of a Northern environment, however, are apparent in both private institutions.

Development at Wilberforce University. At Wilberforce, we return to the familiar pattern of outstanding cognitive development in black institutions. Yet we also face some of the familiar problems of black colleges. In philosophy, Wilberforce stresses attaining excellence and learning to earn a living, and the empirical evidence of intellectual development verifies this concern. Wilberforce is also concerned with helping students face challenges, but several challenges of adolescent development go unmet.

The proof that Wilberforce confers good intellectual development comes from two basic sources: academic performance and intellectual self-concept. Wilberforce seniors make a better showing than freshmen on four of the six measures of academic performance; the seniors also express stronger feelings of intellectual competence. Undoubtedly, this show of intellectual development is closely associated with the many positive feelings that students express about academic life at Wilberforce. Those students became increasingly satisfied with their college choice and with Wilberforce's instructors and courses. Although seniors see the courses as more demanding and experience their share of academic problems, their reports of involvement with faculty and admiration for instructors offset these difficulties. Like students in many of the other colleges, Wilberforce students exhibit strong academic development that is not produced by the desire to get good grades.

Good academic progress at Wilberforce, born of satisfaction with the academic environment, translates into some of the best career development found at any of the fifteen colleges studied. Seniors seek more assistance from faculty members in choosing their careers. They develop more serious plans for graduate school and report less indecision over plans for graduate school. Most important, seniors exhibit higher levels of educational and vocational aspirations. Women develop a preference for continuing their education after graduation rather than working. Seniors more often think that they will be able to integrate marriage and careers successfully, a sign that they envision no conflicts between the two goals.

The rule so far has been that if intellectual development is accompanied by social development, an observable influx of energy benefits the personality. Such is the case at Wilberforce. Seniors seem to feel more socially integrated into campus life, and feelings of social isolation wane over the years. The adjustment value of extracurricular involvements should not be underestimated. As the intellectual and social elements of growth occur together, seniors report stronger feelings of energy, independence, and outspokenness. From a psychological point of view, then, we could not hope for better personality integration than that which occurs at Wilberforce.

While development at Wilberforce is good, even excellent in a psychological sense, it is not perfect. There are at least three areas in which Wilberforce students are not meeting some of the greater challenges of college development. In the first place, differences between the sexes favor males, as in other black schools. At Wilberforce, males achieve the best social adjustment, the warmest feelings for other students, and the most admiration for faculty. Males also show the best satisfaction with their academic lives and report the most positive feelings for instructors and courses.

In the second place, conventional vocational interests are alarmingly higher among seniors. This finding occurs in spite of other ambitious-looking developments in career orientation. Are there still conventional influences in the career patterns, no matter how ambitious the career developments might seem? Or does this trend mean that there are limits to the ambitions of these students? Where are the enterprising career interests so strongly suggested by the developments in the intellectual sphere? One clue is that seniors see the tight job market as an obstacle to their careers; this could signal a fear of competition in the job market. It simply looks as if the stellar growth in the career area is not being channeled as well as it might be.

Third, despite the good development at Wilberforce,

there is still considerable stress. Illnesses become longer and more severe. More life changes occur, and all seniors experience more personal stress. It may be that the normal process of growth in the intellect and personality is accompanied by stress. But it may also be that the North is marked by cross-messages, which tell an individual that it is all right to succeed in college, as long as successful development is channeled along conventional (not entrepreneurial) lines. Perhaps there are fewer outlets for good intellectual growth in the North than we might think.

Development at "Northern University." In contrast to relatively good development at Wilberforce, black students at predominantly white "Northern University" suffer much conflict throughout the developmental profile. These students do indeed develop ambition, but it may be the kind of ambition that falls short of actual fulfillment. If a stronger career orientation were all that mattered, "Northern University" black students would be doing well. Seniors show more involvement in the career selection process. Career plans become more definitive, that is, less ambivalent and more specific. Seniors more often choose careers either on the basis of some competence or to benefit the race. Males in particular develop scientific vocational interests. Senior women worry less about money obstacles to their careers but more about stiff competition in the job market. All in all, black student ambitions are very much intact.

Despite heightened career development, there is no evidence of cognitive growth to support these ambitions. Effects were found neither on any of the measures of academic performance nor on any of the subjective measures of intellectual gain. With no real cognitive gains in sight, suspicion is cast on the validity of career aspirations. The question is, can black students translate their career interests into tangible goals in the absence of cognitive development?

The problems of black students at "Northern University" are by no means confined to academic and career development. The difficulties extend to their adjustment to college life. On the one hand, seniors have developed some resources that they did not have as freshmen. There are faculty members whom they can admire and ask for help, and they have learned to work well under pressure. Their increasing extracurricular involvements offer an important outlet during these years. But these positive indications are undermined by a decline in the level of academic adjustment that extends to disillusionment with the course of instruction, the faculty, and other students. Seniors become more dissatisfied with the teaching methods and experience more academic problems than freshmen. Scores on the social adjustment scale are lower in the senior year, indicating a decline in this area of college life.

Even in personality, evidence of inconsistencies mars the positive developments. While consciousness about black heritage is on the rise, so is evidence of defensiveness surrounding black identity. Males show so many inconsistencies in their self-concepts as to suggest the growth of two different sides to the personality, one positive and one negative. On the one hand, senior males describe themselves as more aggressive and dogmatic; they also report stronger ambition. At the same time, they become more shy and irresponsible. Women seem to become less considerate and more intellectually incompetent.

If we are correct in suggesting that inconsistencies exist in every aspect of development, there should be some evidence of internal strain beyond the stress indications of more life changes and personal stress in the senior year. It appears that males, more affected by the cross-pressures, attempt some resolution of these conflicts in their personal lives. The anticipated difficulties of combining marriage and career lessen over time, and senior males plan to marry at earlier ages than their freshman counterparts. Furthermore, senior males want to have more male children and prefer male children to female children. This is not the first time that males have been observed trying to work out developmental traumas through the family setting. "Traditional University" males in Georgia were a previous example. But, in this context, males seem more intent on having male children to live through than on traditional male dominance within the home. If black men in the North somehow feel blocked from living out their career ambitions, then perhaps

they can channel their frustrations by transferring their hopes
and dreams to male heirs. In this way, sons can be used vicari-
ously to ease feelings of impotence.

While men channel their ambitions into elaborate defensive maneuvers, women do not appear to require these techniques. This is simply because they are less ambitious than men
in the first place. Their fear of job competition and heightened
feelings of intellectual incompetence will surely pose problems.
Yet they plan to use their jobs to benefit the race and perhaps
fulfill frustrated ambitions by working on behalf of others.

In most respects, black student development is far better
at Wilberforce than at "Northern University." Intellectually,
Wilberforce seniors show good improvement in academic efficiency as well as greater intellectual self-confidence. Enhanced
career aspirations follow logically. But, at "Northern University," career ambitions far exceed intellectual growth, a trend
that bodes ill for real-world performance. Wilberforce students
grow more independent and energetic, as expected of students
who effect a good social as well as intellectual adjustment to
college. But, by the senior year at "Northern University," black
personalities begin to reflect inconsistencies in social and intellectual adjustment. These inconsistencies are highly suggestive
of intrapsychic conflict.

In most respects, then, Wilberforce students are better
off as seniors than as freshmen. Wilberforce students improve
intellectually and in career aspirations, although conventional
thinking may restrict the uses to which their cognitive growth is
put. At "Northern University," noble ambitions may fall short
of fulfillment because they are not backed by intellectual
growth. One way or another, black students in Northern private
schools are less likely to develop entrepreneurial skill than their
counterparts in the progressive South.

Impact of Public Colleges in the North

The pattern of better intellectual development among
blacks in black private colleges also holds in public colleges in
the North. However, the differences between the two types of

institutions—black public and white public—are not as great. Furthermore, the cognitive issues in development are overshadowed by evidence of sexist influences at predominantly black Central State (where our study population consisted of 61 male and 63 female freshmen and 57 male and 51 female seniors) and inconsistent development at predominantly white Ohio State (where our population consisted of 57 male and 86 female freshmen and 20 male and 41 female seniors).

Development at Central State University. Sex differences in favor of males at Central State arise in so many areas of development that sexist influences become the major issue. Black colleges in general show sexist influences, but Central State may be the extreme. It is true that both sexes share in the cognitive gains. Grades in the major subject are higher among seniors. More seniors report that college has indeed contributed to their cognitive growth, and seniors suffer less from feelings of intellectual incompetence. Although women share in the cognitive gains, these gains do not have the same career implications for both sexes. Seniors in general are more involved in their career decisions, show less career ambivalence, and study subjects in which there are good job opportunities. But only males develop enterprising career interests. Females lower their aspirations and give up plans to pursue advanced degrees. So, despite career involvement by both sexes, only males get a career boost in the process.

Factors that induce women at Central to lower their ambitions may begin with their poor adjustment to college life. Men experience the best adjustment to college. They develop the most positive feelings for the college and admiration for faculty. They develop the warmest feelings for fellow students and the best social integration. Since personal accomplishments become less important to men, they may derive their greatest benefit from interpersonal liaisons. For women, only the pressures of academic adjustment are salient. For them, instructors become the worst part of college. Although they have learned to work well under pressure, they become dissatisfied with their academic performance. Although seniors of both sexes report more positive feelings about instruction, it looks as if women

feel less supported by faculty. At the same time, women are
strikingly unable to share in the social developments that round
out the college experience for men. Seniors of both sexes complain more about academic problems than freshmen, but males
more often develop faculty attachments and social diversions to
offset these complaints.

Even in personality development, females suffer the
most. Both sexes are more energetic and assertive as seniors.
Men, however, seem to become even more assertive, evidenced
by increasing hostility to white authority. Women report being
less obedient as seniors, which may be their way of trying to assert themselves. But if it is, it may not be the best way, since
they succeed in becoming more unhappy as seniors. Women at
Central State, then, are not content with their second-class developmental status. It is only in the area of psychophysical
stress that women achieve some equality of development. Seniors of both sexes experience fewer bodily symptoms but have
longer illnesses and stronger feelings of personal threat. Again,
stress is a part of college development.

Central State remains true to the black college image of
good intellectual and social development but confers the best of
college development upon its male students. For black women,
black colleges above the Mason-Dixon Line offer no refuge from
male dominance.

Development at Ohio State University. Like the situation
at "Northern University," black students at predominantly
white Ohio State exhibit so many contradictions in development that it is hard to tell where they stand as seniors. Nonetheless, there are many good aspects to development, making
the college one of the more positive environments for black students. Black students at Ohio State show no objective gains in
cognitive growth. There were no effects for any of the six
measures of academic performance. But somehow these students seem to feel that they have developed in this area. They
express more satisfaction with the major subject as seniors and
more often report that college has contributed to their cognitive growth.

Career development is also inconsistent. Despite stronger

evidence of career involvement in the senior year, there is also more ambivalence over the choice of career alternatives. It comes as no surprise that contradictory influences in the developmental profile render students indecisive about their future lives. Furthermore, black women seniors less often choose their careers on the basis of their competence in an area and do not feel that grades are essential to their career goals. It may be that women are trying to cope with the subliminal feelings of incompetence that go along with the absence of objective intellectual gain, despite protestations to the contrary. Another contradiction surfaces in career orientation. Seniors more often claim to choose their careers because they are interested in the area and because of the opportunities to deal with people. Yet, on the only rise in vocational interests, seniors are higher only in mechanically oriented areas that involve the manipulation of objects, rather than people.

The saga of contradiction continues with adjustment to academic life. For black students, there are enough positive aspects to development to suggest a good adjustment. More seniors think that the instructors are the best part of college, and students become more involved in extracurricular activities over time. These are elements of adjustment that have stimulated academic development in a number of other schools. But here, in addition to there being no development in academic functioning, more senior males think that their personal failure is the worst part of college. Furthermore, seniors of both sexes experience more academic problems. Thus, good and bad aspects of academic adjustment exist side by side and seem to have the effect of neutralizing intellectual growth.

The developments in personality functioning, however, are free of contradictions. The changes in this area are all geared to enhance assertiveness. Seniors report that they are less tired, less passive, and less obedient than freshmen, Among seniors, there is more black consciousness and less acceptance of white authority. Seniors report stronger ambition on a cluster of self-concept items, while senior females exhibit stronger militant attitudes. Although we know by now that healthy assertiveness is normally the by-product of favorable intellectual and social development in college, this general rule does not apply to these students. Here, strong assertive development has the ring of defensive rebellion.

Once again, the best intellectual development has been found in predominantly black institutions. At the white colleges, contradictions in development seem sufficient to neutralize real intellectual growth. But, just as Ohio State does not do well by its black students in general, Central State does little for its female students.

Conclusions

Predominantly white colleges of the North are not much better for black students than white schools in any of our Southern states. Indeed, they may even be worse. In each of the Northern white colleges, black students make no real intellectual gains. Despite the fact that data suggest otherwise, these students seem to be under the unsettling illusion that they are making cognitive gains. We fear for the future of their career ambitions, built on false feelings of personal progress. Though unencouraging, is this not a fitting developmental outcome for blacks in the North? Remember, it was the North that promised freedom to blacks but delivered only ambivalence. Ambivalence is insidious. It is harmful, because it produces confusion. Part of the confusion stems from the belief that the North is better for blacks than it is. Another part of the confusion seems to be that black students believe that they are better than they are. By the senior year, the confusing contradictions of the North may become part of the black personality structure—a trend that bodes no good.

9

Differences by Race

The evidence presented makes a straightforward statement about the impact of colleges on black students. In most cases, black students fare better in predominantly black institutions. By the same token, black students adjust poorly to predominantly white colleges and show poor cognitive growth. The hypothesis suggested is that there are problems in interracial contact that make learning difficult for black students in white situations. Without racial barriers, black intellectual development can proceed, even amid poor educational facilities. But is it true that black students have more difficulty in white colleges because of their race? Part of the question could be answered by knowing how white students fare in college. If white students show good intellectual development in college, then the problems that race poses must be understood. On the other hand, if white student development leaves much to be desired, critical universal issues regarding the impact of education may emerge for our consideration.

Fortunately, this study includes data from white students on three of the college campuses: Georgia Institute of Technology, the University of Houston, and "Northern University." (Quotation marks indicate a fictitious name.) These samples include 388 white students (see breakdown in Table 1 in Chapter Three) in three of the four states studied. The most extensive measurements were taken in Texas, providing the most well-rounded picture of development; yet measures administered in the remaining states also yielded black-white comparisons. The

nature of the race differences in development does indeed clarify the issues for black students. It is true that white students
do not always show the kind of development that is cause for
celebration. Intellectual development per se is not always vastly
better for whites. But white students do always show better
overall development than black students. For white students,
white college environments appear to be more supportive of
growth.

Development at Georgia Institute of Technology

Black students at Georgia Tech suffer from some of the
worst intellectual deterioration found in a white college in this
study. Their academic energies are apparently frustrated by
classroom incidents and then withdrawn from the classroom
into extracurricular pursuits that afford no intellectual benefit.
These trends in no way describe the educational experience for
white students. White students at Tech, in fact, show the kind
of development typical of black students in black colleges. With
decent evidence of well-rounded growth, the whole personality
seems to move in the direction of an energetic outgoingness.

By itself, the evidence of objective intellectual gain
among Tech's white students is, however, not great. Indeed,
there is no improvement on any of the six measures of academic
performance, and the importance of grades to these students, as
well as the time put into studying, is less in the senior year. But
these seniors do feel that their class and learning activities are
the best part of college, and they are satisfied with whatever
their academic performance might be. Beyond the fact that
Tech's white students develop a stronger interest in academics
over the years, their academic profile is not far better than that
of black students.

Although the evidence of objective intellectual gain is not
convincing among white Tech students, the remainder of their
developmental profile is. This suggests that there are forces in
the Tech environment that are supportive of college development. Tech students are more ambitious with respect to career
choices and are more involved in their careers by working in

career-related areas and by seeking the help of faculty in making career decisions. More seniors than freshmen have serious plans for further education, and the SES level of career aspirations is higher among them. Furthermore, among seniors, there are fewer plans to marry right after graduation and more plans for continuing with further education. Thus, even if the actual grades of these students do not show improvement during college, there certainly seems to be a convergence of interest in academics and career issues.

Just as was the case for black students in black colleges, academic and career development seem to proceed smoothly when there is evidence of a positive adjustment to institutional life. White students at Tech seem to have effected one of those unambivalent attachments to their institution. As seniors, students report stronger positive feelings about the administration. Not only do seniors show more involvement with teachers, who they feel are interested in them, encouraging, and helpful; they also report more informal contact with professors. Seniors more often hold offices in extracurricular activities, but they do not think that these activities are the best part of college. Unlike black students, who put all their energy into activities outside the classroom, white seniors participate in extracurricular activities but maintain the strongest interest in learning activities in the classroom. Their allegiance to learning may well be catalyzed by the positive relationships that they have established with faculty members.

The positive impact of college for white students at Tech continues with encouraging findings in the area of personality. Almost all the findings in this area indicate that the personalities of these students are taking an outgoing turn. Seniors are less shy, less fearful of confrontation, and more outspoken. Seniors more often describe themselves as being leaders and as enterprising. Seniors also score higher on the extroversion factor of the self-concept scale, further confirming the outward thrust of their energies. On two indicators, however, seniors are experiencing stronger feelings of life stress than freshmen—in their personal lives and in public feelings of personal threat. It does seem to be the case that college students escape feelings of psy-

chophysical stress only in rare instances. More significantly, seniors exhibit lower scores on the genital stage of maturity,
which means that their personalities are less well integrated because of diminishing concern for others. As was the case for
Morehouse College, career success may be developed at the
price of optimal interpersonal orientation.

The feminine version of these findings takes a slightly
different slant, as the interaction effects for sex and class show.
Women turn out to be quite attached to their teachers and to
use them more over time in their efforts to make career decisions. Nonetheless, senior women are less motivated to study to
get good grades or to work in job areas related to their careers.
At the same time, senior women more often describe themselves as not as nice as and more irresponsible than freshmen.
By contrast, senior males are more strongly motivated to study
and work in their career areas, while they describe themselves as
nicer and more responsible than their freshman counterparts.
So, despite female students' apparent involvement with teachers, their apparent losses in motivation may create some rough
spots in their personalities and levels of confidence.

Thus, while black students at Tech are experiencing a
serious academic dislocation, their white counterparts are faring
quite well, despite some loss of confidence for women.

Development at the University of Houston

The University of Houston is a problematical case. White
students seem to be out of tune with the academic experience.
Their psychosocial developments are also far from encouraging.
Nonetheless, the intellectual developments are still better than
they are for black students (see Chapter Six). Black University
of Houston students show excellent improvement on measures
of grade averages. However, their failure to show gains on the
measures of cognitive growth or on measures of competitive
performance is accompanied by a loss of competitive motivation over the four years. In some ways, white students at the
University of Houston are not that much better off than their
black counterparts. They, too, show excellent improvement on

five out of the six measures of grade averages. As with black students, this improvement in grades happens under inauspicious circumstances, in that white students seem generally disenchanted with academics. Seniors are less challenged by courses than freshmen. In addition, more seniors think that instructors are the worst part of college. White students participated in the experimental study of competitive performance. They, like black students, show no superiority on verbal or math indices as seniors. Yet, unlike black students, white seniors have developed a greater capacity for enjoying competition. Furthermore, stronger achievement and power needs are aroused in them as a result of competition, and their absolute level of performance was better than that of black students, even with initial aptitude for the tasks controlled. Finally, on the tasks of cognitive growth, white seniors show higher scores on the measure of thematic analysis, a sophisticated measure of concept formation.

That white students seem disenchanted with academics does not mean that there are no positive aspects to their adjustment to college life. More seniors use faculty as resource persons in making career decisions. Senior males show more admiration for certain faculty members. Yet the sense of the data is that males are more immersed in their extracurricular activities, while females think that the people they meet are the best part of college. Students of both sexes, however, develop stronger needs for affiliation. Part of this stronger affiliative motivation may be home and marriage oriented: seniors of both sexes describe themselves as more domestic than freshmen and also want more children, female children in particular. If the lure of academic stimulation cannot sustain these students, the affiliative attractions of marriage and family may be seizing their attention by the senior year.

There is a side to personality development among these students that seems distinctly out of character for the wild Southwest—a withdrawn, nonconfrontational style. Seniors are more fearful of confrontation and more shy. More seniors describe themselves as lazy, and their lower scores on the phallic stage imply a less intrusive, oppositional style. Whatever the significance of these trends, the signs are not good for whole personality integration, since they reflect a loss of energy.

Like the women at Georgia Tech, University of Houston senior women are the happiest with their major subjects and are the most likely to attain honors. But even so, there seem to be motivational difficulties. As men begin to plan for advanced degrees, women seniors more often choose to terminate their education with the B.A. Senior women also are more dogmatic, lazier, and more fearful of power than freshmen. Indeed, in competition, women suffer from aroused fears of power. They are the only group to show declines in competitive (math) performance from freshman to senior year, as well as increasingly inaccurate estimates of their mathematical abilities. While it is not clear how the struggle will be resolved, their concern for power seems directed not into the outside world but into the arena of home and family life.

Thus, development for white students at the University of Houston is far more involved with affiliative and power issues than with cognitive ones. Unfortunately, the psychosocial and intellectual developments do not complement one another for the good of holistic development in men or women. Instead, energies seem tied up in affiliative and power conflicts that may be played out within the traditional home setting.

Development at "Northern University"

The problem for black students at "Northern University" is the presence of inconsistencies in many areas of development. There are, in fact, so many sources of contradictory development that little faith can be placed in the positive gains indicated. Not so for white students at "Northern University." In this respect, the developmental profile for white students is quite the opposite of that for their black counterparts. "Northern University" 's academic environment provides staunch, unambivalent support for academic and career growth among white students.

Like black students, whites show no obvious improvement in grade averages over the four years. However, unlike black students, they develop interest and satisfaction in the academic experience. For them, class and learning activities become the best part of going to college. While their motivation for doing well has little to do with getting good grades, seniors expend more effort on academics and show more satisfaction with the major subject. By the senior year, students have a higher estimate of their general ability and weaker fears of academic failure. Undoubtedly, their academic enhancement is assisted by increasing informal contact with faculty and culminates in stronger positive feelings about college life.

The relative joy taken in academics is matched by exceptionally encouraging career development. Seniors show more career involvement in career-relevant jobs and with teachers who help with career decisions. Seniors more often plan to pursue further education rather than work, and more seniors have serious plans for graduate or professional school. The level of educational aspirations is higher in the senior year, because more seniors are planning to pursue master's degrees instead of terminating their education with the B.A. The SES level of vocational aspirations is also higher among seniors, and their student vocational interests are more investigative in nature, that is, more oriented to scientific knowing. In assessing their chances for achieving their goals, lack of ability is less of a perceived obstacle among seniors.

The personality findings complement this positive picture of development. From the self-concept items, seniors claim that they are not as nice and considerate as their freshman fellows but that they are more competent. Their claims of being less dogmatic are also an encouraging sign, and the fact that seniors think that they are not as lazy suggests the free use of energy that should come from optimal development in the college years.

If it is possible, development at "Northern University" may be a little too consistent in its encouragement of academic and career growth. By the senior year, meeting people and socializing are no longer seen as the best parts of college, and seniors less often report enjoying social gatherings. Perhaps there is not quite enough emphasis on social development, a lack that may figure in the greater personal stress and illness that seniors experience.

The numerous effects for senior sex-role orientation also suggest a positive reconciliation with the career role. This is, moreover, especially true of women. Putting the most time into academics, they want to become career wives and assign the most importance to a career. Nonetheless, their commitment to a career may entail some stress, and, in fact, senior women are the least happy of "Northern University" students.

Thus, as in other schools where the development is quite positive and the emphasis is on career success, "Northern University" students may be confronted with some emotional and social costs.

Conclusions

The comparison of white and black student profiles tells us that black students have special problems in predominantly white college settings that white students do not share. For the most part, the environment at white colleges supports the development of white students and assists the integration of intellectual and interpersonal energies that is the task of late adolescence. Unlike black students, white students adjust well to the academic institution and have no complaints about alienation or unfairness in the classroom. Even when white students are disenchanted with academics, as they are in Texas, it is for reasons that are less devastating to cognitive functioning than seem to be the case for black students. White students seem to have an available reservoir of relatively stronger positive achievement and power motivations to be called upon when necessary (as in competition). These motivations probably help them sustain a higher concurrent level of cognitive functioning.

Development among white students in white colleges roughly parallels that of black students in black colleges. This parallel makes us think harder about what attributes of the college environment operate to create advantages for individuals in homogeneous environments. We have seen that when both the intellectual and interpersonal sides of the personality are nourished, synergistic personality development is most often the result. While black students are better able to feed more sides of their individuality in black settings, the basic issues are larger than race. Simply recall the fact that women have special problems on black campuses and on white ones as well. What we need, then, is a precise understanding of how to manipulate the college environment for intellectual gain.

10

Differences
by Race and Sex

For most of this book, we have been concerned with the accumulating evidence that black students show better development in predominantly black colleges. Beyond the broad findings of this study, there are issues specific to each of the sexes within each of the races that should be highlighted. In this chapter, we ask, "Who gets the most out of college?" Even in this arena, it turns out to be a man's world. Women usually bring up the rear. In predominantly black colleges, black men gain the most, and in predominantly white colleges, white men take first prize.

The idea that men, on their own turf, dominate the scene is hardly a new one. It is a truism in every area of extrahome life. We know that dominance has many rewards. And we now know that on college campuses those rewards include intellectual gains. Dominance implies competition, and it is certainly true that women and minorities do not compete well in college when there are white men present. It is also true that black women do not compete well when there are large numbers of black men present. But why? Is it that men are simply the villains of the world, from whom everyone else needs protection? Or is there some tacit agreement between the sexes and the races that allows men in general, or white men in particular, to take control and keep it? Does competition for the unique rewards of education begin with the inequities in the childrearing process? Or are we dealing with some vestige of primitive territoriality that evolution has not allowed us to escape?

Do the analyses presented in this book help us learn any more about the obvious battle between the sexes and between the races? Our data certainly confirm that male dominance in general and white male dominance in particular are facts of life even on college campuses. We learn that the college environment is a critical factor in terms of which group it supports most. But we also learn that the current college environment is not the whole answer. There is evidence of cross-pressures, contradictory messages, and motivational conflicts that are a part of the early learning students bring with them to the college setting. When early learning, traditions, and the press of the college environment convey similar messages, the motivational potential of students is more available for use. When those early conflicts are reactivated by nonsupportive college settings, the ability to get the most out of college is compromised.

The White Male

It is the traditional role of men to dominate life outside the home. Indeed, we expect this of men. Through centuries of mutual agreement between the sexes, men have been granted the world at large as their special territory. It is only recently that the occupation of different spheres of activity by men and women has become a competitive issue. The world outside the home has continued to enlarge, offering more and more opportunities for the development of social and cognitive capacities. The world inside the home has shrunk to minute, unsatisfying proportions that leave little room for the critical manipulation of things and people. Despite the battle over women's (and minorities') rights to participate in the world of men, the current trends are still dictated by expectations so old that they are no longer conscious. It is completely in accordance with these expectations that white men take first prize for college development on predominantly white campuses.

In a real sense, the longevity of traditional expectations for men acts as a kind of support system for them and their dominance activities. This system helps yield intellectual gains. Indeed, the ways in which social expectations are supportive of the white male are evident in their college development. It is not that intellectual development per se is vastly better for white men than for others; the fact is that the college environment seems more supportive of their overall development. The actual cognitive improvements for men during the college years were not that much better than for other groups. Improvement on grade averages was better for whites than blacks in only one out of three samples. In the Texas sample, improvement on the measures of cognitive growth was better for whites on only one of three indices. In the study of competitive performance, also carried out in Texas, whites showed no more improvement than blacks.

Thus, actual cognitive development is not the unique advantage of white males. Yet the general developmental profile for white males is always better, because the intellectual and psychosocial sides of college life complement one another and give the impression of good adjustment to a supportive environment. Furthermore, in two out of three samples, well-rounded personality development is accompanied by increasing energy—a sign of good personality integration. White males also have the ability to translate cognitive functioning into unambivalent educational, vocational, and career ambitions. They seem relatively free from downward pulls on their aspirations and from motivational conflicts that douse ambition. The difference between white males and other groups was especially clear in direct competition. Here, white males were able to call up stronger reserves of positive achievement and power motivations that help them enjoy their tasks and sustain a higher level of performance at any given time. Perhaps more than anything else, it seems that stronger positive motivations are the legacy of consistent expectations for the white male's dominant role in the world.

This is not to say that the white male role does not have its share of strains. According to social scientists such as Nancy Chodorow (1978) and Joseph Pleck (1981), the male role strains begin all too early. The characteristic male inability to achieve satisfying intimacy in relationships may begin with too much mothering and not enough fathering. Males then come to deny their dependence on women, devalue them, and become driven by needs to be superior to them. At the same time, they become inclined toward competitive rather than cooperative relationships with other males. Remnants of this early dilemma were, of course, evident in the college profiles. Lack of mutuality, avoidance of social involvements, and conflicts between intellectual and affiliative demands were features of male college development. Yet, in a world that has come to value male activities to the extent that it has, these costs of masculinity may go unnoticed.

The Black Male

It seems safe to continue saying that males dominate and that their dominance activities have a payoff in developmental gains during the college years. If this is true of white males, are black males any different? Certainly, black males behave similarly on their own turf in black colleges and reap similar gains. But on predominantly white college campuses, black male development suffers most. Clearly, black males are hardest hit by the stress of interracial educational environments. What is it that happens to their dominance tendencies, and what happens to their intellectual gains? The idea that racist influences hit black males the hardest is not new. However, the phenomenon is such an interesting one that it invites at least several levels of analysis. On the most immediate level, the fact that black students must matriculate in an atmosphere that feels hostile arouses defensive reactions that interfere with intellectual performance. But the element of interpersonal hostility does not explain why black males are the hardest hit.

A second level of analysis leads us to suspect that male-male interactions are the most laden with hostility. We recall from our discussion of early learning that males are the victims of insufficient fathering, so that they learn to be competitive rather than cooperative with other males. Since black, as well as white, males are similarly deprived, they are predisposed to interact competitively. The racial difference serves to intensify the basically hostile nature of male-male interactions. Black males are then excluded from participation in a wide range of activities and restricted to small groups of all-black social and political organizations. Apparently, the restricted role that black males play, both within the classroom and without, acts to constrict the intellectual gains that issue from being an actor in campus goings-on.

Upon entering what is in some sense alien territory, black males fall into the category of subdominant males by virtue of their visibility and small numbers. Interestingly, observers of primate dominance hierarchies such as Robert Rose and his colleagues (Rose, Holaday, and Bernstein, 1971; Rose, Gordon, and Bernstein, 1972) find that subdominant males lapse into a nonconfrontational, lethargic state of behavior that can only be described as depression. In many ways, the developmental profiles of black males in white colleges can also be described as depressed. They become unhappy with college life. They feel that they have been treated unfairly. They display academic demotivation and think less of their abilities. They profess losses of energy and cease to be able to enjoy competitive activities. To be sure, there are ways in which these males do not act depressed, inasmuch as they become assertive and may participate energetically in certain campus activities. Nonetheless, these developments are defensive and do little to remedy their plight.

Black males on black campuses exhibit behavioral profiles that are indistinguishable from those of white males. Though they are sometimes disenchanted with the classroom atmosphere, they maneuver around their dissatisfaction by forming informal attachments to faculty and by participating in extra-classroom activities. They experience cognitive growth as well as a release of their assertive energies. Their competitive abilities improve as they come to enjoy competition and find expression for their power motivation in black settings. In short, they display a social and intellectual ascendance that looks like great fun.

The role strains from which black males suffer are in the same interpersonal arena as those influencing white males. But the strains among black males are more visible, perhaps because we are able to observe their behavior in two vastly different settings. In the supportive environments of black colleges, where black men feel accepted, interpersonal issues become almost irrelevant to them. They show far less concern for others. They use the many opportunities for comforting relationships to reach a state of interpersonal detachment. Thus, in a warm environment where there are many opportunities for relatedness, black males strive to remain unaffected by people. Perhaps this maneuver helps them feel in control of their emotional needs for intimacy.

But in stressful environments such as white colleges, where they do not feel warmly received or secure in the comfort of many relationships, black males are unable to maintain controlled feelings of detachment. Their feelings of being surrounded by a hostile environment hit them where they hurt the most, in the denied needs for friendship and intimacy. The threat to needs for relatedness creates a vast interpersonal void that they must spend time and energy trying to fill—energy that has to be siphoned off from intellectual pursuits. Black men often try to work the problem out through their interpersonal lives. They may attempt to attain dominance over women or to live through children. In each of these important relationships, they are striving to become central or indispensable in the lives of others. This may be a way of trying to establish new interpersonal anchors to offset the feelings of being rejected. First and foremost, then, black men on white campuses are responding to feelings of competitive rejection that have consequences for their capacity to muster intellectual motivation. Although black males in white colleges suffer intellectual losses, the problem is not essentially an intellectual one. The problem for black males in white settings is very much an interpersonal issue that rearouses the usually unnoticed strains of being male. The hostile reception given to them on white campuses acts to trigger interpersonal vulnerabilities and initiates a depressive withdrawal from the situation. In black settings, which offer so many opportunities for social ascendance, these interpersonal strains can be ignored.

The Black Female

We have been arguing that males on their own turf dominate and, in so doing, manage to get the most out of the college experience. But rumor has it that black women are unusually

adept at domination. Thus, they have been revered as unnatural-
ly superior by sociologist Jessie Bernard (1965) and indicted as
matriarchs by others (see Staples, 1970; Fleming, 1983a, 1983b).
As with most rumors, this one is only partly true. The question
is, under what conditions does the rumor come closest to the
truth? The data here indicate that the rumor is least likely to be
true when black women are around black men who are enjoying
their own dominance. That is, it is least likely to be true on
black campuses. Among black women, the degree of development seems to hinge on whether or not they are able to nurture
and use their own latent assertive abilities.

Whereas men have more trouble achieving a satisfying degree of interpersonal relatedness, women have more trouble
with their feelings of competence. Black women are no exception. The in-depth study of competitive performance in Chapter
Six reveals that whether black women attend a black or white
college they are anxious about their own competence. They invariably set lower goals than men. They perform more poorly in
math. They experience more anxiety during competition and
express more dissatisfaction with their performance than men.
But black women's competence anxieties are out of proportion
with some of the objective facts of their competitive abilities.
While it is true that they perform worse than men in math, they
do perform well in verbal tasks and show the most improvement
in their verbal skills from freshman to senior year. In fact, it is
because of women's performance gains that the freshman-senior
comparisons for black colleges look so good. Although black
women have higher initial levels of fear of success, which act to
depress feelings of competence, in competition they are inspired
with strong needs for achievement. Furthermore, this study
shows that competition does not have the deleterious effect of
raising blood pressure among women that it has for men. Thus,
there is an important sense in which black women's feelings of
incompetence are just that—feelings, not well supported by the
facts. What we need, then, is to understand the nature of competence anxieties that detract from performance in experimental situations as well as intellectual gain in the college years.

In our analysis of sex differences in the impact of colleges in Georgia (see Chapters Four and Five), the big issue for black women on black campuses is their fear of using assertive skills. Indeed, the most striking aspect of personal development for women in black schools is the alarming drop in social assertive skills. Social passivity may be why exceptionally good academic development does not lead to energetic postgraduate ambitions, as it does for men. In short, stifling the assertive tendencies also stifles intellectual abilities.

It seems that when there are men around who are flexing their assertive muscles, there is no room for black women to do the same. This basic pattern of women failing to translate their academic gains into good career development holds true in most of the black colleges studied. In some of the other black schools, the degree of social passivity is not so great. But there are clearly costs to women who do not try to hide their assertiveness. In the North, women who become a little more assertive in college, but not as much as men, suffer from feelings of unhappiness. In Texas, women who give little thought to suppressing assertiveness find that they are less popular by the senior year. It looks, then, as if women invest in not asserting themselves so that they can maintain the approval of men. Perhaps this is our root of female competence anxiety.

If black women suppress their assertive selves to please men, then we can understand why it is easier for them to develop their assertive abilities on white campuses. The data indicate that on most predominantly white college campuses, there are few black men, especially among seniors. Furthermore, we know that on predominantly white campuses, black males are often undergoing depressive reactions that cause them to withdraw academically and psychologically. In other words, they are not men enjoying dominance, social ascendance, or their own assertive abilities. In this context, black women may very well be able to develop the assertive capacities that help them hold their own intellectually.

In Georgia, black women in white schools become outspoken, articulate, and able to deal with people. At the same time, they are able to get more out of the academic experience than their black male counterparts. In Texas, assertiveness among black women is also related to their capacity to protect their developing psychological independence. In the Northern schools, black women are less successful in self-development, apparently because black men are trying to use them as vehicles for assuaging feelings of frustration.

Despite the admirable development of assertiveness in white colleges, there is always the clear sense that black women are suffering from emotional pain, social isolation, or aroused fears about their competence. The pain may have to do with the lack of support in white colleges; but it may also have to do with the difficulty of overcoming inhibitions surrounding assertiveness. Because of their early histories as women, black women may not want to use all of their talents. They, like other women, may prefer to lean on dominant men and stifle their own abilities. They call upon their latent resources only when they have to and only when there are no men to rely on.

The White Female

As long as there are men around who are enjoying their dominance, women seem to have a harder time reaping intellectual gains. But if men are in short supply or otherwise indisposed, black women can then begin to tinker with their latent dominance inclinations. Are white women any different?

In any number of studies that directly compare black and white women, white women turn out to have lower aspirations and more conflicts surrounding those aspirations (see Fleming, 1983b). It may be, however, that black and white women are not so fundamentally different. It may be that black women have had more experience with men so preoccupied by stress reactions that there has been more room for female exploration and exertion of assertive skills. Perhaps when and if white women are left to their own devices in relatively male-free settings, they too discover more of themselves and rise to whatever the occasion calls for. From the reports that we have on how white women develop in single-sex colleges (of which none were included in the present study), this certainly seems to be the case.

Tidball's (1973) study of notable American women is

clear in finding that women are twice as likely to end up in *Who's Who of American Women* if they have gone to a women's college. Even low-caliber women's colleges are at least as successful in catapulting a woman to prominence as elite coeducational schools. What's more, Tidball locates responsibility for the trends in two facts about the college environments of women's institutions. First, the number of notable women increases with the presence of women on the faculty, indicating the opportunity to watch role models maneuvering among men (who are always present on the faculty of women's institutions). Secondly, the number of notable women increases as the proportion of males in the student body decreases. Thus, it is the total or relative absence of male peers that helps to free their capacities and inclinations for the nontraditional. Thus, black and white women are alike in functioning best without men.

We are fortunate in having several psychological studies that tell why white women have a harder time in coed settings. The upshot of these studies is that motivational conflicts, which pose no problem in female settings, become aroused and then interfere with performance in the presence of males. Researchers such as Marybeth Shinn (1973) and Matina Horner (1973) find that the effects are immediately noticeable upon putting men and women together in classrooms and that the longer women have been educated with men, the more serious is the debilitation.

Something very similar happens to the white women in this study, who are all in coed college environments. Motivational conflicts are aroused in two of the three samples of women. Men in Georgia become more motivated to study and to work in their career areas, while women become less motivated to do so. Indeed, women even begin to see themselves as less responsible by the senior year. These apparent losses in motivation create definite rough spots in their personalities, specifically in their inability to be nice to other people. Likewise in Texas, motivational difficulties are evident as women terminate their educations prematurely and become lazy, fearful of their own power motivations, less adept at abstract thought, and inaccurate in estimating their own abilities. Only in Ohio is there

no evidence that women are suffering from motivational problems. Quite the opposite. These women end up putting the most
time into academics, desiring to become career wives who place
the most importance on a career. But we can now assume confi-
dently that when women are bold enough to want what men
want, they pay a price. In this case, career-oriented women in
Ohio are the unhappiest group of seniors.

It is not entirely fair to blame the motivational conflicts
of women on the mere presence of males in any given educational setting. It is not simply that males compete with women
to relieve them of their responsibilities for assertiveness and
thereby take away much of the intellectual gain that comes
from dominance activity. It is also that women give up their
rights to self-assertion because of their heightened fears of not
being liked. In a sense, a tacit agreement is reached that works
to the motivational and intellectual disadvantage of women but
perhaps has a marriageability advantage. Yet women might not
be susceptible to the latent pressures they feel from men if it
were not for the fact that their motivational conflicts begin so
early in life. These conflicts are rooted in many early experiences that give the double-binding message that it is all right to
be intelligent, so long as no practical use is made of that intelligence.

Conclusions

In looking at the four sex and race groups, we wonder if
there are similarities between the battle between the sexes and
the battle between the races. It does seem clear that what the
groups are fighting over is the right to opportunities for social
manipulation. It is almost as if all the players know that mere
exposure to education is not sufficient by itself. In order to
achieve that energetic personality fusion that is the task of adolescence, the interpersonal side of the personality must also be
developed. When this is done, exposure to education then results in observable intellectual gains.

In the presence of men, women of both races suppress
their rights to self-assertion (which would lead to social manip-

ulation) and submit to male dominance. If they refuse to submit to positions of social passivity, they may be ostracized to
the extent that they feel unhappy and/or unpopular. Between
the races, there is clearly not the same heterosexual incentive to
submit to the dominant group, so that a process of competitive
rejection and exclusion takes place instead. The consequences
for intellectual and social development of the subdominant
group are serious.

Our attention is focused on the game being played on
these college campuses. Yet we should not lose sight of the fact
that the need to dominate and the fear of not dominating are
conditioned during primary relationships with all-powerful parents. It may also be that, because our world view and very evolution stress the value of competition, it is difficult for us to
see the value of cooperation and friendship. Valuing competition as we do, we would never believe that there are enough opportunities for intellectual and social manipulation to go
around. Until we manage to incorporate cooperative acceptance
into our value system, separate colleges for special interests may
be necessary for optimal development in the college years.

11

Implications
for the Education
of Black Students

Implications for Black Colleges

Our findings that black colleges have the capacity to positively influence cognitive development certainly argue for their continued existence. There are many reports of vastly poorer educational resources at black institutions. Clearly, these assessments are correct in evaluating the relative standing of black colleges on any number of objective grounds. The findings of this report do not alter the objective realities of black college resources. They only suggest that their deleterious impact on intellectual development is overestimated and that the significance of opportunities for academic progress, social participation, and interpersonal belonging is underestimated. We can be sure that the poor resources of black colleges must set some limits on how much they can do for black students. Nevertheless, our understanding of these limits has so far been inaccurate.

The Supportive Community. Despite their poorer resources, black colleges still possess the capacity to permit the expression of natural adolescent motivations for cognitive growth. This appears to be so because the black college environment offers a student a wider network of supportive relationships. According to developmental theorists such as Loevinger (1976), supportive interpersonal relationships are not only desirable but necessary for development during the college years. This study confirms that, on the average, the presence of a supportive community may well be a sine qua non for development, while an alienating atmosphere limits possibilities for growth. The critical essence of a supportive community is not easy to define in precise terms. In all probability, it does not mean a place where everyone loves and accepts one another. Indeed, in the black colleges, there are numerous indications of racial struggles, interpersonal clashes, unfairness, and favoritism. A supportive community may well provide a variety of experiences, both good and bad, friendly and hostile; it may challenge at the same time that it provides some measure of security.

This investigation can pinpoint three aspects of supportive community. Perhaps most important, the individual must have many opportunities for friendship. These friendships should not be confined to one's peers but should include teachers, staff members, and professional counselors. It would appear that a friendship network composed not only of peers but also of role models is essential. Informal relationships with role models, relationships that continue outside the classroom setting, are an important source of support. The interviews in Texas tell us that it is important not only to know many people but to have enough people with whom to talk, especially in times of stress. The mere opportunity to talk to people about our troubles constitutes a buffer against the impact of trauma, particularly against interpersonal trauma. This kind of support is reminiscent of Freud's cathartic "talking cure." It does seem that to a great extent the troubles of adolescence can be talked away. The absence of opportunities to turn to friends in times of need can create a dangerous vulnerability to stress, the kind of vulnerability so apparent among black students in predominantly white colleges.

Secondly, students must have the opportunity to participate in the life of the campus. They must feel some connection to current goings-on. In other words, there must be opportunities to satisfy adolescent needs to participate, to be seen, and to be recognized. Black colleges afford more opportunities for black students to assume leadership roles in extracurricular activities, thereby providing them with a rehearsal for the roles they are expected to assume in society. This kind of experience offers some of the informal learning that is an essential part of the educational process. From the experimental evidence in Texas, we find that black students' power motives are more likely to be aroused and expressed in black work settings. This means that they are satisfying their desire to have an impact on others and attain the esteem that comes from being recognized. On predominantly white campuses, black students' power needs are more likely to be frustrated. This is because they feel abandoned by the institution, rebuffed by fellow students, and inhibited from taking part in any but all-black organizational activities. This state of affairs creates feelings of invisibility.

Third, students must have the opportunity to feel some sense of progress and success in their academic pursuits. Feelings of success are an aspect of an affirmed identity, so that a sense of failure becomes a disconnecting experience that places the search for identity in jeopardy. The perceived inability to make progress undercuts the esteem that comes from doing something well. On predominantly black campuses, black student successes are more likely to gain the attention of faculty. Students are more likely to acquire the help they need in overcoming those achievement-related deficiencies that are brought to the college setting. Conversely, on white college campuses, black students' feelings of progress are thwarted. These students feel that instructors are not interested in them, do not give encouragement, and use unfair grading practices. By the senior year, many black students are suffering from feelings of failure and lack of academic motivation. While it is not possible for all students to receive A's or the highest academic honors, it should be possible for all students to feel some sense of improvement throughout their academic careers.

To the extent that an individual can achieve feelings of progress, gain a sense of recognition, and know that there are people who will provide an attentive ear, the ingredients of social connectedness are present within black college settings. As a consequence, these settings promote intellectual development among black students. It is probably no accident that these three ingredients parallel the achievement, power, and affiliative incentives that are the basis of motivational theory. The ingredients we pinpoint also parallel humanistic theory's security and esteem needs, which act as the prime motivators for human endeavors.

A Blow for Integration? Perhaps one of the most troubling issues surrounding the findings for black colleges is that they may seem to argue in favor of segregation at a time when the concept is contrary to our nobler ideals. Rather than acting to maintain segregation, black colleges appear to effectively impart the orientation and skills that allow black students to function well in the larger society: aspiration, confidence, motivation, and the ability to enjoy competition in the integrated world. Good intellectual skills would seem to constitute the most effective coping mechanisms for the modern world. For black students, our concern should be not where intellectual skills are gained but whether they are gained. If we allow black colleges to serve as a stepping-stone for those who wish to become part of the larger society, these institutions might become a stronger aid to integration than ever imagined.

Black colleges provide the closest approximation to racially balanced educational institutions that can be found. Indeed, research findings in both Georgia and Texas uncovered tension-fraught dealings with whites on black campuses; these findings remind us that the faculty and staff of many black schools are well integrated. However, at black colleges, race-related tensions occur in the context of (and may actually be related to) positive developmental outcomes. Because black schools offer something closer to racially balanced teaching environments, they may allow students to adjust more gradually to the realities of integrated settings. This may be especially true for students hailing from segregated secondary schools. Instead of being overwhelmed by frustration, these students develop appropriate coping mechanisms in preparation for more difficult challenges. This line of reasoning certainly fits the findings of enhanced competitive performance by black college stu-

dents in white work settings. It would seem that if the positive
factors found to be operative for women in women's colleges
also apply to black colleges, the presence of black and white
role models provides a balance lacking in many institutions.

Conformist Influences. The learning environments within
black colleges still leave something to be desired, inasmuch as
this study finds suspicious evidence of conformist influences
that merit examination. Historically, black colleges have been
pressured to conform to values and curricula imposed on them
from the larger society. It should be of little wonder, then, that
residual conformist or overconformist tendencies remain. Indeed, overallegiance to white values as well as intolerance of different viewpoints and individualism are aspects of black colleges
most abhorrent to Ann Jones (1973) and Tom Sowell (1972).
What is interesting from our data is that conformist tendencies
may grow at the same time that independence and enterprise
flourish. Perhaps students come to play either the leader or fol-
lower roles. Also relevant is the Jencks and Riesman (1968)
allegation that many black college presidents rule in the authori-
tarian manner of feudal lords. The organizational psychology
literature warns that the price for tyranny, even when it serves a
constructive purpose, is listless conformity. As a state of mind,
conformity suggests a cognitive rigidity that the process of education strives to overcome. It may be time for black institutions
to indulge in some self-education that might free some of their
energies for an attitude of flexibility in educational environments.

On the Matriarchate. If the present investigation were
concerned more with the impact of college environments on
black women than with the development of black students in
general, the black college advantage would be less certain. Our
analysis suggests that black women in black college environments suffer from many of the latent difficulties that beset
blacks in white educational settings. While the black-white competition appears to be waged largely in the intellectual arena,
that between black women and men on black campuses appears
to be hottest in the social arena. Black women thus compromise
their social assertiveness and find stereotyped passive ways of

gaining recognition and control. Should they resist the pressure to do so, they risk their popularity. This is fine for femininity, but the undermining of assertiveness will eventually take its toll in the intellectual arena as well. Because cognitive and socio-emotional energies are connected, loss in one area will eventually be felt in the other. Indeed, the aggressive action underlying intellectual accomplishment cannot be fully utilized if its assertive components are paralyzed in social interactions. As the subdominant group in white environments, black men harbor certain conscious and unconscious fears. Perhaps, in black educational settings, black males also harbor conscious or unconscious fears of being overtaken by the ranks of the dreaded matriarchate. If so, evidence presented in Chapter Ten that there is no immediate danger will undoubtedly not assuage these fears. Problems of dominance and submission and their consequences for individual development in college are as difficult to work through as are latent hostilities between races. This is because both have deep emotional roots. Suffice it to say that the most observable male needs for dominance over women are directly linked to strong personal insecurities. If black colleges could bring sufficient resources to bear in helping insecure individuals grow beyond the need for dominance, women would have greater room to maneuver.

Implications for White Colleges

The Plight of Black Students. Inasmuch as the gains for black students in white schools are not as great as we would like, we are confronted with a problem in need of a solution. Our findings should not be taken as an indictment of predominantly white colleges as learning environments for black students. Nor should our results be taken to mean that black students should not attend white colleges. The data simply underscore the need for continued efforts on both sides. From the evidence provided by black students themselves, the problem is one of institutional abandonment, isolation, and bias in the classroom —factors that create a hostile interpersonal climate. In all fairness, poor racial interaction has always been a marked characteristic of American society, one that is not likely to disappear. It is also a problem that manifests itself long before black students reach the freshman year. Singling out educational institutions for blame that belongs to us all will clearly not turn the tide. Furthermore, the problem involves an *interaction* between the factors that black students bring to white colleges and the conditions that they find within these institutions.

White colleges and universities have only recently been faced with the presence of significant numbers of minority students. The conflict, brought to a head by the institutional lack of experience and by mutual misunderstanding, is just beginning to yield strategies for more effective communication. Completed studies underscore the need for more black faculty and staff members, a maximum of black students with a balanced sex ratio, curricula relevant to the black experience, and responsive counseling services. To the extent that institutions are willing and able to meet these basic requirements, the problems of black students will be lessened.

The Challenge of Predominantly White Colleges. Since 1954, black students have been trying to exercise their right to attend predominantly white colleges, but the average black student at many white schools has not yet learned how to achieve the full intellectual development that goes with the territory. Black students share half the responsibility for what happens to them during the college years. Their activities during the sixties certainly helped to focus attention on the general concerns of students vis-à-vis universities. We hope that black college students continue to guard their educational rights and speak out when necessary. Yet the tendency to withdraw from academics and divert frustration into less constructive outlets—a tendency so prominent in the study's findings—serves to keep intellectual gains at a minimum. The task for black students on white campuses is to direct frustration into, not away from, academic activities; to challenge rather than retreat from unfairness in the classroom; to find constructive means of encouraging helpful peer contact rather than mutual avoidance. Undoubtedly, the latent fear and hostility game works best when two play. Keeping the struggle against racism in education in the appropriate arena might well obviate the need for compensatory strategies that have little educational value.

Development in Modern American Colleges. In the search for comparative understanding, the inclusion of white students is valuable in two respects: it clarifies the educational status of blacks in white colleges and also underscores the fact that white students do not fare as well as they should. In large, impersonal universities, where instructors are paid to do research rather than teach, there are definite costs to white students. While this system of benign neglect affects all students, it happens that the intellectual consequences are more devastating for black students. An orientation to subject matter, rather than student development, characterizes many universities. These colleges select students who need no special assistance. Colleges in general, however, may need to rethink their orientation, since so many college students are uninspired. We have found that the problems of white women in white colleges parallel those of black women in black institutions. Obviously, there is plenty of work for us all to do in the future.

A Question of Options

The question of importance is not whether black colleges are to continue to be, and not whether black students should go to white colleges, but how to maintain viable options for the vast number of students with a multitude of needs. Where black students go to college will continue to be a matter of individual choice, dictated by family, finance, geography, educational readiness, and personal preferences. We hope that prospective black students will become more aware of what college environments have in store for them, so that they can muster whatever resources are necessary for a successful tenure. The task for public policy is to insure the best educational options that we as a society can provide.

Too often, one educational policy alternative becomes a blanket solution or a precedent from which it becomes difficult to depart. The issue of forced school busing is relevant because of the operative word *forced.* The problem has received intense attention because white parents have rebelled against an educational policy that serves the needs of only some students. But, from the point of view of black children, the question of choice is unexpectedly critical as well.

It should come as no surprise that studies of black children in desegregated schools show exactly the same pattern of findings as did our investigation of college functioning (see Coles, 1963). When conditions characterizing the early years of a desegregation experience are unfavorable, Coles reports that *most* children experience some fear or stress reaction, including marshaling defenses against emotional pain and behavior to surmount it. Black students carry realistic fears of educational inadequacy into more demanding desegregated environments. But Katz has evidence of unrealistic fears conditioned by "an emotional accommodation to the demeaning role in American culture that has been imposed . . . by the dominant white majority" (1964, p. 387). Even under favorable conditions, those in which there is a mutual desire for desegregation to work, Yarrow (1958) finds that black children experience more tension in integrated than in segregated environments. In integrated settings, Yarrow pinpoints more social and emotional tension, as well as more covert signs of distress, such as enuresis, fears, nightmares, withdrawal, and physical symptoms among children.

Desegregation reports often contain evidence that black children fail to keep pace with their white classmates. In one such case, Day (1962) attributes the failures to lack of motivation and a disadvantaged home background. However, Wyatt (1962) ascribes most of the difficulties to poor social adjustment on the part of black children, and particularly older black children. Studies of integration show clearly that novel contact situations with whites possess a potential social-threat component for blacks. In view of studies showing that blacks do desire friendly relationships with white counterparts (Horowitz, 1936; Radke, Sutherland, and Rosenberg, 1950; Yarrow, 1958), we can assume that the effects of desegregation are more favorable in an atmosphere of social acceptance. Acceptance is accompanied by displays of black leadership (Tanner, 1964). Perhaps the lesson here is that college is not the place to start if we desire to achieve mutual racial acceptance. The success of our efforts at the college level will depend on the extent to which students learn as children to seek interracial exposure and to benefit from the richness of understanding that goes with the effort.

The bulk of the desegregation literature presents a favorable view of black adjustment in white schools, but a closer look at some of these studies reveals that the situation is far more complex. Consider, for example, a study of the effects of legal desegregation on achievement tests in Louisville, Kentucky. Stallings (1959) reports that gains are made by all students at all grade levels tested but that black students show greater gains than white students. Another report notes further that, since black teachers in this city have not been assigned to desegregated classrooms, the greater gains are displayed by black children who remain in segregated classrooms (Knowles, 1962). Note, however, that gains are greater where blacks remain with black teachers *by choice* (Stallings, 1959). These studies are noteworthy in showing that factors other than desegregation itself are responsible for general gains, since desegregation is usually accompanied by a general improvement in educational standards. Thus, the combination of all-black classrooms *freely chosen* and improved facilities makes the biggest difference for some black children. Similar situations have been reported for other school districts (Hansen, 1960).

Thus, in secondary school, as well as in college, educational benefits accrue to black students in predominantly black environments, especially if they are in them of their own volition. On this evidence, the policy implication that follows is that black colleges ought to exist as long as black students choose to attend them. For black students, the significance of the 1954 victory is not only the right to enter white schools but also the right to choose which educational environment is best for a given individual. Who can deny the value of a black college option if it constitutes a stepping-stone from one level to another and provides the tools necessary to function in a wider, integrated world that holds the next set of choices to be made? For those who understand and are ready to meet this wider

challenge *at an earlier age,* the right to compete for a place in
the best of predominantly white colleges is uncontested.

As far as we have come in understanding the contributions of black colleges to black education, there is still no way
of knowing how much these schools might accomplish with the
educational resources most white schools possess. It must be
clear that the choice of a black college with facilities scorned
by the world is no choice at all. With the unique resource of a
potentially facilitative educational climate, black colleges seem
able to accomplish far more than they have been given credit for
doing. In important respects, it appears that they are able to
overcome the dual handicap of poor facilities and insufficient
funds to pay the best teachers. Yet we gain this perspective only
after careful observation of the failings of predominantly white
schools in the realm of black higher education. If black colleges
do not become content to surpass comparable white schools,
they might demand a chance to show what they could deliver
with equal resources. For, at this time, black students are still
faced with an unhappy compromise between superior educational resources at white schools and the best chance for social
participation at black institutions. Their potential for intellectual growth at a black college notwithstanding, why is it that
they cannot have both, all in the same college?

12

Summarizing
the Impacts
of College
on Students

Rationale for the Study

Since 1954, when de jure segregation in school systems became illegal, the continued validity of black colleges has been challenged many times. More and more often, the future of colleges established for the education of blacks has become a subject of debate, journalistic inquiry, federal deliberation, and court battle. Thus, the subject of the research reported in this volume is whether black colleges make a contribution to black education that white colleges are not better able to assume.

At first blush, the case against the survival of historically black colleges seems overwhelming. These colleges, it is said, are testament only to another age, characterized by castelike segregation in education, while the current ideal of racial progress stresses integration as the path of the future. As we work toward integrated living and working patterns, it is inescapable that the classroom is as good a place as any within which to begin coping with an integrated world. With this goal in mind, can the continued existence of so many black colleges be seen as

161

anything other than an anachronism? If our new ideals are not reason enough to question the contribution of black colleges, there is evidence that they provide an inferior education that allegedly does an intellectual disservice to black students. Witness the reports of their weaknesses: inadequate financial resources; underpaid and presumably less competent teachers; the prevalence of teachers as opposed to research scholars; a semiliterate student culture created by individuals whose test scores and high school preparation are far below average, and whose social backgrounds are considerably less privileged (McGrath, 1965; Jencks and Riesman, 1968; Sowell, 1972; Carnegie Commission on Higher Education, 1971; Jones, 1971). In addition to having been described as fourth-rank institutions at the tail end of the academic procession, none of which ranks with a decent state university, black colleges are charged with favoritism and sexual blackmail in grading. It is said that tyrannical presidents preside over these colleges as if they were their personal feudal property.

It seems almost anticlimactic to add that black schools are said to represent gross waste and inefficiency in educational expenditures, since they duplicate the services offered at nearby white institutions. Almost three fourths of black students have already elected to go to predominantly white colleges. In the face of such compelling evidence of the intellectual crisis facing black colleges, the issue seems to be quite closed. To continue the discussion feels much like beating a dead horse.

However, further examination reveals that there are, indeed, other issues to be considered. For example, social scientists have amassed a considerable body of literature indicating that all is not well with black students in predominantly white colleges. The recurrent problems of hostility and racism, poor rapport with faculty, feeling left out of the curriculum, inadequate social lives, exclusion from campus activities, the conflict of a comforting but demanding black subculture, and the experience of academic failure are said to be indications of a crisis in social adjustment symptomatic of a more serious identity crisis (Gibbs, 1974; Willie and McCord, 1972; Davis and Borders-Patterson, 1973). If the possibility of aroused conflicts in ego identity is taken seriously, there may be more basic questions concerning the educational inputs necessary to assist students through the tricky but critical stage of adolescence—the stage that coincides with the college experience.

In this broader light, there seem to be many questions warranting an investigation of the relative contributions of predominantly black and white colleges for black students. What are the patterns of adjustment that can be observed within each kind of college experience? Do black colleges indeed do an intellectual disservice to black students, or do they make a contribution to black education unlikely to be equaled by white institutions now or in the near future? Is a crisis in intellectual input or a crisis in social adjustment more devastating to the college experience of black students? These are the questions that inspired a major four-year, Carnegie Corporation–funded research effort to provide concrete data capable of informing policy decisions.

Going About the Study

In order to inform policy, this investigation attempted to address several basic requirements: that it attend to the issue of student outcomes without ignoring institutional issues; that it provide a comparative picture of the progress that individuals make in black and white colleges; that it be intensive enough to approximate a case study but large-scale enough to approximate a survey; that it address the issue of general student development but give specific readings of the importance of sex, race, and individual differences in the college experience; and that it be accomplished in a manner that allows reasonable inferences about development during the late adolescent years in college. These considerations guided the study design.

The study employed a cross-sectional design in which samples of freshmen and seniors were recruited at each of the colleges. They were compared on a number of measures, so that the differences between them were used to make reasonable inferences about developmental outcomes during the four-year experience. Although a cross-sectional approach is less preferable than a longitudinal design, the cross-sectional approach is a far more practical one as a first step, and many authors find that results obtained from both procedures yield comparable information (for example, Feldman and Newcomb, 1969). While developmental psychologists prefer the use of both cross-sectional and longitudinal studies, where the former provide reasonable inferences about developmental processes and the latter provide confirmation, this study attempts to begin at the beginning with the first most practical step of a cross-sectional study. In taking this first step, the groundwork is thereby laid for future longitudinal verifications.

Several considerations went into choosing the fifteen colleges (seven predominantly black and eight predominantly white) that make up the sample. They represent four geographical areas with distinct mores and attitudes toward black education: Georgia, Texas, Mississippi, and Ohio. The exploratory research was conducted in Georgia because of the presence of many colleges that attract a large number of black students. Three predominantly black and four predominantly white colleges participated in the exploratory research. Because the predominantly black institutions in Georgia are among the best in the country, they attract some of the best black students and allow a good match of students' background characteristics in black and white schools. Thus, the focus in the exploratory year was on the matching of student characteristics. The succeeding years of the study were devoted to the matching of institutional characteristics. The year of research in Texas was devoted to comparing the progress of black students in two large, state-supported urban universities. Because large numbers of black students were enrolled in these universities, a series of four projects was undertaken to confirm the initial findings: (1) readministration of the standard test battery; (2) a closer examination of cognitive growth; (3) an experimental study of competitive performance; and (4) personal interviews on the college experience. The remaining task was to choose areas that would allow us to determine the generality of the findings from the first two states. In Mississippi, a state that offered a more rural contrast and one more traditional in its relationship to blacks, the progress of black students in two small private institutions was assessed. Then, in order to determine whether the results from three Southern states were also true of the North, four colleges in Ohio joined the sample: a pair of black and white private colleges and a pair of public colleges. Finally, in three of these states, Georgia, Texas, and Ohio, samples of white students were recruited. Thus, the study sample includes almost 3,000 black students and 500 white students, who underwent from four to eight hours of testing.

The measurement goal was to assess global student functioning on academic/intellectual and psychosocial levels. The idea was to find out as much as possible about the functioning of these students by administering an unusually large battery of instruments. The assessments of many areas of functioning allow patterns of adjustment to emerge, so that the conclusions rest not on the strength of a single finding but on the consistency with which a series of findings suggests a conclusion. The assessments included measurements of adjustment to academic life, academic performance, vocational interests, educational and vocational aspirations, sex-role orientation, social adjustment, self-concept, psychophysical stress, personality, and motivation.

The analytical task was to determine whether freshman and senior differences on each of the measures were statistically significant and could not have occurred by chance (at the .05 probability level). An analysis of variance procedure was used to determine statistical significance. We know that freshman and senior students, as well as students in black and white colleges, are usually different with respect to social-class background and scholastic aptitude scores. So that the results would not be confounded by background differences, each dependent variable was submitted to as many as two additional analyses of covariance (that is, when the dependent variable was significantly correlated at the .05 probability level with a covariate) in order to control for any background differences. Also, the exploratory research variables were routinely submitted to all three analyses, whether or not they were required by significant correlations with covariates. Thus, the results reported are true of the general population and hold even after controls for social class and aptitude are instituted. The statistical approach, then, is conservative and requires a robustness of effects not usually found in research. Finally, assessment of effect sizes—that is, the magnitude or meaningfulness of the results—was calculated according to the method described in Cohen (1969). The patterning of significant differences determined was aided by correlational and factor-analytical techniques. At the very least, the combination of measures and methods should leave us with a rich source of ideas to consider in the debate over what will happen to black colleges and the options for black students.

The Exploratory Research

The exploratory field work began in January 1977, and, during the next five months, the basic questionnaire and a Thematic Apperception Test were given to 874 students from the seven target colleges: predominantly black Morehouse (N = 146), Spelman (N = 185), and Clark (N = 209) and predominantly white "Southern" (N = 38), "Traditional University" (N = 125), Georgia Tech (N = 89), and "County College" (N = 78). (Quotation marks indicate a fictitious name.)

The results show that the patterns of intellectual development are consistently more positive for students in black schools. These students exhibit stronger personal attachments to faculty, enhanced involvement in the career process, greater satisfaction with their academic lives, improvement on measures of academic performance, more enterprising vocational interest patterns, and maintenance of higher occupational aspirations. Black students in white schools, however, show quite the opposite, with increasing dissatisfaction with academic life, negative attitudes to teachers who use unfair grading practices, little return on time and effort invested in schoolwork, and no net improvement in academic performance. Among students in white schools, there were a few positive indications of attachment to a role model and high educational aspirations. Nevertheless, students in black colleges seem to have a virtual corner on intellectual satisfactions and outcomes during the college years.

In the subjective, psychosocial domain, the findings are more complex. In black schools, students complain about strained relationships with incompetent instructors and classroom favoritism but nonetheless express greater satisfaction with social and extracurricular activities, institutional quality and responsiveness, contact with faculty, and perceived intellectual growth. For these students, the major psychosocial developments are better social adjustment, gains in social assertiveness, and consistent gains in intellectual self-concept. Women in black schools, however, become more passive and may come to express power motivation through sex-role stereotypical behavior. So, despite some complaints, their psychosocial developments parallel those in the intellectual domain, with some problematical findings for women.

Students in white schools become increasingly dissatisfied with the formal and institutional aspects of the college years and point to a lack of institutional support, negative interactions with instructors, and feelings of abandonment. In their social lives, they experience increasing racial tension as well as interpersonal stresses within the black subculture. Thus, they more often come to see cultural and political activities that allow the opportunity for protest (that is, tension release) to be the best aspect of college. Given their less than encouraging evaluation, it is not surprising that these students show declines in social adjustment and increases in stress. However, these students also show an arousal of even stronger assertive and manipulative desires than their counterparts in black schools. These desires are linked to the kinds of interpersonal confrontation that characterize their daily existence.

Thus, the investigation isolates intellectual development as the domain of experience in which students at black and white schools differ most strikingly. While the psychosocial findings are less consistent, they tend to parallel this pattern, with positive developments in black schools and discouraging ones in white schools.

Sex Differences. Within black populations, the issue of sex differences is of particular interest, because much has been written about the presumed dominance of black women (Moynihan, 1965; Staples, 1970). In fact, black colleges have been accused of perpetuating a black matriarchy (Jencks and Riesman, 1968). Note that the most conservative controls for social class and aptitude have been instituted for this and remaining analyses of the exploratory data.

Males in black schools exhibit the happiest adjustment to college life that can be found. Despite some ambivalence surrounding their interactions with teachers, their experience is more strongly characterized by absorption with role models, greater satisfaction with and positive outcomes from the educational experience (including perceived cognitive growth), and gains in assertiveness of self-expression and in dealing with others.

The development of females in black schools is most notable for the strong improvement in academic functioning (on five of six indices) associated with subjective gains in intellectual self-confidence. However, women also show consistent losses in social assertiveness and more submission to external authority. The results are striking, because the intensely positive academic development occurs side by side with losses in social assertiveness; the latter may well undermine female students' ability to translate academic gains into postgraduate accomplishments. Thus, contrary to allegations of a matriarchate in black colleges, there is really empirical support for the suspected presence of sexist influences. There is a clear sense that the heartening psychosocial ascendance of males occurs at the expense of female development. The male ascendance implies hierarchal dominance over others, and an increasingly submissive social posture among females is evident from the data. It may be that the presence of large numbers of men and women on black campuses creates a situation conducive to the traditional sex-role conditioning associated with psychosocial disadvantages for women.

The profile for black males in white schools is perhaps the most grim. The distressing feature of this profile is that men, initially competitive and career oriented, undergo excessively frustrating experiences that thwart virtually every evidence of academic drive. To be sure, there are gains in educational aspirations, but these gains occur in the context of falling grades in the critical major subject, diminishing feelings of intellectual ability, declining social adjustment, and losses in perceived energy level suggestive of emotional strain. These students become less concerned with academic failure and institutional abandonment; they turn their attentions to extracurricular activities that provide tension release. The fact that few statistical effects can be found for these males creates a sense that they become lost in the data—a phenomenon symbolic of their psychological withdrawal.

The picture for black females in white schools, while not quite as grim, suggests an even more painful process of adaptation. Aroused feelings of failure are evident by the senior year, along with an overwhelming sense of painful frustration in every domain of experience. Their plight is further exacerbated by feelings of academic stress and institutional abandonment. Women who are initially noncompetitive and nonassertive show little academic improvement but are able to effect gains in coping skills, working under pressure, role modeling, assertiveness, and career orientation. There are also indications that these women are able to redirect their energies from frustrated social lives into academics. They develop a facility for surviving, however unhappily. For them, a relatively male-free environment has positive consequences for career development. Thus, any perpetuation of a matriarchate can be observed only in white college environments, supporting the familiar observation that racism has a greater impact on black males. The general conclusions of better intellectual gains in black schools are still valid, but the added dimension of sex differences allows a better understanding of potent sexist and racist influences that are clearly operative.

School Differences. We consider the unique variance contributed by each college in order to see more concretely how the total picture has emerged. While the previous results draw on year-cohort analysis (for example, freshmen in white schools compared to freshmen in black schools) and developmental analysis (that is, from freshman to senior year), the impact of a given college is determined only from freshman-senior developmental comparisons. The development within black colleges remains largely positive, while adverse effects can be observed in most of the white schools. The variations, however, are illuminating.

Morehouse College is, in many ways, the most interesting of the predominantly black schools, because of its apparent inculcation of professionalism and leadership. In concentrating on these elements, the school sacrifices many of the frills of well-rounded development in favor of developing a masculine orientation to future attainment. While students perceive general cognitive growth in themselves, it is clear that any gains are strictly in the service of career and leadership development. The price, of course, looks very much like one many success-oriented men pay—a loss in concern for and/or interest in others.

At Spelman College, the greatest gains are observed in an exceptionally positive picture of academic adjustment, in which students show greater satisfaction with academics, better performance, more constructive relationships with teachers, involvement in the selection of careers, and gains in motivation. Nevertheless, it also appears that career options become more constricted. There is also a tendency toward less assertiveness by the senior year. These two seemingly independent developments may bear some relationship to the reputation of Spelman women: they are said to employ intellectual skills on behalf of others in community service. College development at Morehouse and Spelman is strongest within the intellectual domain.

Clark College, on the other hand, seems to exert a less generalized impact on the intellectual arena. Good academic adjustment is evident, but there are no observable changes in postgraduate plans. Instead, the most important gains seem to revolve around the development of interpersonal coping skills, feelings of competence, and self-assertion in interpersonal situations. In short, Clark students seem to be far more preoccupied with interpersonal development.

Black students matriculating at "Southern University" are, from subjective reports, at best ambivalent about their college experiences. The most distressing features of intellectual changes from freshman to senior year are the absence of academic improvement and a decline in aspirations, especially among males. While there are gains in the development of social assertiveness, the loss in identity affirmation suggests that the college experience is most strongly characterized by a sense of isolation and disconnectedness.

"Traditional University" provides one of the most complex pictures of black student development observed so far. Despite increasing subjective discontent and lack of academic improvement, the aspirations of these students (at least for males) adjust upward; there is also evidence of continued desire for future education. On the other hand, complex psychosocial changes seem to be taking place among males: an apparent acquiescence to white authority accompanies an aroused need for dominance in personal relationships. At the same time, "Traditional University" women appear to be gearing for a more submissive role in relation to men.

At Georgia Tech, the experience of racial conflict and institutional abandonment becomes increasingly apparent. Perhaps as a consequence, these students show little intellectual development and marked deterioration in academic performance, especially in the major subject. Because the time put into studying also decreases, it would seem that there is a gradual decathexis of academic energy that may be routed into nonacademic activities. The data also suggest that the majority of student energies become involved in a struggle for psychological survival. This struggle yields gains in coping and survival skills, self-assertiveness, and leadership status in extracurricular pursuits. However, these gains seem to come at the expense of optimal intellectual functioning.

"County College" presents the most encouraging picture of development at predominantly white Georgia schools. Black students here show gains in the subjective sense of academic adjustment but little objective evidence of intellectual growth. There is evidence of a crisis-oriented mode of dealing with academic life. The inconsistent nature of this mode may equip students characterized by it for the business interests they express. Despite the lack of consistent intellectual development, the psychosocial results indicate personality development along more outgoing and less conventional lines. There is, however, some evidence of the achievement-related conflict that seems unavoidable among black students in white environments, despite sympathetic institutional auspices.

Just as interesting as the examination of school variance is the fact that institutional goals are often strongly related to the kinds of results found. Two of the three black schools show clear evidence that institutional missions have observable outcomes. The leadership emphasis at Morehouse is realized among its seniors, and the Clark interest in people is reflected in the interpersonal development found. Only at Spelman is there very little correspondence between the institutional veneration of accomplished leadership and the objective results. Given the exceptional level of academic development at Spelman, the data seem to suggest that this phenomenon is due not to the institution itself but to nonacademic influences in the environment. These influences may act to override or reduce the intended institutional impact.

None of the academic goals described in the catalogues of the predominantly white schools are realized for black students. Indeed, it would seem that academic achievement is the one area in which these schools do not or cannot support the development of blacks. However, it is interesting that the institutional purposes of these schools often seem to shape the nature of the nonintellectual adjustments, or maladjustments, seen among black students. The "Southern University" catalogue's cold concern for academic excellence is certainly consistent with the feelings of isolation expressed by black students. Indeed, this aspect of "Southern" has prompted its own officials to improve the quality of student life in general. The emphasis on tradition at "Traditional University" helps to explain the emergence of hierarchical relationships of black women to black men as relationships involving traditional notions of dominance and submission. The extensive discussions of well-rounded development in the "County College" statement of purpose do have clear empirical analogues and seem to account for the most positive aspects of black students' development within this school. In addition, "County College" pays less attention to imparting academic subject matter than it does to helping its less competitive students reach college-level competencies—a goal not unlike that of many black colleges.

Individual Differences. Finally, we attempted one last way of looking at the data. Instead of comparing groups of students, we analyzed the relationship between the motivational characteristics and the college development of individual subjects. We take this approach to assure ourselves of deriving more than understanding of average differences. This kind of analysis allows us a more internal look within the college environment. This approach allows us to probe beyond average differences and to consider the question "Who benefits most from each college environment?" We observe the range of behaviors associated with need for achievement, fear of failure, and fear of success. Responses from the 61 men at Clark College and the 43 men from "Traditional University" are analyzed, with correlates corrected for differences in social class and aptitude. These liberal arts colleges are coed, have similar institutional climates, and have large enough male subject pools to permit meaningful correlational analysis.

The need to achieve, to do things well, usually predicts successful competition against standards of excellence, with a future-oriented entrepreneurial style. Of the two populations, Clark students show more achievement-oriented behavior, including better performance on four of six academic measures, higher educational aspirations, and higher vocational aspirations. They are, however, more dissatisfied with campus racial tensions.

Students with a fear of failure usually avoid competitive activities. However, at Clark, such individuals look more like their achievement-oriented counterparts displaying better academic performance (on four of six measures), ambition, and leadership orientation, as well as frustration with racial pressures. This wholly unexpected set of findings indicates that, in a supportive environment that reduces rather than arouses achievement anxieties, even insecure individuals can show good progress. Fear of success is an almost nonintuitive dilemma surrounding the unconscious expectation of negative consequences of success; it is theoretically associated with desires for success coupled with an inability to actualize these desires. This avoidance motivation is virtually inactive at Clark. The few results found indicate less defensiveness surrounding prestigious male-dominated occupations. Thus, the Clark College environment not only permits the satisfaction of achievement drives; it also encourages the development of those men who suffer from potentially self-defeating achievement conflicts.

In contrast, at "Traditional University," need for achievement accounts for very few findings, while the avoidance motives predict more aspects of the college experience. At this institution, the achievement motive is associated with feelings of fatigue that suggest frustration. An aroused fear of failure is indicated by a number of significant correlations, indicating a withdrawal from participation in academics, lack of ambition, and sex-role traditionality. Correlates of the motive to avoid success suggest a heightened activity level (that is, extroversion) that fails to bring constructive gains. Thus, the "Traditional University" environment acts to discourage positive achievement behaviors and at the same time arouses the most nonproductive achievement anxieties. From this subinvestigation, one can only conclude that everyone stands to gain something from a black college environment such as Clark, even if men motivated by strong needs for achievement benefit most. In a white environment such as that of "Traditional University," aroused feelings of insecurity and frustration limit the achievement potential of all concerned.

Having examined the data provided by almost 900 students from a number of perspectives, using several statistical tools, we can identify academic/intellectual development as the domain of experience in which students in black and white college environments differ most sharply. Now we must determine the extent to which this initial conclusion holds as the investigation proceeds.

Confirming the Findings

Texas was chosen as the field site for a replication of the Georgia research, as well as for an additional series of intensive studies designed to confirm or deny the initial impressions. The previous results indicate that cognitive, intellectual, and career-related functioning seem to be the critical areas in which black students at predominantly white and predominantly black schools differ. Subsequent work considers additional measures designed to test the validity of these findings. The measures used in Georgia to assess intellectual development are "soft" in several respects. Some variables, such as those assessing academic adjustment, tap inner thoughts and feelings of students (that is, perceptions) that measure subjective rather than objective reality. Other measures, such as vocational orientation and postgraduate plans, assess interests and aspirations that may not always bear a one-to-one correspondence to future behavior. Finally, while grades have good objective validity within institutions, the varying standards on which they may be based make them less useful in cross-institutional comparisons. "Hard" measures, on the other hand, are those that assess objective behavior and are standardized to the extent that they have meaning beyond a particular subjective environment. The inclusion of a series of more objective measures seems warranted, given the central importance of cognitive issues in education. In addition to the use of harder measures of intellectual development, the Texas data also probe more deeply into the subjective reactions of students through personal interviews.

First, the battery of instruments used in Atlanta was repeated among the 779 students in Texas (455 at Texas Southern University, 324 at the University of Houston). Significant among the findings from these measures is the fact that UH students come to college with many more advantages in the intellectual and psychosocial realms than their counterparts at TSU. University of Houston students enter with much better test scores, higher levels of intellectual self-confidence, better study habits, and more marked social assertiveness. Most of these initial advantages are maintained during the college years, such that in any cohort comparison, the results are in favor of UH students. The development analyses, however, tell a different story.

At TSU, there is evidence of developing academic and intellectual confidence. Consistent with student appraisals are positive gains in such areas as academic efficiency (on two of six measures), academic involvement, commitment to education, and desire for future challenges. Although TSU students begin college with significantly poorer psychosocial adjustment, they show gains where improvement is most needed. The personality gains in achievement motivation and assertiveness are paralleled by self-concept gains in intellectual confidence and verbal expression. While positive changes occur for both sexes, these changes may be somewhat more painful for women, who experience more internal stress and loss of popularity.

At UH, despite the many advantages that students bring to the college, the increasing impact of racism and a lack of camaraderie among black students frustrate personal initiative. While these students feel that they have made cognitive gains, the objective intellectual impact of college is less than encouraging. The increasing dissatisfactions and frustrations of academic life lead to ambivalence about future goals and reduced levels of aspiration, especially in males. On the other hand, there are strong gains in academic functioning (five of six measures) and the development of an orientation to knowledge. While UH students do show more development in their social assertiveness, career orientation, and sense of independence, their experience also appears to result in substantial psychosocial stress. They experience declines in social adjustment, diminishing identity affirmation, and increasing unhappiness.

The fact that TSU and UH are large urban universities with substantial commuter populations must in some way contribute to the pattern of results. A review of the literature and the findings from Georgia seems to suggest that the stresses of social and racial isolation tend to thwart academic development and redirect academic energies into nonintellectual pursuits. However, instead of losing interest in learning, UH students come to focus their attention on grades and knowledge. It may be that, if many students are able to leave campus and return to a family atmosphere supportive of their goals, the effect of racism and isolation may be lessened.

Cognitive Growth. Three nontraditional measures of cognitive skill have been included to test the impressions gained from less objective indices. These new tests are nontraditional in that they require students to generate their own responses to cognitive problem-solving tasks, rather than selecting answers from prearranged options. Because the tests are not geared to particular subject matter, they have a general relevance that makes them even better measures than growth estimates from GRE scores (which have been taken by too few students to provide a reliable analysis).

The results are, of course, consistent with the general picture. At TSU, students show gains on two of three measures, while at UH, males suffer a loss on one of the measures. UH women, however, show evidence of intellectual gain on this same task. It is unlikely that UH students become less intelligent while in college, but these findings do, indeed, provide a testament to the effects of frustration on behavior and motivation.

Competitive Performance. An experimental study of the impact of college on competitive performance constitutes the most ambitious (and revealing) aspect of the entire project. The idea is to see how well students can integrate the intellectual skills gained in black and white colleges for more practical use in a simulated work setting that previews real-world performance—at least to the extent that a laboratory situation can. Each student competes on achievement tasks against a same-sex peer in either a black or white working environment created by an older experimenter and a confederate peer. The study incorporates a unique combination of measures that assess more or less cognitive reactions to competition (that is, performance tasks and subjective reactions). It also includes measures providing a more internal look at the organism's involuntary reactions (that is, pulse, blood pressure, and motivation). Again, the usual controls for SES and aptitude are instituted, along with even more accurate controls for baseline levels of the abilities and measurements under consideration.

The effects of competition on basic math performance are minimal, but a number of results have been found for verbal performance. Although TSU freshmen do not fare as well in competition as their UH counterparts, there are no differences by the senior year; seniors at both schools are performing at the same level, provided that verbal aptitude is roughly similar. What, then, makes up the difference from freshman to senior year? As might be expected, considering the previous results for these schools, the only gains made in ability to compete are found at TSU. Furthermore, these gains are strongest for students working in white environments. So, oddly enough, the experience at a black school equips students to function better in integrated work settings. TSU students also come to enjoy working in white environments more over time, while UH students actually begin to like competition less. The motivational incentive underlying these results is that TSU students are more likely to see competition as providing the opportunity to satisfy power needs.

There is, however, another side of this rosy picture for students in black schools. There is evidence that the stress of competition arouses stronger achievement-related anxieties (that is, fear of success) and produces elevated physiological readings at TSU. There is some evidence that the physiological impact of competition is progressive over time, with males in general displaying the adverse effects of competition more than women. The tendencies are strongest at TSU. It has long been recognized that certain "special needs" may influence some black students to choose predominantly black colleges. One aspect of these needs appears to involve deeply rooted achievement conflicts with physiological consequences under stress. TSU may not *solve* the underlying conflict, which is by definition inaccessible to consciousness. Unlike UH, however, TSU *channels* this conflict constructively.

It is worth mentioning that women exhibit some interesting patterns during the competitive experience. They exhibit higher levels of achievement motivation and faster physiological recovery from competition. Women at TSU show the most dramatic gains in competitive ability. So far, so good. However, questioning about their performance reveals that women's stronger motivation to do well is accompanied by more nervousness and less satisfaction with their performance. Thus, at a conscious level, women display anxieties not consistent with more significant measures of their capabilities and fortitude. In short, their relative shortcomings are more apparent than real and amount to attitudinal fictions that may be self-defeating. Perhaps giving lip service to competitive distress helps to ward off the costs to women of successful competition—namely, the loss in popularity evident from the first study of TSU women.

Sources of Stress and Satisfaction. From the personal interviews, we are able to examine student opinion more closely. We ask students to talk about sources of stress and satisfaction. Despite the attention to academic development observed in previous analyses, the interpersonal domain of experience reflects the impact of college on student states of contentment or distress. Interpersonal stress (that is, stress revolving around significant others) increases over time at UH but decreases at Texas Southern. Further, TSU students more often use other-directed means of handling stress, such as talking to people, while UH students more often resort to mental distraction, in such forms as forgetting. Thus, a college environment that encourages sharing burdens acts as a buffer against interpersonal sorrow. In contrast, repressing unhappiness creates a special vulnerability to the impact of impaired relationships. For many black students, the white college is a lonely environment, one offering no buffer against interpersonal stress. In such a context, these students experience threats to interpersonal ties more acutely.

College exerts a similar impact on the interpersonal unhappiness of both men and women. However, for males, interpersonal happiness (that revolving around intimates and the social environment) is a special case. In addition to increasing interpersonal unhappiness, UH males report more interpersonal happiness over time. This suggests that, in a lonely college environment, one's strongest positive and negative emotions revolve around the interpersonal void. At TSU, on the other hand, males report less interpersonal stress *and* less interpersonal happiness over time. So, in a positive environment that provides freedom from interpersonal longing, males seek to rise above and deny all interpersonal feeling, perhaps to reach the macho ideal of detachment.

The preceding chapters clearly show that black colleges provide greater academic/intellectual gains. This addition underscores the gains in interpersonal adjustment and suggests that such gains are a critical mediator of intellectual development. From the results of personal interviews, we could argue that the opportunity to develop sound, primary interpersonal anchors is a precondition for students' secondary, higher-order cognitive development.

Generality of the Findings

In the Deep South: Mississippi. With nine colleges having been investigated, convincing evidence has been marshaled to confirm that black students do indeed show greater intellectual gains in predominantly black colleges, gains not apparent in predominantly white institutions. So far, the investigations of the impact of predominantly black and predominantly white colleges have been conducted in two major cosmopolitan areas of the Southern United States. These cities are notable as centers of business as well as of educational and cultural activities. They are consequently growing and changing rapidly. It is expected that, in the process of adjusting to rapid growth, traditional attitudes and mores would also undergo change. Regional influences are already apparent in the results reported, and those results must, in some way, reflect the social and economic changes in each region. The question now arises: What is the impact of college on black students in a more remote area of the Deep South? Will the general pattern thus far established hold up in an area where life in general and the traditional status of blacks in particular have changed less dramatically? For this investigation, students from two small private colleges in Mississippi are chosen—predominantly black "Freedmen College" (N = 80) and predominantly white "Magnolia College" (N = 51). These students received the basic battery of measures.

Relative to counterparts at "Magnolia," students at "Freedmen" come to college with lower standardized test scores. Nevertheless, the social-class backgrounds of the two groups are very similar. When asked to assess their college experience, "Freedmen" students express relatively more positive sentiment about both the general school experience and their student peers. They do, however, complain more about the functioning of the administration and the quality of the institution. From freshman to senior year at "Freedmen," students show increasing satisfaction with teachers, become more likely to choose careers on the basis of their competence, and assume more leadership roles in campus activities. However, the positive aspects of development at "Freedmen College" end here. Not only is there an absence of gain in academic performance from freshman to senior year; there are also significant losses in investigative and enterprising vocational orientations, indices of desires for scientific knowledge, and outgoing business entrepreneurship. We find diminishing ambition and social orientation, losses in identity integration, and increases in psychophysical stress. These findings suggest a social withdrawal and desire to avoid knowing, investigating, or confronting aspects of their broader reality. In the process, certain elements of students' identity integration seem to suffer. Is it possible that such a development prepares these students to function in their traditional roles as blacks in Mississippi? The empirical findings for "Freedmen" are quite contrary to the school's established reputation as a valiant leader during the civil rights era and producer of many distinguished alumni. Although the "Freedmen" results suggest a discouraging lack of ambition, it may well be that such a demeanor is really a dissimulation strategy, of hidden value to those coping with the realities of black existence in Mississippi.

At "Magnolia," black students complain more about racism, the faculty, courses, and a sense of personal failure. As a result, the best aspects of college become nonacademic. These students do show gains on one of six indices of academic performance as well as enhanced career orientation and feelings of intellectual competence. As freshmen, they exhibit higher aspirations than "Freedmen" students, but this edge disappears by the senior year. Their psychosocial development is marred by greater stress and identity disintegration. In short, the positive outcomes for these students are in academic functioning, career orientation, and feelings of competence. However, the ambitious-career set found in the data may be misleading, since it is not consistent with educational and career aspirations. It may be that "Magnolia" students proclaim career ambitions that are somehow inhibited (or hidden) in actual practice. In a sense, this pattern is a reversal of the "Freedmen" strategy.

Thus, the general findings for these two Mississippi colleges are not consistent with the previous results, which show greater gains in the intellectual domain in predominantly black schools. However, the sleepy "Freedmen" facade may cloak and protect strivings toward achievement, sheltering them from both external threat and internal anxiety. At "Magnolia," a declared desire to achieve may summon those obstacles and inhibitions the "Freedmen" strategy eludes.

In the North: Ohio. It is conceivable that the pattern of findings, richly varied as it is, could be the result of Southern mores. It does not necessarily point to a more general dilemma for the majority of black students who attend predominantly white colleges in the North. To rule out this possibility, students were recruited from predominantly black Wilberforce University ($N = 222$) and Central State University ($N = 232$)

and from predominantly white "Northern University" (N = 153) and Ohio State University (N = 204). They were subjected to the Mississippi battery of tests.

The development results from Wilberforce create one of the rosier pictures found. Students become more likely to express satisfaction with the college and the quality of instruction. They feel that their identities have taken shape during college. Their intellectual development is overwhelmingly positive in that they express satisfaction with many aspects of academic life, improve in their academic efficiency (on four of six measures), and have higher educational and occupational goals. These positive developments seem to be consistent with personality changes indicating greater expressiveness, stronger feelings of competence, and stronger constructive drive levels. Such developments, however, are accompanied by some internal discomfort.

At Central State, there is some evidence of positive development in that students express positive feelings about their courses and the intellectual aspects of college over time. Students feel that they have shown cognitive growth as a result of the college experience. They show more academic improvement (on one of the six measures), positive attachment to role models, and increasing career and extracurricular involvement. In the psychosocial realm, students also show growing feelings of intellectual competence and social assertiveness. The academic/intellectual gains are, however, far from dramatic in that college has little impact on future plans, and students actually show more career ambivalence over time. Over time, men express the most positive sentiment about the college, their peers, and the instructors. Men also show the best social development and enhanced black ideology. Women, on the other hand, show increasing dissatisfaction with teachers, more academic problems, stronger fear of failure, and more unhappiness over time. At the same time, however, they describe themselves as less obedient and show gains in enterprising vocational orientation. It would seem, then, that women are experiencing more difficulties in their academic lives.

At "Northern University," the findings give the peculiar impression of contradictory development. In spite of low ratings of the faculty, classroom instructors, and peers, students perceive more personal motivation. While they show decreasing interest in grades, minimal academic improvement, and decreasing educational ambitions, they show more interest in their careers and stronger enterprising vocational interests. These students perceive themselves as more aggressive, dogmatic, and ambitious. However, they also become more shy, irresponsible, and intellectually incompetent.

Like the development results for "Northern University," the findings for Ohio State indicate a number of contradictions in that students' subjective reactions seem to be out of sync with the more objective evidence. Students are more likely to praise their instructors, show more involvement with instructors over time, and express feelings of enhanced cognitive growth during the college years. The objective evidence, however, shows no improvement in grades, no increases in educational or vocational aspirations, and ambivalence surrounding career goals as well as the interests and abilities behind them. As students tell the story, they have shown positive changes in their self-concepts surrounding enhanced energy and ambitiousness. Yet they also complain of personal failure and show evidence of more personal stress. In short, the subjective sentiment seems to serve to disguise the absence of real gain and possible evidence of internal conflict.

The results, of course, support the general pattern of better intellectual and psychosocial development in predominantly black schools. Indeed, the overall pattern shows that black colleges are twice as likely to encourage improvement in academic functioning and gains in intellectual self-confidence. In the psychosocial realm, black colleges are twice as likely to encourage greater energy in the senior year and four times as likely to promote good social adjustment.

Comparing Black and White Students

The conclusions so far have been drawn from comparisons of only black students in black and white colleges. Limiting the analysis in this way does not enable us to determine whether the pressures on black students in white schools are peculiar to the black experience. Do white students also show a different kind of development from that found in predominantly black colleges? Some norms against which to judge the progress of black students in white colleges would round out our understanding of the processes at work. To this end, samples of white students are recruited from Georgia Tech (N = 134), the University of Houston (N = 109), and "Northern University" (N = 145).

Compared to black students, white freshmen come to Georgia Tech with stronger mechanical vocational interests, suited to engineering. They also exhibit stronger needs for power and influence. Despite lower work-related ambitions, lack of intellectual confidence, and somewhat lower performance in the major subject, these students express more satisfaction with college. Over time, white students show consistent evidence of positive development in the three areas investigated. Their subjective reactions show a convergence of interest in the cognitive/academic side of college life. While there is no improvement in academic functioning, students become more involved with role models and become more preoccupied with the end products of education, such as higher educational and occupational goals. Their psychosocial changes revolve around enhanced expressive and leadership abilities, which go along with reductions in symptoms of physical stress. Compared to black students, white seniors show better social adjustment and better grades. Recall that black students in this institution make some psychosocial strides in the areas of coping and assertiveness but show important intellectual losses, particularly in academic functioning. White students, on the other hand, show both psychosocial and intellectual gains during the college years. While white students at Georgia Tech may not show dramatic intellectual gains, they certainly display more positive growth in this area than can be observed among black students.

White students at the University of Houston become more negative about the academic experience, especially class activities and poor instructors, such that the most positive aspects come to be nonacademic. While white students are more casual than black students in their approach to grades, they nonetheless receive better grades. White students show more (though not dramatic) evidence of cognitive growth, positive development in terms of constructive involvement with faculty, higher educational goals, and fewer perceived obstacles to future goals. In spite of dissatisfaction with academics, white students show a number of intellectual gains. The development picture is not bright for any group of students at the University of Houston. Both black and white students are disenchanted with the academic experience, but for different reasons. While black students face the challenge of racism in the classroom, white students seem simply uninspired. Clearly, though, racism has a more devastating effect on intellectual growth than does simple lack of inspiration.

At the University of Houston, white students are also involved in the practical test of abilities provided by the experiment in competitive performance. Neither black nor white students at the University of Houston show performance gains on either math or verbal tasks. In fact, white women show a loss in math performance from freshman to senior year. But, even with initial level of ability controlled, white students perform better on verbal tasks, while white women perform better than black women on the math test. Analysis of subjective ratings suggests that the problem is one of motivation, since motivation to do well in competition is most depressed among black students. The motivational analyses confirm that positive incentives for the attainment of achievement and power satisfactions are more strongly aroused in white students. Power-related anxieties are, however, aroused in women. The relative absence of physiological effects following competition is distinct from the previous observations of black students; it suggests a weaker physiological impact of competition among whites. The differences in black-white competitive performance thus appear to have strong motivational components, with white students having stronger positive incentives for competition. These incentives may well be related to the absence of progressive physiological effects. College has very little impact on this basic black-white difference in orientation to competition.

There are so many inconsistencies in the development of

black students at "Northern University" that little faith can be placed in the positive gains indicated. Not so for white students. For them, the academic environment provides staunch, unambivalent support for academic and career growth. Like black students, they show no obvious improvement in grade averages over the four years. Unlike black students, they develop interest and satisfaction in the academic experience. For them, class and learning activities become the best part of college; they expend more effort in academics over the years. By the senior year, white "Northern" students have a higher estimate of their own ability, higher aspirations, and weaker fears of failure. Psychosocial developments for these students are also positive, contributing to a greater energy level by the senior year.

In short, white students do not always show the kind of development that makes a university proud. Nevertheless, compared to black students, whites face fewer hostile pressures and thus show substantially greater gains, particularly in the intellectual domain. Thus, the college gains shown by white students in white schools look much like those shown by black students in black schools.

Validity of the Findings

This investigation was conceived in response to the increasingly serious pressures on predominantly black colleges to justify their continued existence in the face of relatively poor institutional resources. Teachers at black colleges are less competent by research standards. The student culture within black institutions is semiliterate. The efficiency of maintaining separate institutions at public expense is questionable. All these factors suggest that white colleges are better able to assume the intellectual responsibility for educating black students. These, then, are some of the strong prevailing assumptions about black colleges that the present study has shown to be faulty as far as student outcomes are concerned. Better facilities in and of themselves do not necessarily translate into a better education; by the same token, inferior resources do not ensure an intellectual disservice to students. The most consistent finding of this study is precisely the one least expected by critics of black institutions: that black colleges produce greater gains in the cognitive domain. There is more widespread belief that black colleges provide greater social-psychological supports, a belief that is indeed borne out in the results of this study. In many instances, the academic/intellectual gains are not dramatic, but they stand in contradistinction to the direction of development in predominantly white schools.

Limits of Cross-Sectional Designs. It is well worth considering why the prevailing assumptions about the failings of black colleges are so at odds with this study's actual findings. Indeed, could the present findings be in error? Could the fact that a cross-sectional design is a less preferred method than a longitudinal one have produced results that are misleading? If we had tracked the development of the same individuals over four years instead of comparing different students, would our results have been different? It is true that, according to the most recent consensus of developmentalists, a cross-sectional study constitutes only part of the evidence for growth. Longitudinal research helps to place the final picture in context, define the magnitude of the effects, and separate the effect of cohort. However, if a longitudinal verification of our results yielded vastly different findings, it would be the first time. According to Feldman and Newcomb (1969), cross-sectional findings of college impact parallel those from longitudinal findings in both nature and direction. In his review of college impact studies, Pace (1979b) tells us that the two methods yield complementary, not contradictory, information. Studying the impact of college on liberal arts competence, Winter, McClelland, and Stewart (1981) also find that a longitudinal test of their cross-sectional study confirms their findings. If the conclusions of the current investigation were based on cross-sectional differences (or even longitudinal changes) from a small sample of 30 subjects (not uncommon in social science research), the results might be misleading if extrapolated beyond an idiosyncratic data base. Yet the present conclusions rest on not one sample but on fifteen different subject pools, combined and dissected in various ways. This study represents experience in four states and among contrasting types of colleges. The odds that a similar pattern of findings would emerge consistently across the various comparisons by chance are highly unfavorable.

Magnitude of the Findings. Perhaps, then, the fact that the magnitude of the research findings is relatively small suggests that the findings should not be taken seriously. The magnitude of the research findings has central relevance to the question of validity. According to Cohen (1969), it is possible to calculate the size of a given effect from "small" (barely visible to the naked eye) to "large" (a highly visible effect). There is no denying that, with few exceptions, any given result in the study is of small magnitude. Although of small magnitude, our results are statistically robust. The fact of consistency across so many findings of small magnitude, tapping relatively independent aspects of experience and behavior (as indicated by the factor analyses performed), suggests that the results may be cumulative and noticeable, especially for the individual. Also, the magnitude of the effects for black students is much the same as it is for white students. Thus, the gains of black students in black schools are as large (or small) as the measurable impact of education itself. Indeed, Moos (1979) also reports that the findings in his research and in educational research in general tend to be of small magnitude. Winter, McClelland, and Stewart (1981) suggest that the reason lies in the nature of the measurements. Instruments that presume to measure stable traits such as intelligence, abilities, and personality are purposely constructed with a built-in bias against showing change. Consequently, many of the available measures may underestimate the real impact of college. This study, of course, has many limitations, but there are two fundamental questions to be asked in considering its validity: (1) Are the study's limitations capable of producing findings vastly in error? (2) Could the observed patterns of adjustment have emerged if they did not really exist? The many sources of validation internal to and external to the study suggest not.

Fit with Empirical Research. The findings are very much in agreement with the bulk of previous empirical research in the area. The factors that have already been identified by Gurin and

Epps (1975) as constituting positive intellectual climates at predominantly black colleges have been found to be largely absent or unavailable to black students in predominantly white schools. Good evidence is already available that racial tension and inadequate social lives combine with racism in the classroom to create feelings of alienation and abandonment, as well as serious adjustment problems for black students in white schools (Davis and Borders-Patterson, 1973; Willie and McCord, 1972; Gibbs, 1975; Monroe, 1973). Adjustment problems have been found to lead students to a series of coping reactions having negative consequences for intellectual functioning (Erikson, 1968; Gibbs, 1974; Clark and Plotkin, 1963; Hedegard and Brown, 1969). In total agreement with this conclusion are the results of our personal interviews. They strongly indicate that the interpersonal climate lies at the heart of differences between academic functioning at black schools and that within white institutions.

Fit with Experimental Studies. The study's conclusions are in remarkable agreement with a long series of experimental studies by Irwin Katz and associates, showing that the productivity of black males is seriously disrupted in white work environments (for example, Katz, Goldston, and Benjamin, 1958; Katz and Benjamin, 1960). Their results read much like our description of the plight of black students in white colleges. The researchers find that black subjects display a distinctly compliant orientation to whites, are less active in communication, direct remarks mainly to whites, and overestimate white task performance. Blacks are less participatory in problem-solving tasks, even when matched with white subjects for intelligence. They have less influence on team decisions and make more errors in biracial work groups than they do when working alone. According to Katz, there is good reason to think that anxiety is aroused in black subjects over the consequences of displaying competence and assertiveness, especially when there is a high degree of interaction with whites on work-related tasks. Because of these fears, black students are likely to avoid highly interactive situations when they can or to compliantly alter their behavior when they cannot. Performance in the mere presence of whites, without even a high degree of interaction, can also generate anxiety when the climate is hostile or the students disadvantaged. This particular observation reminds us of the performance of certain black subjects during our experiments in interracial competition. Black performance is not necessarily disrupted in white environments, and not to the same degree in all individuals. It can be enhanced when the atmosphere is relaxed, the tasks nonthreatening, or the students high achievers. Katz finds that strong achievement motivations actually seem to equip blacks for the challenge of competition with whites but that strong needs for approval and fears of success are distinct liabilities. Originally inspired by Katz's work, the present investigation echoes his findings.

Not only are Katz's cumulative findings too much like the pattern of blacks in white colleges to be accidental; his experimental work on black performance in all-black environments leads to the same conclusion as this project. With black testers, black performance is invariably enhanced in black environments and by the use of black comparison groups. In Katz's work, the more educationally disadvantaged students are, the more susceptible they are to the effects described. This speaks very directly to the mission of black colleges. Yet, in both sets of research, the demotivating effects seem difficult to escape. This observation is easier to comprehend if the effects are, indeed, rooted in conditioned fears that surround black intellectual assertiveness on both sides.

Fit with Comparative Studies. The few comparative studies that precede the present one are limited in both number and scope. Nevertheless, they suggest, first, that black-white differences in academic functioning, while present, are not as great as might be expected, given the initial problems (Bayer and Boruch, 1969). The present study finds that black and white students tend to be more similar than different. The gap in academic performance tends to become greater over time, suggesting the enhanced influence of nonintellectual factors. Secondly, previous studies suggest different consequences for men and women in white environments (Bayer and Boruch, 1969; Hughes and Works, 1976). This study confirms sex differences in adjustment not only to white college environments but to black environments as well. Black women clearly face different stresses in each kind of college environment, while black environments can foster an ascendance of males that may come at the expense of women.

The provocative study by Centra, Linn, and Parry (1970) finds no average differences in cognitive growth in a sample of black and white schools. The present study, however, clearly demonstrates greater gains in black schools in the cognitive domain, although this evidence comes from a different set of measures (as well as colleges) than the Centra, Linn, and Parry study. Cognitive growth seems not to be a unitary phenomenon; it appears to have many different facets, all of which are undoubtedly influenced by a variety of nonintellectual factors. The picture of cognitive development gained from academic functioning is by no means the same as that obtained from the nontraditional measures of cognitive growth, from measures of educational and vocational aspiration, from measures of competitive performance, or, for that matter, from measures of achievement motivation. Each of these instruments does have different methodological properties—some with greater favor than others. However, each measure contributes something valuable to an understanding of how college environments affect students. The use of several measures provides us with an insight into developmental complexities that no single measure can convey.

The findings by Anderson and Hrabowski (1977), showing no differences in graduate school performance among black students from black and white colleges, raise general questions about the implications of our results for life after college. This, of course, is a matter entirely separate from the issue tackled by the present study. The one certain conclusion to be drawn is that black students show greater gains in black colleges than in white schools. While we cannot say with any certainty what happens thereafter, the probable consequences are of interest.

Without question, black students entering black colleges come from further behind than do their counterparts in white schools. Yet they make greater strides during the college years.

On some measures, such as cognitive skill, the intellectual gap is not closed even for individuals of roughly similar testable abilities. By other standards (most importantly, competitive performance), the performance gap can be closed, so that seniors at black schools and those at white institutions function at about the same level, given a rough parity of aptitude. On still other indices (such as achievement motivation, aspiration, and confidence), students in black schools overtake their counterparts in white institutions. The probable consequences of these gains may depend on the circumstances facing graduates of each school and which of their abilities will be called into play in the future. Where pure cognitive skill is at issue, graduates of some white schools may make a better showing. Where the integration of many skills is required for competitive potential, graduates of black schools may be indistinguishable from others. Where confidence and drive make the difference—at this point we can only guess the outcome. Black college graduates must, of course, leave the predominantly black environment and cope with the largely white world. The mere fact that the world is white could act to neutralize further progress. On the other hand, having made the transition from adolescence to adulthood in a positive setting could, à la Erik Erikson, bring these students to a stage of maturity strong enough to see them through the hard times ahead. The pertinent evidence provided by this study is that black colleges seem to equip students to compete effectively in white environments and to enjoy the competition more, in spite of prior "disadvantages" brought to the integrated situation.

Fit with Studies of Women's Colleges. That "something extra" accruing to women with baccalaureate origins in women's colleges so fits the pattern for black students that we might have foretold the outcome. Lee Tidball's (1973) study of notable American women calls attention to the fact that female achievers of *Who's Who of American Women* status are twice as likely to have graduated from an all-women's college. This is so not because these women have been unable to attend male schools but because they have had the opportunity to watch female faculty role models function effectively in a mixed-sex educational arena—a preview of the real world. With male and female adult models but an absence of male peers, female students derive something special, something that they are far less likely to gain in the presence of male classmates. As in the present study, Tidball finds that poor-quality women's colleges are at least as effective in producing achievers as elite coed institutions. Black students, then, are not the only students who benefit from institutions specially geared to their needs.

Future Research

Comprehensive as the present volume is on the subject of black college students, there is much that one volume cannot do. There has been no discussion of how predominantly black or white experiences in secondary school influence preparedness for black or white college, although we are sure that they do. The influence of social class is statistically controlled in all comparisons reported, meaning that the results are not confused by SES differences among students. Yet how would the results look if the impact of college on low-SES students could be viewed separately from college impact on higher-social-class students? Surely, patterns not now apparent would surface. Likewise, is the differential impact of black and white schools different for very-low-aptitude students as opposed to those higher in the abilities measured by standardized tests? Our examination of sex differences is cursory, considering the wealth of data left unanalyzed by gender. It goes without saying that many individual differences in strengths and weaknesses, factors that make or break the college experience, must remain a mystery. For those interested in particular dimensions of development in college, such as the development of black ideology, it is not possible here to give due attention to the factors that detract from or enhance healthy black identities. Our attention has been focused on a larger pattern of development. Such is the loss of information when so many measurements are taken. Yet all of the remaining questions can still be answered; it is easy to imagine future volumes looking at college life from vastly different perspectives. The developmental view expects college to have a far-ranging impact, precisely because the special inputs of college coincide with a special period of adolescence for the individual. The college/adolescent period is one in which critical choices are made for the future. Clearly, the events that occur during the college years are expected not to constitute a transitory phase but to shape the course and nature of future development.

What is the differential future for black students who attend predominantly black or white colleges? In general, the black college environments are more effective, because they are "supportive." But what will happen to students when they leave the black college protectorate and enter the less supportive and perhaps even hostile environments that they will surely encounter thereafter? Will the gains made survive, or will further development become neutralized or thwarted, as has often been the case for white college counterparts? Without the constancy of a supportive environment, can the developmental progress continue? Are students in black colleges becoming dependent on a style of experience that they cannot realistically expect to find in the real world? If so, how well are these colleges preparing them for later realities? More practically, will a black college education be a ticket to a better life when discrimination is still such a reality? Will a black college B.A. be given the credit it deserves? Will it open as many doors as a white college B.A.?

According to developmental theory, college is a critical period, because adolescence comes to an end during this time. The accomplishments of the adolescent period culminate in a crystallized sense of identity. This new structural identity then becomes the organizing principle, capable of directing the future course of one's life. In developmental terms, then, good progress during the black college years is expected to provide a new level of maturity, capable of acting as a buffer against harder times ahead. This appears to have been the case for Tidball's eminent women of female colleges. What the future really holds for black graduates of black and white colleges only future research can tell.

Appendix A: Measures Used in the Study

Socioeconomic Status

It was anticipated that a measure of socioeconomic status would be used as a covariate, that is, to adjust certain of the research findings for initial sample differences in background status. In addition to the specific background items, the Hamburger (1971) Revised Occupational Scale for Rating Socioeconomic Status was used to provide a summary measure of background status. Hamburger's measure provides a continuous *vertical* scale (which best fits the statistical requirements for a covariate) composed of seven levels (with one the highest level). In addition, it differs from other scales in providing a *horizontal* scale with seven occupational categories within the levels. Hamburger's revision of previous scales resulted in this class-status, multidimensional scale with occupational prestige as the most heavily weighted factor (see Warner and others, 1949). The occupational categories are professional; semiprofessional; proprietors, managers, and business officials; clerical and sales; manual; protection and service workers; and farmers.

The assessment of socioeconomic status of blacks (especially in comparison to whites) has met with some criticism because of the discrepancy among occupation, income, and prestige typically found among blacks, such that years of education do not translate into occupational status or income level similarly for whites and blacks. Thus, a number of authors have found education to be the best single index of social class among blacks (Rose, 1956; Kahl, 1957; Simpson and Yinger, 1972; Frazier, 1962). However, the fact that most of the comparisons in the present study would be performed *within race* seemed to argue in favor of using an existing scale rather than an approximate measure based on years of education alone.

Aptitude

Beyond socioeconomic status, aptitude test scores are the next most important background variable along which black students in black and white schools are found to differ. Thus, standardized scores were obtained for as many students as possible for use as a covariate, that is, to further adjust findings for initial differences in aptitude. Since both SAT and ACT scores were used by some colleges, ACT scores were converted to their SAT equivalents according to a formula made available by the American Colleges Testing Program (Langston and Watkins, 1976). It was, in many cases, difficult to obtain test scores, because some students had not taken the tests (or been required to take them) and because the colleges often had no record of them (especially for students who had transferred in after the first semester of the freshman year).

Subjective Assessments of the College Experience

The concept of college (or institutional) climate refers to the perceived or experienced qualities of the total configural environment. As such, it differs from the usual environmental concepts, which refer to specific discrete qualities often measured by physical (or interpersonal) objects and stimuli. Theoretically, an institutional climate influences people by arousing different kinds of motivation, generating distinctive attitudes about a person's relationship with others, and strongly influencing feelings of satisfaction and performance level (see Litwin and Stringer, 1968). Thus, patterns of behavior can be expected to change, often dramatically, with changes in institutional climate.

While several questionnaire methods of assessing *perceived* climate have been attempted (Litwin and Stringer, 1968; Pace, 1979b; Stern, 1965), they suffer from the fact that it is difficult to determine a priori what the important subjective dimensions may be. Thus, for the purposes of the present study, perceived college climate was assessed by the open-ended method used by Stewart (1975) in her longitudinal follow-up of college educated women. From several questions about the positive and negative aspects of the college experience, Stewart was able to distinguish strong perceived differences between two ostensibly similar college environments—differences that were found to be useful in interpreting differential findings and as important moderator variables in predicting life outcomes after college.

The following three open-ended questions were presented to students, with sufficient space for elaboration:

1. What is the single most enjoyable thing that you do in college, or the most enjoyable event? In other words, when do things really seem to go well for you? Please describe as fully as possible, explaining the significance of this positive aspect of college.
2. Similarly, what do you think is the most disappointing thing that occurs or that has occurred in college? Please fully describe the significance of this disappointing aspect of college life for you.
3. At the present time, how much and in what ways would you say college has influenced or changed you?

A content analysis of the responses to these questions resulted in the following thirty-five variables:

Best Aspects of College

Class activities: Learning, studying, being prepared for class, class participation, working in my major, working in a subject matter I like.

Personal accomplishment: Anything done well or excel-
lently, as opposed to simple involvement in class activities, getting an A, performing well.

Extracurricular activity: Fraternity, sorority, tutoring,
glee-club.

Opposite sex: Boyfriend/girlfriend, men/women, dating
situation.

Socializing: Partying, seeing friends, social gatherings, social closeness.

New people: Meeting different kinds of people, sharing
ideas and life-styles with people, communication with
people, relating to people, learning to understand people.

Instructors: Rapport with teachers, a teacher who enjoys
teaching.

Student involvement: Involvement in general, cultural involvement, interest in politics, demonstrations, black
involvement.

Nothing.

Worst Aspects of College

Financial problems: Lack of money, having to work and
go to school.

Opposite sex: bad incident with opposite sex, no boy-
friend/girlfriend.

Social isolation: Social rejection, lack of sororities, loneliness, missing out on campus activities, not being close
to roommate, "people don't like me," lack of social
life.

Interpersonal tensions: Bad roommate, being used by
friends, dull or immature people, phony people, com-
petitiveness, lack of concern for one another, need for
privacy

Personal failure: Flunking, doing poorly on a test, lack of
motivation or discipline.

Poor decisions: "I should not have majored in English."

Lack of student involvement: Apathy, lack of student interest in politics, culture, or academics, lack of participation, lack of intellectualism.

Race-related tensions and pressures: Racism, racist students, teachers, or administrators, racial isolation, racial tension, all-white classes, white roommate.

Unfairness, favoritism: A grade unjustly given, teachers who play favorites, "I deserved to make honor society."

Instructors: Incompetent teachers, no rapport with instructors, archaic teaching methods, lack of honesty or integrity among teachers.

Administration: Attitude of administration, students being treated badly, being placed in wrong class, registration, poor management of school, dorm mothers, curfews.

Institutional quality: Poor curriculum, closing of my department, shutting down the swim team, large classes.

Lack of institutional support: No one cares, lack of support for blacks.

Class activities.

Confusion, indecision: "I'm more confused now; I can't figure out what to do with my life."

Influence of College

Generally negative: Statements that cannot be coded elsewhere; mention of negative impact—more selfish, for instance.

Generally positive: Statements that cannot be coded elsewhere.

Not much.

Self-development: More mature, more independent, stronger, more responsible, more assertive, self-confidence, self-expression.

Cognitive growth: "I learned a lot"; exposed to many ideas; "I developed my mind."

Identity formation: "I found myself," "It added direction and depth to my life," "I realize who I am," "I discovered the things I'm good at and like to do."

Personal motivation: "I'm more determined to succeed," willingness to compete, realization of importance of education, desire to continue education, desire to be rich.

Racial motivation: "Blacks need to succeed," need for economic power, ability to compete with whites.

Coping and survival: "Learned how to get over," learning what life would be like, "I have to look out for myself," gaining realistic view of the world, ability to deal with trouble, ability to adjust to situations, becoming less naive, "I am able to cope with a job."

Ability to deal with people: Ability to relate to all kinds of people, "Taught me a lot about people," learning to judge people, learning to tolerate people, "I understand how people are."

Cultural broadening and exposure: "I'm more concerned about world events, more aware of things outside my sphere," awareness of people and things, "I discovered culture, black culture."

Although Stewart was able to factor her original variables into four major dimensions of environmental press, in the present study the low intercorrelations among variables (probably due largely to categorical coding) yielded extremely low factor loadings. Thus, each of the variables was used individually. Although these variables cannot be further aggregated, they do reflect dimensions of significance from the subject's own point of view.

Ratings of the College Experience

In order to direct the students' attention to a series of specific aspects of the college experience, several scales were provided so that students could rate the nature of their feelings (from very dissatisfied to very satisfied) on five dimensions:

In general, how do you feel about the college?

How do you feel about the college's administration?

How do you feel about the college's faculty?

How do you feel about the quality of instruction at this college?

In general, how do you feel about the other students at this college?

In addition, they were asked:

> How much contact do you have with faculty members or members of the administration outside of class (from none at all to quite a bit)?

The advantage of using both the climate questionnaire and rating scales is that, on the climate variables, any given student may receive a (present) score only for a small number of variables—a procedure that results in relatively small means that are reflective of the spontaneous awareness of some subjects. Ratings, on the other hand, while limited in scope, require each student to make a judgment on each dimension of interest.

Academic Adjustment

A series of twenty-four questions was designed to probe the nature of students' adjustment to academic life in college. They were concerned not with the specifics of what students were studying (for example, the precise major) but with their feelings about the course of instruction, their degree of satisfaction with their academic performance, their perception of the faculty's responsiveness to their needs, and so on. In essence, then, their degree of subjective involvement and active participation in academic and campus activities was the focus of the investigation. The specific items were:

> So far, are you happy with your decision to come to this college?
>
> Are you planning to take time off from school before you graduate?
>
> Are you planning to drop out of college?
>
> Are you planning to transfer to another college?
>
> Is there a particular problem that you are now facing in some aspect of your college life?
>
> Are you satisfied with the courses you are now taking?
>
> Are you satisfied with the teaching methods of your courses?

Is there a person on campus who you feel has been particularly helpful to you?

In general, do you feel that your teachers are interested
in your welfare and provide encouragement?

Do you feel that your teachers have used fair grading procedures?

Have you ever sought assistance from a teacher or administrator in choosing your courses or in planning your
future? If so, what were the circumstances and the outcome?

Have you had an academic problem? If so, what was the
problem, what did you do about it, and what was the
outcome?

Have you ever sought assistance from the college's counseling services? If so, describe the circumstances and
the outcome.

Is there a faculty member or member of the administration whom you particularly admire?

What extracurricular activities do you actively participate
in? Indicate whether you hold a leadership position in
any of them.

Are you happy with your major?

Irrespective of your own grade-point average, where do
you think you stand in relation to your fellow students
in general ability (that is, verbal and quantitative ability)?

Are you satisfied with your academic performance?

During a typical week (not during exams), how many
hours a week do you usually spend studying?

When exams are coming up, how many hours a week do
you usually spend studying?

Do you work well under pressure?

Are good grades essential to your career objective?

Are good grades in your major subject essential to your
career objective?

How important is it to you to get good grades?

In addition, the following factors extracted from the above variables were used:

Academic Effort
   Number of hours studied in a typical week.
   Number of hours spent studying in an exam week.
Extracurricular Involvement
   Number of extracurricular activities.
   Number of offices held in extracurricular activities.
Importance of Grades
   Feeling good grades to be essential to career goal.
   Feeling good grades in the major to be essential to career goal.
   General importance of getting good grades.
Satisfaction with Teaching Methods
   Satisfaction with courses.
   Satisfaction with teaching methods.
   Feeling that teachers grade fairly.
Involvement with Faculty
   Finding campus person to have been helpful.
   Admiration of a person on the faculty or administration.
Adjustment Problems
   Facing a problem in college life.
   Having an academic problem.
Career Involvement
   Seeking career assistance.
   Having job related to career plans.
Satisfaction with Major
   Being happy with the major.
   Having no plans to change the major.
General Academic Adjustment
   Being happy with the college choice.
   Finding teachers to be interested and encouraging.
   Positive feelings about the college.
   Positive feelings about the administration.
   Positive feelings about the faculty.
   Positive feelings about the quality of classroom instruction.

Academic Performance

While grade averages were reported on the questionnaires, the potential distortions in self-report data in areas as ego-involving as grades, as well as students' inability to report the specific details of their academic histories, argued for reliance on official records. From the transcripts, six measures of academic performance were used:

> Overall grade-point average for the most recent semester or quarter available;
> Grade-point average in the major for the most recent semester;
> Cumulative overall grade-point average;
> Cumulative grade-point average in the major;
> Honors status in the most recent semester;
> Academic probation status in the most recent semester.

For coding purposes, a four-point system was used uniformly, and differential weighting of letter grades was discarded.

Postgraduate Plans and Career Aspirations

Several questionnaire items pertained to the nature of students' plans after college:

> Are you seriously planning to go to graduate or professional school after college?
> If yes, what degree and course of study will you pursue?
> What obstacles might prevent you from carrying out your plans?
> If you do not plan to go to graduate school, what are your career plans?
> What is your vocational objective? That is, what are your career plans?
> Why have you chosen this particular career? That is, who or what has influenced you?
> What obstacles might prevent you from carrying out your plans?

Again, the primary focus was not the specific career choices made by students but was rather the direction and level of their aspirations. From the above questions, the following series of sixteen items was extracted:

Plans graduate or professional school after graduation.
Is ambivalent about plans for graduate school, that is, gives two or more alternatives.
Postgraduate plan is work.
Postgraduate plan is work, then school.
Postgraduate plan is work way up in some business.
Postgraduate plan is marriage.
Postgraduate plan is relaxation, exploratory activities.
Is undecided about career plans.
Is ambivalent about career plans, that is, gives two or more alternatives.
Has specific career plan.
Traditionality of Career Choice Scale
   Chose male-dominated career.
   Chose neutral career.
   Chose female-dominated career.
Educational Aspirations Scale
   Highest degree planned is the B.A.
   Highest degree planned is the M.A.
   Highest degree planned is advanced.

In addition, it seemed important to gain some knowledge of why and how students were making their plans for the future. Therefore, another series of measures was extracted from a content analysis on the reasons for choosing the major subject and on reasons for career and perceived obstacles to the career:

Reasons for Major

Interest: Enjoyment, love.
Knowledge: Exposure, learning something.
Competence: Doing well, best subject.
Challenge: Difficult.
Instrumental to work goal: Needed for graduate school, for good job.

To make contribution: Skill needed, blacks needed, social change.
Good job market: Open market, money.
Race-related: Blacks needed, help blacks.
Dealing with people: Working with people.
Helping others: Others need help.
Liking children.
Family members: Support, encouragement from; role modeling.
Mother: Support, encouragement from; role modeling.
Father: Support, encouragement from; role modeling.
Person outside family: Support, encouragement from; role modeling.
Plans for graduate school undecided.

Reasons for Career

Status: Respect of profession.
Interest: Enjoyment, love.
Knowledge: Exposure, learning something.
Competence: Good at it, will do good job.
Challenge: Difficult.
To make contribution: Skill needed, blacks needed, social change.
Good job market: Open market, money.
Race-related: Need blacks, blacks doing it, help blacks.
Working with people: Meeting people, dealing with people.
Helping others: Others need help, help blacks.
Liking children.
Family members: Support, encouragement from; role modeling.
Mother: Support, encouragement from; role modeling.
Father: Support, encouragement from; role modeling.
Person outside family: Support, encouragement from; role modeling.

Obstacles to Career

Number of obstacles.
No obstacles.

Ability: Grades, acceptance to school.

Indecision: Changing interest, lack of interest, motivation.

Tight job market: Competition.

Marriage: Children, sex-role pressures.

Death: Bad health.

Race-related: Acceptance of blacks.

Assessment of Vocational Interests

In addition to the information specific to career aspirations, the study included a broader assessment of students' vocational interests. A modified version of the Holland (1970) Self-Directed Search (SDS) was employed to assess vocational interest patterns. The instrument consists of 200 yes/no items, which assess a person's interests, competencies, and vocational interests. From these items, it is possible to characterize people by their resemblance to each of six personality types: realistic, investigative, artistic, social, enterprising, and conventional. Within interest, competency, and vocational-interest items, equal numbers of items are given representing each of the six types:

The Realistic Type. This type prefers activities that entail the explicit, ordered, or systematic manipulation of objects, tools, machines, and animals and has an aversion to educational or therapeutic activities. Such persons see themselves as having mechanical and athletic ability and lacking ability in human relations.

The Investigative Type. This type shows a preference for the creative investigation of physical, biological, and cultural phenomena. Such persons avoid enterprising occupations or situations and perceive themselves as scholarly, intellectually self-confident, and lacking in leadership ability.

The Artistic Type. They tend to avoid the activities demanded by conventional occupations or situations and perceive themselves as expressive, original, intuitive, feminine, nonconforming, introspective, independent, and disorderly, having artistic and musical ability (acting, writing, speaking).

The Social Type. Predisposed toward the manipulation of

others to inform, train, develop, cure, or enlighten, such persons perceive themselves as liking to help others, understanding others, having teaching ability, and lacking in mechanical and scientific ability.

The Enterprising Type. Enterprising persons prefer the manipulation of others to attain organizational goals or economic gain. Such persons perceive themselves as aggressive, popular, self-confident, and sociable, possessing leadership and speaking abilities and lacking scientific ability.

The Conventional Type. This type shows a preference for systematic manipulation of data, such as keeping records, filing materials, and so on. Such persons tend to be conforming and orderly, to have clerical and numerical ability, and to avoid artistic activities.

Sex-Role Orientation

The sex-role items included in the study were chosen in order to determine the extent to which students were oriented toward marriage/family/home as opposed to career and the extent of perceived conflict or compatibility between the two sets of goals:

How important is it for you to marry?

At what age would you ideally like to get married?

To what extent do you consider yourself a domestic person, that is, interested in cooking, sewing, interior decorating, homecrafts, and so on?

How important is it for you to have a family?

Would you like to have children? If so, how many children would you like to have?

At what age would you ideally like to have children?

The following items were combined into the Woman's Role Preference Scale:

If you could have your way, what would you like to be? (females only)

A housewife, who is able to devote her full energies to her home and family.

A working wife, who would work to supplement the
family income or to stay active but whose primary
interest is her home and family.

A career wife, who is able to devote major energies to
her career, for whom a home and a family are important but secondary to a career.

A single woman.

If you could have your way, what would you like your
wife to be? (males only)

A housewife.

A working wife.

A career wife.

How difficult do you think marriage and a family would
make it for you to have a full-time career?

The following items made up the career orientation scale:

Please rate the relative importance of marriage/family versus career goals by checking the appropriate choice:

Career goals are definitely more important to me.

Career goals are somewhat more important to me.

Marriage and family are definitely more important to
me.

Marriage and family are somewhat more important.

Marriage, family, and career goals are equally important.

The following items were extracted from the question to form
the Effect of Marriage on Career Scale:

How do you think marriage will affect your career plans?

Marriage will interfere with career.

Marriage will delay career.

Marriage will make career harder.

Marriage will have no effect on career.

Marriage will help career.

Social Adjustment

Six items addressed some of the aspects of interpersonal
and heterosexual adjustment faced by students in college. The

previous literature suggests that the potential significance for the individual of each of these aspects of social living is such that a poor resolution would generate powerful feelings of loneliness and isolation (see Clark and Plotkin, 1963; Hedegard and Brown, 1969):

> Do you have a roommate?
> Do you get along with your roommate?
> In general, do you like the people you have met in college?
> Are you satisfied with the dating situation on campus?
> Do you feel you are excluded from any activities on campus?
> Do you have a boyfriend (or girlfriend)?

Along with "feelings about other students" from the subjective rating scales, these items were combined into a general social adjustment scale where all items were summed (with the exception of one item, which was subtracted). The correlations of these seven items with the total scale score show that they are substantially correlated in the expected directions. Thus, this analysis provides justification for treating these items in scale form.

Self-Concept

A measure of several aspects of the self-concept was included, both because the previous literature indicates that there may be differences in self-concept among black students as a function of race of school environment (Hughes and Works, 1976) and because self-concept theory is clear in suggesting that the self (or environment) *as the subject sees it* has important consequences for behavior. However, the self-concept as an area of research is more problematical than many others in psychology because of the vagueness of the theories themselves and the wide variety of methodological shortcomings found in the studies (Wylie, 1974; Christmas, 1973). In addition to inadequate demonstrations of construct validity, the method used in many studies suffers from a vagueness of terms that renders interpretations of "low" or "inadequate" self-concept suspect. Thus, such research has met with considerable difficulties in operationalizing concepts and in demonstrating the predicted relationship to behavior.

With these reservations in mind, the self-concept measure utilized in the present research was a modification of the Adjective Checklist (see Wylie, 1974). Subjects were instructed to indicate on a six-point Likert-type scale the extent to which each of the thirty-six adjectives (or adjective phrases) described them. The list consists of both positive and negative self-descriptions, selected to assess factors such as intelligence ("intelligent," "ambitious"), assertiveness ("outspoken," "aggressive"), incompetence ("inarticulate," "have a poor memory"), introversion ("shy," "quiet"), and other-directedness ("polite to others," "friendly"). Thus, while this selection of adjectives does not allow a simple dichotomous assessment of a good/bad, high/low self-concept, it locates the nature of self-descriptions in specific content areas. The thirty-six items were submitted to a factor analysis, from which five clusters were extracted:

Social Decorum

well-mannered
obedient
a lady/gentleman
friendly
nice
polite
considerate of others

Incompetence

scatterbrained
poor memory
slow-witted
irresponsible
incompetent

Ambition

competitive
energetic

enterprising
happy
ambitious
adventurous

Fatigue

lazy
tired

Extro-/Introversion

outspoken
talkative
shy
quiet

Recent Life Changes Questionnaire

The present study incorporated an adaptation of the Life Adjustment Scale developed by Rahe and colleagues to assess the number and significance of life changes, or alterations in life-style (Rahe and others, 1964; Rahe, McKean, and Arthur, 1967; Holmes and Rahe, 1967). The questionnaire attempts to examine every area of significant life change, regardless of whether the change is considered to be desirable, undesirable, volitional, or not under the person's control. Higher than normal levels of life changes are associated with the onset of illness. Use of the Life Adjustment Scale then provides a measure of the psychosocial stress being experienced by an individual, stress that has been found to have physical consequences.

The present Recent Life Changes Questionnaire is a twenty-one-item self-report scale, adapted for the specific circumstances of college life, that asks whether they have experienced certain life changes *since entering college*. The items range from changes in eating habits, drug consumption, legal troubles, and achievement to problems in personal relationships. If the student indicates that he or she has experienced a change, he or she is asked to rate the amount of adjustment needed to cope with the event on a scale from 1 to 100. Thus, the following measures were derived from the scale: absolute number of recent life changes and average life adjustment score. Three additional factors were extracted from the twenty-one items of the Recent Life Changes Questionnaire:

Academic Stress

Change in sleeping habits.
Change in alcohol or drug consumption.
Increase in unhappiness.
Change in study habits.
Failure in a course.
Disagreement with an instructor.
Competitive event.

Personal Threat

Violation of the law.
Legal troubles.
Change in political beliefs.
Physical attack.

Personal Stress

Personal achievement.
Change in personal habits.
Change in social activities.
Major decision.

Illness Report

The decision to include an illness report in the study was based on the unambiguous finding in the literature that disease is a response to social stress (see Graham and Stevenson, 1963). The illness report asked students to list the illnesses they have had since entering college and further asked them to indicate the year(s) in which the illness(es) occurred, in addition to the severity (on a scale from 1 to 6) and the duration of the illness. The report provided the following measures: (1) absolute number of illnesses experienced since college (not used in freshman-senior comparisons); (2) average severity of illness; and (3) average length of illness (in weeks).

Psychosomatic Symptoms

Students were asked to indicate whether they were currently experiencing any of a list of nineteen "common complaints" that are commonly diagnosed as having psychosomatic origins (Lachman, 1972). The list included disturbances such as migraine headache, ulcer, insomnia, asthma, and diarrhea. Students were also asked to indicate the severity of the complaint (the degree to which it interfered with normal functioning) on a scale from 1 to 6, the age at which they first began to experience the complaint, and whether medical assistance had been sought for the problem. While the questionnaire may not effectively distinguish between psychosomatic reactions and disease, it should provide an index of the individual's physical reactivity. The following measures were used: (1) absolute number of psychosomatic symptoms; (2) number of symptoms with onset since college; (3) average severity of symptoms; (4) number of times medical assistance was sought for symptoms. Measures based on absolute numbers were not used in freshman-senior comparisons.

Hypochondriasis Scale

The twenty-three items from the Minnesota Multiphasic Personality Inventory (1943) comprising the Hypochondriasis Scale were extracted from the larger inventory as a stress indicator because the items focused on bodily disturbance. This scale was included in the present study in light of consistent research evidence that scores on it are elevated among blacks. There is also some evidence based on MMPI research of a generalized tendency for blacks to report more physical symptoms. And it has further been suggested that a common kind of adjustment in blacks is a denial of disturbing inner feelings and a focus on physical symptoms (Miller, Knapp, and Daniels, 1968).

Personality Scales

Several scales were utilized that provide measures of personality orientations particularly relevant to the problem area, namely, social assertiveness, black ideology, and fear of failure.

These scales rely on a relatively large number of items that appear to have consistent face validity relative to the construct under investigation. The items show a high level of internal consistency in that they are well intercorrelated and thus appear to be measuring the same phenomenon. Such scales have good test-retest reliability such that subjects tend to answer the questions similarly at time 1 and time 2.

Social Assertiveness Scale. The need for a measure of assertiveness was in particular suggested by the work of Irwin Katz and colleagues. In this study, the Rathus (1973) Social Assertiveness Scale was used, which permits a self-report assessment of assertiveness or social boldness. The thirty items are presented in the form of statements to which subjects responded as characteristic or uncharacteristic of them according to a six-point Likert-type scale. The following five factors extracted from this scale were also used:

Fear of Confrontation

"I will hesitate to make phone calls to business establishments and institutions."

"I would rather apply for a job or for admission to a college by writing letters than by going through personal interviews."

"I find it embarrassing to return merchandise."

"I have avoided asking questions for fear of sounding stupid."

"During an argument, I am sometimes afraid that I will get so upset that I will shake all over."

Emotional Suppression

"I am careful to avoid hurting other people's feelings, even when I feel that I have been injured."

"If a close and respected relative were annoying to me, I would smother my feelings rather than express my annoyance."

Openness

"I enjoy starting conversations with new acquaintances and strangers."

"I am open and frank about my feelings."

"I am quick to express my opinion."

Shyness

"Most people seem to be more aggressive and assertive than I."

"I have hesitated to make or accept dates because of shyness."

"I often don't know what to say to attractive persons of the opposite sex."

Submissiveness

"If a salesman has gone to considerable trouble to show me merchandise that is not quite suitable, I have a difficult time in saying no."

"To be honest, people often take advantage of me."

"I often have have a hard time saying no."

Black Ideology Scale. A review of the literature suggests that the saliency of "blackness" and black issues in general will vary partially as a function of attending a white or black college. While Ramseur's (1975) scale has not been utilized extensively, he does report that these items form clusters of personal saliency and group ideology factors and that students' positions on these factors correlated with past history and present behavior. With minor modification, Ramseur's scale was utilized in this study to measure the extent of black ideology and subsequently determine how this relates to college environment, achievement, and expectations. The scale is a twenty-five-item, five-point Likert-type scale, with "1" representing "not at all like me" and "5" representing "extremely important to me." Six factors emerged from the items of the Black Ideology Scale:

Black Heritage

What happens in Africa.

Reading Afro-American authors.

Traveling to black Africa.

Afro-American music.

Learning an African language.
The Southern African liberation struggle.
Black children should learn African languages.

Identity Integration

Where the United States will be in five years.
Academic success.
Feeling I have close friends.
Feeling socially successful.
Thinking where I'll be in five years.
Feeling part of the entire community.
Feeling able to compete against others.

White Culture

European literature.
Learning about white culture.
Getting into classical music.
Much of white culture is of interest.

Black Defensiveness

Blacks are more intelligent than whites.
Thick lips look better.
Whites can't get "down."

Acceptance of White Authority

Afro-Americans should not buy guns.
Police protect the black community.
Black schools do not need a black principal.
Services need not be community-controlled.

Militance

Feeling able to stand up to whites.
Feeling free to date people of my own race.
Fighting white racism.

Test Anxiety Questionnaire (Fear of Failure). The Test
Anxiety Questionnaire (TAQ), constructed by Mandler and
Sarason (1952), has been used in motivation research as a mea-

sure of fear of failure (Atkinson and Litwin, 1960). When used in conjunction with a measure of need for achievement, the TAQ improves motivational predictions (Atkinson and Feather, 1966).

The test is composed of items that assess the students' emotions and attitudes towards tests. The present research utilized an abbreviated version of the Mandler-Sarason scale. The test consists of fifteen items arranged on a five-point Likert-type scale. Examples of items are: "If you know you are going to take a group intelligence test, how do you feel beforehand?" and "To what extent do you feel that your performance on the college entrance test (SAT), or a similar test, was affected by your emotional feelings at the time?"

Thematic Apperception Test. Subjects were given a version of the Thematic Apperception Test according to standard neutral instructions (see McClelland and others, 1953). Subjects were given twenty seconds to look at each picture and five minutes to write brief imaginative stories to each one. This version of the TAT consisted of the following six pictures of black people in everyday scenes: (1) a man and woman in a laboratory; (2) a mother and child seated; (3) close-up of a boy and girl; (4) a father and child walking along the street; (5) a businesswoman on the telephone; (6) a black businessman and a white businessman in an office scene. Counterbalanced versions were given to white students.

The following eleven variables (including the four stages of maturity) were derived from the TAT. The references cited contain discussions of the reliability and validity issues specific to each one.

> *Need for Achievement*—a competitive disposition surrounding the desire to do things well (McClelland and others, 1953; McClelland, 1961; Klinger, 1966).
> *Need for Affiliation*—the desire to establish and maintain relationships with others; also interpreted as the need for social approval (Shipley and Veroff, 1954; Atkinson, Heyns, and Veroff, 1958; Boyatzis, 1973).
> *Need for Power*—a desire to have an impact on others

that has approach and avoidance components (Winter, 1973; McClelland and others, 1972; McClelland, 1975).

Hope of Power—approach orientation indicating a desire to have a personal impact on others.

Fear of Power—avoidance orientation indicating a sensitivity to but avoidance of power situations.

Fear of Success—an approach-avoidance conflict surrounding fear of instrumental competence in areas perceived as role-inappropriate (Horner, 1972, 1974; Zuckerman and Wheeler, 1975; Fleming, Beldner, and Esposito, 1979).

Self-Definition—a tendency to think purposively in terms of causal relationships, associated with an inclination to act independently (Stewart and Winter, 1974).

The remaining variables are TAT-derived measures of Freudian psychosexual stages of maturity developed and validated by Abigail J. Stewart (1977b). Each stage is defined as follows:

Oral Stage of Maturity: Behaviorally oral individuals in fantasy showed a tendency to perceive authority figures as benevolent and other persons as sources of immediate gratification of their wishes. Their feelings showed a preoccupation with the issues of loss and abandonment, including both confusion and despair, and their orientation to action was entirely passive-receptive.

Anal Stage of Maturity: Behaviorally anal people showed a fantasy view that other people in general would *not* gratify their wishes and that authority figures would be critical and reprimanding. In addition, their predominant expressed affect was in the area of anxiety about competence, including both anticipatory anxiety and indecisiveness. Finally, fantasy characters' actions were oriented toward clearing up disordered or chaotic situations.

Phallic Stage of Maturity: Behaviorally phallic people expressed an attitude of rebellious opposition to authority and exploitation or flight in relationships with non-authority figures. In general, the approach to others seemed to involve a desire to use others for one's own purposes or to attempt to get away from them when using them was impossible.

Genital Stage of Maturity: Behaviorally genital people show, in fantasy, a sense of the limited power of authorities, as well as an orientation to other people involving differentiation of others as clear external others, and a desire for sharing and mutuality in relations with others. In addition, they showed a tendency in expression of feelings to clearly express ambivalent or apparently contradictory feelings without any sense of tension about this ambivalence and an orientation to actions indicating an emotional involvement in or commitment to work.

Measures of Cognitive Skill

Three tests were added to measure the effects of a liberal arts education: (1) Test of Concept Formation; (2) Test of Effectiveness of Argument; and (3) Test of Thematic Analysis. These new tests, as reported in a nontraditional study of liberal arts education by David G. Winter, David C. McClelland, and Abigail J. Stewart (1981), were found to have a number of advantages over traditional measures.

Traditional tests of aptitude have generally failed as adequate measures of cognitive growth or of the effectiveness of higher education for several reasons (Winter and McClelland, 1978; Winter, McClelland, and Stewart, 1981). First, aptitude tests require the knowledge of specific facts that are forgotten as soon as continued exposure to them ceases. Secondly, such measures are never correlated with knowledge or skill imparted by educational institutions but rather are correlated with the initial intelligence of the subjects. Third, such tests utilize forced-choice response formats that are easily precoded for computer scoring and that require students only to guess which of the alternatives set before them is correct. Thus, students are never required to generate answers of their own, and the individual thought process is never directly assessed. Finally, the existing aptitude tests were never developed for the specific purpose of assessing cognitive development in the college years.

The stated goals of higher education are said to be to teach students (1) to think effectively; (2) to communicate effectively; (3) to make relevant judgments; and (4) to discriminate among values. Relevant tests would, then, be those with these stated goals in mind. Thus, the new tests do not assess knowledge or facts, because specific facts are never asked for, and the tests are independent of whatever college major the students may happen to be pursuing. Students are required to generate their own answers in response to a problem so that the relevant thought processes can be investigated. The problem-solving ability then demonstrated is not correlated with the amount of information at a student's disposal.

Test of Concept Formation. Edna Heidbreder (1948) of Wellesley developed a measure of concept formation that never became part of the mental testing movement. It is a learning task in which nine different objects are presented visually, each of them associated with a nonsense syllable, such as "narp." The student is expected to recall which nonsense syllable goes with which object. He or she is then presented with an entirely new set of objects and asked to record which nonsense syllable goes with each one. Gradually, the student learns that the nonsense syllable "narp" is correct whenever two objects have the same spatial configuration and that another nonsense syllable is correct when the objects are of the same sort, such as automobiles. Three of the objects presented in different configurations are similar by number, three by spatial configuration, and three by class of object. Subscores are available in terms of how many of the numerical, spatial, or object configurations the student gets correct on the final trial, but for this report the total concept formation score was obtained by summing the number correct in all categories.

Test of Analysis of Argument. This test (Stewart, 1977a)

asks students to read a controversial article about Dr. Spock, blaming permissive childrearing practices for widespread moral laxity. They are asked to argue against the ideas presented, which is fairly easy for them to do. But they are then required to defend the article, including, if necessary, arguing against their own statements. This aspect of the task becomes much harder for undergraduates in that it is a test of ability to argue effectively without emotional intrusion. Reflecting on the intuitive rationale for such an ability, it would seem that emotions are, by their very nature, often irrational and directly linked to one's self-interest. Society, on the other hand, attempts to control irrational forces by attending to reason and logic. The method of scoring the responses to such a test was empirically derived by comparing the freshman and senior protocols. Those elements of argument found most often among seniors were taken as the basis of the scoring procedures. The research did indeed find that scores on this test increased from freshman to senior year at all of the three colleges studied and that the higher the quality of the institution, the greater the gain in scores during the undergraduate years. Because the research is still under way, it is difficult to say what real-life outcomes might be associated with such an ability.

Test of Thematic Analysis. In this test (Winter and McClelland, 1978), students were given two sets of imaginative stories and were asked to describe the differences between them in any way they liked. The stories were actually written by different people under a neutral testing condition and an aroused power condition. The test requires the ability to form and articulate complex concepts, as in compare-and-contrast essay examinations. Thus, the use of concepts in drawing the contrasts is a key element of the test. Furthermore, there are no right or wrong answers, as the ability does not depend on facts. However, an additional point is given for recognizing the difference in power imagery.

As for the previous test, there was no a priori scoring system, so that the comparison of freshman/senior differences constituted the basic scoring procedures. Again, in each of the three schools, seniors were dramatically better, and the gains increased with the quality of the school. The fact that there are differential gains depending on school quality indicates that the changes are not due to age or maturation. With practice, high interscorer reliabilities can be attained in scoring the protocols. While the real-life outcomes associated with this ability are not yet known, it is clear that such an ability can be taught by emphasizing essay examinations that call for the kinds of comparisons scored in this test. Indeed, the same scoring system can be applied to the scoring of college essay exams.

Experiment in Competitive Performance

Subjects. From the initial subject pool (that is, from Session I), students were recruited by telephone to participate in a third session of the research project, conducted in February and March of 1978. A total of 259 black subjects from Texas Southern and the University of Houston and 60 white students from the University of Houston participated in a session lasting one hour and fifteen minutes, for which they were paid $5.

During Session I of the research, subjects received five pages of the Lowell Scrambled Words Test (Lowell, 1952), described as a test of facility with words. Each page consisted of twenty-four scrambled words; two minutes were allowed to work on each page. This task was given to provide a noncompetitive measure of verbal performance to be used as a baseline for comparing verbal performance in a competitive situation.

Procedure: Session III. As each subject arrived for this session, he or she was greeted by a member of the project staff (a qualified nurse), who told the student that a blood pressure check would be taken and that it required five minutes' resting. During the five-minute interval, inquiries were made about any exercise immediately before the session and the length of time spent walking to the session. After a full five minutes (or more, if exercise preceded arrival), the first pulse reading was taken for a whole minute, followed by the first blood pressure reading.

The subject then read and signed the Session III consent form. The consent form was given after the pulse and blood pressure readings to avoid any effect from the anticipation of competition. The subject was then led to a testing room and randomly assigned to one of two conditions with the appropriate partner (confederate): (1) a white environment, created by a white male experimenter and a white peer, where the experimenter was always an older-looking male and the subject worked with a same-sex peer, or (2) a black environment created by a black male experimenter and a black same-sex peer. These conditions were designed to approximate the most usual real-world conditions, in which males work and compete with other males and in which women most often work with other women but under a male supervisor—a situation that is generally true even in female-dominated occupations.

When the subject entered the testing room, the experimenter greeted him or her and asked that both participants be seated opposite a table, where the instruments in folders were set out. Subjects were asked to open the folders and take out the first task, entitled "National Scholastic Aptitude Examination: Numerical Ability" (in the white environment) or "United Negro College Fund Scholastic Aptitude Examination: Numerical Ability" (in the black environment). This arithmetic test, consisting of 100 two-step problems, was used primarily as a competitive arousal measure. The experimenter then said:

> This is part of a *new* series of tests that have recently been developed by the National Scholastic Testing Service [or the United Negro College Fund] for research and evaluation efforts with college students [black college students]. These tests have been administered to thousands of college students [black college students] throughout the country. The subtests that you will take today will be used to evaluate your intellectual ability by comparing your performance with the norms that have been developed. You recently had a tryout on one of these subtests during the group testing session.
>
> I now would like you to compete against one another on these arithmetic problems. Your scores will be compared with one another *and*

against the national norms. From the previous information you have given us, we have tried to match you two students for general ability. Thus, each of you should have a fair chance of winning. We will let you know how you do on these tests.

After the arithmetic problems, the experimenter administered a counterbalanced, four-picture version of the Thematic Apperception Test given in Session I. Opponents then competed once more on an anagram task, introduced as a measure of intellectual ability, where they were required to make as many smaller words as possible from the master word *generation* (Clark and McClelland, 1956). Ten minutes were allowed for the total test, and subjects checked the last word completed every two minutes. This task was entitled "National Scholastic Aptitude Examination: Verbal Ability" (white environment) or "United Negro College Fund Scholastic Aptitude Examination: Verbal Ability" (black environment).

The testing instructions were designed to accomplish several purposes: (1) to create a clearly competitive atmosphere; (2) to let the subject know that his or her performance would be evaluated against national norms (either white or black) *and* against the performance of a competitor; (3) to make it clear to the subject that the tests were measuring *intellectual* abilities, on which there was a 50/50 chance of success. From past research in this area, it was clear that these features of the testing session were necessary to induce maximum effort as well as to maximally arouse inhibitive or facilitative anxieties. While highly interactive work settings have produced the strongest effects, time constraints limited the present investigation to noninteractive competition. A short debriefing session was given to explain why competition was necessary and to allay any fears, suspicions, or resentments that might have been generated.

Immediately following the session, the subject was escorted back to the waiting room, where the second pulse and blood pressure readings were taken. Subjects were then told that a fifteen-minute rest period was required before the last reading could be taken. During this interval, subjects filled out the postsession questionnaire, in which they rated their performance, their emotional state, and the effectiveness of the experimenter. After about fifteen minutes, the third pulse and blood pressure readings were taken, and the subject was paid.

Procedural Changes for White Students. White students did not take a Scrambled Words Test in time 1 such that an alternate baseline was required (see the following section). All white students participated only in the white environment with a same-sex peer and a white male experimenter, so that comparisons are made only with black students who also worked in a white environment. Thus, all tests taken were labeled "National Scholastic Aptitude Examinations." No counterbalanced set of TAT pictures was available, so that the first four pictures for time 1 were readministered with appropriate instructions to reduce the effects of recall on the second administration.

Treatment of Data. From Session III, four measures were related to competitive performance: arithmetic test, arithmetic level of aspiration, level of aspiration discrepancy, and anagram. From the arithmetic test, a level-of-aspiration score (the estimated number of problems, out of 100, that could be solved) and a level-of-aspiration-discrepancy score (level of aspiration minus actual performance) were obtained. For the arithmetic test itself, as well as the anagram test, one point was given for each correct solution to the respective problem. No wholly adequate baseline control was available for measures derived from the arithmetic test. None of the Session I measures involved similar mathematical abilities that might serve as a noncompetitive control. The general aptitude measure (math plus verbal SAT) did not correlate well with any of the measures. However, the math SAT score is well correlated with the arithmetic score for black students ($r = .533$, $p = .000$) and for UH black and white students ($r = .496, p = .000$). These correlations are based on only 145 of the total black sample of 259 and 82 of the UH sample of 124, a loss of 44 percent of the black data and 34 percent of the UH data. To avoid the loss of data, the mean math SAT (that is, the best estimate) was substituted for missing data. Appropriate means were determined for TSU freshmen and seniors, as well as for UH freshmen and seniors. A regression line was plotted, with arithmetic scores from the competitive condition as the Y variable and the math SAT as the X variable. A regressed score $(y - y')$ was then calculated for each subject. To the extent possible, this regressed score provides a measure of changes in math performance owing to interpersonal competition, and its use avoids the methodological problems associated with change scores (Hummel-Rossi and Weinberg, 1973). The math SAT shows variable correlations with the two arithmetic aspiration scores, so that these measures are submitted to the usual series of corrections for SES and aptitude when required, but without a baseline control.

For the anagram test, the Session I measure of scrambled words provides a good noncompetitive baseline, inasmuch as both are verbal tasks measuring similar abilities and are, in fact, well correlated $(r = .542, p = .000$ for TSU and UH combined; $r = .588, p = .000$ for UH; $r = .54, p = .000$ for TSU). Furthermore, both sets of test scores are available for 252 of 259 subjects. Thus, for black student comparisons, scrambled words performance was used to control the anagram results for initial individual differences in verbal ability. In the absence of Session I verbal data for white students, the verbal SAT was used as a baseline control in UH black-white comparisons, since it was well correlated with anagram performance $(r = .449, p = .000)$.

On the postexperimental questionnaire, subjects were asked to rate eight aspects of the session on a scale that was later reduced to five intervals. Thus, scores ranged from 1 to 5. No baseline control was appropriate for subjective ratings, although these variables were correlated with SES and aptitude to determine whether corrections for each of these background variables were required.

The physiological measures used as dependent variables were the second and third readings of pulse rate and blood pressure. For each blood pressure reading, two measures were used: systolic pressure and diastolic pressure. For all the physiological measures, the correlations between initial and postcompetition rates were very strong in both samples $(.66 < r < .85)$, and it was necessary to control for individual differences in baseline rates. Thus, the first readings of these measures taken before competition were used to control the second and third readings according to the regression procedure described. Thus, the corrected measures are indications of changes in physiological rates attributable to competition and recovery from competition after fifteen minutes of resting.

The effects of the TAT-derived motivational variables theoretically linked to competition that were considered were need for achievement, fear of success, hope and fear of power, and need for affiliation. The TAT variables are sensitive to situational changes and are thus appropriate for the assessment of changes in these motivational states as a function of competition. The measure of fear of failure, assessed from a questionnaire, was not included. Only four TAT pictures were given in Session III, so that scores from these stories are compared with scores from the first four of the six pictures given in Session I. Even with appropriate retest instructions, motive scores from time 1 to time 3 are not well correlated. Nonetheless, regressed scores were calculated where possible.

Analysis. For purposes of black student analysis, a 2 X 2 X 2 X 2 factorial design was used, with school (predominantly black Texas Southern University, predominantly white University of Houston); condition (black environment, white environment); class (underclassmen, upperclassmen); and sex (males, females) as independent factors. The 259 subjects were distributed across the 16 cells created by the design, with near-equal Ns in each cell (that is, from 14 to 17). For UH comparisons, a 2 X 2 X 2 design was required with race (black, white), class, and sex as factors, with near-equal Ns in each of the 8 cells.

The experimental design required that the data for black students be submitted to a four-way analysis of variance, while a three-way design is required for black-white comparisons at UH because of the absence of a condition factor. As has been the practice throughout this report, an attempt is made in this investigation to institute statistical controls for sample differences in socioeconomic status and aptitude where required. Furthermore, the design of this experiment, with its baseline measures of verbal ability, pulse, and blood pressure, allows even more accurate controls for certain critical measures.

Appendix B:
Summary Tables

Deciding what tables should accompany this manuscript was a perplexing problem, stemming from the project's having generated an exceptionally large mass of data. Hundreds of variables were submitted to comparison tests for each school population. To qualify for discussion, each variable had to pass three significance tests in the exploratory studies and up to three more tests of significance in the remaining studies. Reproducing the tables that contain the voluminous numbers involved in these tests would have made the cost of this book prohibitive. Instead, I have chosen to present only listings of variables that passed all the significance tests for each population. The purpose of the tables is limited: to show which variables distinguished freshman and senior students at each school.

　　Most of the tables list variables that indicate the impact of a school on its students. These tables consist of lists of labels of variables, that is, indicators of the items, factors, and measures used in our surveys. The variables are explained in Appendix A, where the measures are described and are somewhat further elaborated in the chapters where the schools are discussed. Labels marked with this symbol † indicate variables for which freshman students' mean score was significantly higher than seniors' mean score. Unmarked labels indicate variables for which seniors' mean score was significantly higher than freshmen's. For example, if the label "Influence of college is cognitive

growth" appears without the symbol †, significantly more seniors than freshmen indicated that college had spurred them to
grow intellectually. (Anyone interested in understanding this
item further can read the description of the measure from
which this item comes, that is, "subjective assessments of college," in Appendix A.) The label "GPA in major for last semester," without a †, means that seniors' grade point averages in
their academic majors were significantly higher than were fresh-
mens' grade point averages. (To understand the meaning of
this index, the section on academic performance in Appendix A
should be read.)

A few other points should be mentioned:

- Variables with the notation "factor" are drawn from academic adjustment, social assertiveness, and black ideology
  measures.
- Variables preceded by the words "described as" are self-concept items.
- The subheadings in the tables are means of grouping the significant variables for each school; because not all variables or
  groups of variables were significant in every school, the subheadings are not the same in every table.
- Except when specifically stated otherwise, tables refer to responses from black students.
- If an entire table consists of responses from students of only
  one sex, this fact is indicated in the table title or notes.
- The designation "males" or "females" after a listed item
  indicates an interaction effect, usually class by sex, that was
  most pronounced for the indicated sex.

The factor analyses that assisted interpretation were of inconsistent usefulness and no attempt is made to present them. Interested readers may request the complete tables from the
author.

Table 1. Impact of Morehouse College.

Academic Adjustment	Adjustment to College	Career Development	Psychosocial Adjustment
Influence of college is cognitive growth	Best of college is extracurricular activities	Gives specific career plan	Importance of family
Importance of grades (factor)[†]	Worst of college is unfairness and favoritism	Enterprising vocational interest	Life adjustment score[†]
Good grades in major essential[†]	Informal contact with faculty	Conventional vocational interest	Personal threat (factor)
Good grades essential to career goal[†]	Extracurricular involvement (factor)	Difficult to combine family and career[†]	Fatigue (factor)[†]
Importance of getting good grades[†]	Number of extracurricular activities	Positive effect of marriage on career	Described as tired[†]
	Offices held in extra activities		Described as passive[†]
			Described as incompetent[†]
			Described as enterprising
			Black ideology
			Black defensiveness (factor)
			Shyness (factor)[†]
			Genital stage[†]

$N = 146$ males (freshmen = 92; seniors = 54)

[†]Indicates freshmen scoring higher.

Each variable is significant at .05 level for three analyses of variance.

Table 2. Impact of Spelman College.

Academic Adjustment	Adjustment to College	Career Development	Psychosocial Adjustment
GPA for last semester	Informal contact with faculty	Career involvement (factor)	Life adjustment score
GPA in major for last semester	Satisfied with courses	Sought assistance with career	Described as argumentative†
Cumulative GPA in major	Works well under pressure	Nontraditionality of career choice†	Described as liking social gathering†
Honors status for last semester	Extracurricular involvement (factor)		Described as incompetent†
Academic effort (factor)†	Number of extracurricular activities		Text anxiety (fear of failure)†
Time spent studying†	Offices held in extra activities		Acceptance of white authority (factor)
Time spent studying during exams†			Fear of confrontation (factor)
Importance or grades (factor)†			Shyness (factor)
Importance of getting good grades†			Submissiveness (factor)
Estimate of general ability			Emotional suppression (factor)†
Satisfied with academic performance			

$N = 185$ females (freshmen = 102; seniors = 83)

†Indicates freshmen scoring higher.

Each variable is significant at .05 level for three analyses of variance.

Table 3. Impact of Clark College.

Academic Adjustment	Adjustment to College	Career Development	Psychosocial Adjustment
GPA for last semester	Best of college is socializing[†]	Sought assistance with career	Ideal age for marriage: males
GPA in major for last semester	Worst of college is social isolation[†]		Number of life changes
Satisfied with courses	Worst of college is interpersonal tensions[†]		Intellectual incompetence (factor)[†]
Satisfied with academic performance	Worst of college is racial tension		Described as scatterbrained[†]
Having academic problems	Worst of college is instructors		Described as slow witted[†]
	Influence of college is self-development: males		Described as incompetent[†]
	Influence of college is cultural broadening: males		Extroversion (factor)
	Influence of college is ability to deal with people: females		Described as outspoken
	Informal contact with instructors		Described as well mannered
	Involvement with faculty (factor)		Described as lady or gentleman
	Faculty person proved helpful		Described as inarticulate[†]
	Admires faculty person		Social assertiveness score
	Extracurricular involvement (factor)		
	Number of extracurricular activities		
	Offices held in extra activities		

$N = 209$ (freshmen = 141; seniors = 68)

[†]Indicates freshmen scoring higher.

Each variable is significant at .05 level for three analyses of variance.

Table 4. Impact of "Southern University."

Academic Adjustment	Adjustment to College	Career Development	Psychosocial Adjustment
Importance of grades (factor)†	Feelings about course of instruction†	SES of career choice: males†	Severity of illnesses: females†
Importance of getting good grades†	Feelings about fellow students†	Career orientation: males†	Having domestic interest†
			Described as passive†
			Emotional suppression (factor)†
			Identity integration (factor)†

$N = 38$ (freshmen = 19; seniors = 19)
†Indicates freshmen scoring higher.
Each variable is significant at .05 level for three analyses of variance.

Table 5. Impact of Georgia Tech.

Academic Adjustment	Adjustment to College	Career Development	Psychosocial Adjustment
GPA in major for last semester†	Happy with college choice†	Sought career assistance	Number of life changes
Cumulative GPA in major†	Best of college is student involvement	Conventional vocational interests	Academic stress (factor)
Academic effort (factor)†	Influence of college is coping and survival		Personal threat (factor)
Time spent studying†	Worst of college is racial tensions		Black Ideology (scale)
Time spent studying during exams†	Extracurricular involvement (factor)		Black heritage (factor)
Cramming index†	Offices held in extra activities		Submissiveness (factor)†
Having academic problems			Emotional suppression (factor)†
			Phallic stage
			Fear of power

$N = 89$ (freshmen = 68; seniors = 21)
†Indicates freshmen scoring higher.
Each variable is significant at .05 level for three analyses of variance.

Table 6. Impact of "Traditional University."

Academic Adjustment	Adjustment to College	Career Development	Psychosocial Adjustment
Fair teaching methods (factor)†	General academic adjustment (factor)†	Investigative vocational interests: males†	Social adjustment (scale)†
Teachers grade fairly†	Feelings about the administration†	Ambivalent plans for graduate school	Number of life changes
Satisfied with teaching methods†	Feelings about fellow students†	Sought career assistance	Academic stress (factor)
Importance of grades (factor)†	Teachers are interested and encouraging†	Plans to attend graduate or professional school†	Personal stress (factor)
Importance of getting good grades†	Influence of college is coping and surviving	Educational aspirations (scale)	Personal threat (factor)
Good grades essential to career†	Extracurricular involvement (factor)	Plans to work after college	Black ideology (scale)
	Number extracurricular activities	SES of vocational aspiration: females†	Acceptance of white authority (factor)†
	Offices held in extra activities	Positive effect of marriage on career	Anal stage†
		Nontraditional woman's role preference: females†	

$N = 125$ (freshmen = 82; seniors = 43)
†Indicates freshmen scoring higher.
Each variable is significant at .05 level for three analyses of variance.

Table 7. Impact of "County College."

Academic Adjustment	Adjustment to College	Career Development	Psychosocial Adjustment
GPA for last semester	Extracurricular involvement (factor)	SES of vocational choice: males†	Length of illnesses
Importance of grades (factor)†	Number of extracurricular activities	Enterprising vocational interests	Extroversion: females (factor)
Importance of getting good grades†	Offices held in extra activities	Conventional vocational interests	Described as talkative: females
Time spent studying during exams: males			Described as outspoken: males
Cramming index: males			White culture (factor)
Works well under pressure			
Teachers grade fairly†			

$N = 78$ (freshmen = 48; seniors = 30)
†Indicates freshmen scoring higher.
Each variable is significant at .05 level for three analyses of variance.

Table 8. Impact of White Colleges in Georgia on Males.

Academic Adjustment	Adjustment to College	Career Development	Psychosocial Adjustment
Cumulative GPA in major[†]	Feelings about the administration[†]	Plans to attend graduate or professional school	Social adjustment (scale)[†]
Importance of grades (factor)[†]	Feelings about the faculty[†]	Career orientation (scale)	Academic stress (factor)
Importance of getting good grades[†]	Feelings about fellow students[†]		Personal stress (factor)
Teachers grade fairly[†]	Worst of college is personal failure[†]		Personal threat (factor)
	Best of college is student involvement		Described as energetic[†]
	Extracurricular involvement (factor)		Emotional suppression (factor)[†]
			Black ideology (scale)
			Acceptance of white authority (factor)[†]

$N = 131$ (freshmen = 83; seniors = 48)

[†]Indicates freshmen scoring higher.

Each variable is significant at .05 level for three analyses of variance.

Table 9. Impact of White Colleges in Georgia on Females.

Academic Adjustment	Adjustment to College	Psychosocial Adjustment
GPA for last semester	Adjustment to college (factor)[†]	Social adjustment (scale)[†]
Fair teaching methods (factor)[†]	Feelings about the administration[†]	Personal stress (factor)
Teachers grade fairly[†]	Feelings about faculty[†]	Described as energetic[†]
Importance of grades (factor)[†]	Feelings about fellow students[†]	Described as outspoken
Importance of getting good grades[†]	Admires member of faculty	Described as inarticulate[†]
	Worst of college is opposite sex	Social assertiveness (scale)
	Influence of college is self-development[†]	Emotional suppression (factor)[†]
	Influence of college is coping and survival	Black heritage (factor)
	Influence of college is cultural broadening	
	Extracurricular involvement (factor)	
	Number of extracurricular activities	

$N = 199$ (freshmen $= 143$; seniors $= 65$)
[†]Indicates freshmen scoring higher.
Each variable is significant at .05 level for three analyses of variance.

Table 10. Impact of Texas Southern University.

Academic Adjustment	Adjustment to College	Career Development	Psychosocial Adjustment
Cumulative GPA	Worst of college is administration	Career involvement (factor)	Personal stress (factor)
GPA in major for last semester: males	Feelings about the college	Sought career assistance	Intellectual incompetence (factor)†
Works well under pressure	Informal contact with faculty	Plans to attend graduate or professional school	Described as incompetent†
Cramming index: females	Involvement with faculty (factor)	Educational aspirations (scale)	Described as energetic
Estimate of general ability	Admires faculty member	Highest degree planned is B.A.†	Described as ambitious
	Extracurricular involvement (factor)	Conventional vocational interests: females†	Described as competitive
	Number of extracurricular activities	Reason for career is challenge	Described as polite
	Offices held in extra activities	Reason for career is good job market	Described as arrogant†
			Described as outspoken: males
			Described as argumentative: males
			Described as a leader: males
			Described as popular: females†
			Militance (factor)
			Openness: males (factor)
			Need for achievement

$N = 230$ (freshmen = 170; seniors = 60)

†Indicates freshmen scoring higher.

Each variable is significant at .05 level for up to three analyses of variance.

Table 11. Impact of University of Houston.

Academic Adjustment	Adjustment to College	Career Development	Psychosocial Adjustment
GPA for last semester	Worst of college is racial tension	Sought career assistance	Severity of illnesses
Cumulative GPA	Worst of college is institutional quality†	Reason for career is to make contribution	Length of illnesses: males
GPA in major for last semester	College has not had much influence†	Reason for career is race related	Academic stress (factor)
Cumulative GPA in major	Influence of college is negative	Plans to attend graduate or professional school	Personal stress (factor)
Academic probation status†	Influence of college is personal motivation†	Obstacle to career is tight job market	Personal threat (factor)
Influence of college is cognitive growth	Influence of college is cultural broadening		Social decorum (factor) †
Reason for major is knowledge	General academic adjustment (factor) †		Described as obedient†
Reason for major is competence: females†	Teachers are interested and encouraging†		Described as passive†
Fair teaching methods (factor) †	Feelings about the administration†		Described as independent
Satisfied with teaching methods†	Feelings about faculty†		Described as inarticulate
Teachers grade fairly†	Feelings about quality of instruction†		Described as ambitious†
Satisfied with academic performance: females†	Informal contact with faculty		Described as happy†
Works well under pressure	Admire faculty member		Social assertiveness (scale)
Importance of grades (factor) †	Adjustment problems (factor)		Black heritage (factor)
Importance of getting good grades†	Having academic problems		Black defensiveness (factor)
Good grades essential to career†	Extracurricular involvement (factor)		Identity integration†
	Number of extracurricular activities		Need for achievement: females
	Offices held in extra activities		Need for affiliation†
			Oral stage†

$N = 228$ (freshmen = 148; seniors = 80)

†Indicates freshmen scoring higher.

Each variable is significant at .05 level for up to three analyses of variance.

Table 12. Impact of Public Colleges on Cognitive Skills.

School	Test	Freshmen	Seniors
Texas Southern			
N = 455			
Freshmen = 329	Concept Formation[a]	21	23
Seniors = 126	Thematic Analysis[b]	.01	.27
	Analysis of Argument	−2.68	−2.63
University of Houston			
N = 324			
Freshmen = 195	Concept Formation[c]	28.2	27.3
Seniors = 129	Thematic Analysis	.33	.38
	Analysis of Argument	−2.66	−2.77

[a]Significant effect for class (.05 < p < .058)
[b]Significant effect for class (.02 < p < .03)
[c]Significant class × sex interaction (.02 < p < .066): freshman males (27); senior males (23); freshmen females (28.9); senior females (30.7)

Table 13. Cell Means for Corrected Anagram Performance for Black Students.

	Condition	Texas Southern (N = 124)		University of Houston (N = 127)	
		White Environment	Black Environment	White Environment	Black Environment
Underclassmen	Male	18.89 (8.86) 15	17.52 (8.498) 17	20.73 (6.12) 15	22.49 (9.25) 17
	Female	12.89 (8.83) 17	19.54 (5.94) 16	20.96 (9.29) 17	21.06 (6.41) 15
Upperclassmen	Male	22.44 (8.34) 15	18.73 (9.49) 14	18.37 (8.51) 15	18.499 (7.96) 17
	Female	17.61 (7.19) 15	20.60 (7.83) 15	19.97 (8.09) 16	20.75 (7.096) 15

Note: Standard deviation appears in parentheses, followed by numbers of subjects.

Table 14. Impact of "Freedmen College."

Academic Adjustment	Adjustment to College	Career Development	Psychosocial Adjustment
Importance of grades (factor)[†]	Worst of college is unfairness and favoritism	Investigative vocational interests[†]	Ideal age for marriage: males
Importance of getting good grades[†]	Admires faculty member	Enterprising vocational interests[†]	Length of illnesses
Reason for major is competence	Adjustment problems (factor)	Career orientation (scale)[†]	Social decorum (factor)[†]
	Extracurricular involvement (factor)		Described as nice[†]
	Offices held in extra activities		Described as dogmatic: males[†]
			Ambition (factor)[†]
			Identity integration (factor)[†]
			Militance (factor)[†]

$N = 80$ (freshmen = 50; seniors = 30)
[†]Indicates freshmen scoring higher.
Each variable is significant at .05 level for up to three analyses of variance.

Table 15. Impact of "Magnolia College."

Academic Adjustment	Adjustment to College	Career Development	Psychosocial Adjustment
Overall GPA for last semester	General academic adjustment (factor)[†]	Job is related to career plans	Social adjustment (scale)[†]
Academic effort (factor)[†]	Teachers are interested and encouraging: females[†]	Artistic vocational interests[†]	Severity of illnesses
	Feelings about faculty[†]	Investigative vocational interests: males	Personal threat (factor)
	Feelings about quality of instruction[†]	Reason for career is family member	Intellectual incompetence (factor)[†]
	Feelings about fellow students[†]		Described as having a poor memory[†]
	Best of college is extracurricular activities		Fatigue (factor)[†]
	Number of extracurricular activities		Described as lazy[†]
			Described as passive
			Described as aggressive
			Described as shy[†]
			Black ideology (scale)
			Acceptance of white authority (factor)[†]
			Identity integration[†]

$N = 51$ (freshmen = 29; seniors = 22)

[†]Indicates freshmen scoring higher.

Each variable is significant at .05 level for up to three analyses of variance.

Table 16. Impact of Wilberforce University.

Academic Adjustment	Adjustment to College	Career Development	Psychosocial Adjustment
Overall GPA for last semester	Worst of college is social isolation[†]	Sought career assistance	Social adjustment (scale): males
Cumulative GPA	General academic adjustment (factor)	Undecided graduate school plans[†]	Severity of illnesses: females
GPA in major for last semester	Feelings about the college	Plans for graduate or professional school	Length of illnesses
Cumulative GPA in major	Feelings about the quality of instruction	Educational aspirations (scale)	Number of life changes
Having academic problems	Satisfaction with college choice	Highest degree planned is B.A.: females[†]	Personal threat (factor)
Satisfaction with courses	Feelings about fellow students: males	Highest degree planned is M.A.	Personal stress (factor)
Demanding course of instruction	Involvement with faculty	Plans to work after graduation	Extroversion (factor)
Importance of grades (factor)	Admires faculty member	SES of vocational aspirations	Described as quiet: males[†]
Importance of getting good grades	Extracurricular involvement (factor)	Conventional vocational interests	Fatigue (factor)[†]
	Number extracurricular activities	Obstacle to career is tight job market	Described as lazy[†]
	Offices held in extra activities	Positive effect of marriage on career (scale)	Described as energetic
			Described as independent
			Described as outspoken
			Described as irresponsible[†]
			Described as incompetent[†]
			Described as nice
			Black heritage (factor)

$N = 222$ (freshmen = 129; seniors = 93)

[†]Indicates freshmen scoring higher.

Each variable is significant at .05 level for up to three analyses of variance.

Table 17. Impact of "Northern University."

Academic Adjustment	Adjustment to College	Career Development	Psychosocial Adjustment
Satisfaction with teaching methods (factor)	General academic adjustment (factor)[†]	Career involvement (factor)	Social adjustment (scale)[†]
Importance of grades (factor)[†]	Feelings about faculty[†]	Sought career assistance	Ideal age for marriage: males[†]
Grades essential to career[†]	Feelings about quality of instruction[†]	Investigative vocational interests: males	Number of male children desired: males
Grades in major essential to career[†]	Feelings about fellow students[†]	Ambivalent career plans: males[†]	Preference for male children: males
Importance of getting good grades[†]	Adjustment problems (factor)	Specific career plans: females	Number of life changes
Works well under pressure	Admires faculty member	Reason for career is competence	Personal stress (factor)
	Extracurricular involvement (factor)	Race-related reason for career	Described as considerate: females[†]
	Number extracurricular activities	Obstacle to career is money: females[†]	Described as having a poor memory: females
	Offices held in extra activities	Obstacle to career is tight job market	Described as aggressive: males
		Difficult to combine marriage and career[†]	Described as dogmatic: males
			Described as shy: males
			Described as irresponsible: males
			Ambition (factor): males
			Black heritage (factor)
			Black defensiveness (factor)

$N = 153$ (freshmen = 80; seniors = 73)

[†]Indicates freshmen scoring higher.

Each variable is significant at .05 level for up to three analyses of variance.

Table 18. Impact of Central State University.

Academic Adjustment	Adjustment to College	Career Development	Psychosocial Adjustment
Cumulative GPA in major	Best of college is personal accomplishment[†]	Career involvement (factor)	Social adjustment (scale): males
Influence of college is cognitive growth	Worst of college is interpersonal tensions[†]	Sought career assistance	Length of illnesses
Satisfaction with academic performance[†]	Worst of college is instructors: females	Enterprising vocational aspirations: males	Hypochondriasis (scale)[†]
Works well under pressure	Feelings about the college: males	Educational aspirations (scale): females[†]	Personal threat (factor)
Reason for major is good job market	Feelings about fellow students: males	Highest degree planned is advanced: females[†]	Incompetence (factor)[†]
	Feelings about quality of instruction	Ambivalent career plans[†]	Described as incompetent[†]
	Admires a faculty member: males		Described as scatterbrained[†]
	Adjustment problems (factor)		Described as tired[†]
	Having academic problems		Described as obedient: females[†]
			Described as happy: females[†]
			Acceptance of white authority (factor): males[†]
			Fear of confrontation (factor)[†]
			Emotional suppression (factor)[†]

$N = 232$ (freshmen = 124; seniors = 108)

[†]Indicates freshmen scoring higher.

Each variable is significant at .05 level for up to three analyses of variance.

Table 19. Impact of Ohio State University.

Academic Adjustment	Adjustment to College	Career Development	Psychosocial Adjustment
Influence of college is cognitive growth	Best of college is instructors	Career involvement (factor)	Ideal age for marriage
Importance of grades (factor)†	Informal contact with faculty	Sought career assistance	Ambition (factor): males
Importance of getting good grades†	Worst of college is personal failure: males	Job relevant to career: males	Described as ambitious: males
Good grades essential to career†	Adjustment problems (factor)	Realistic vocational interests	Fatigue (factor)†
Satisfaction with major	Having academic problems	Career ambivalence: males	Described as lazy†
Reason for major is interest: males	Extracurricular involvement (factor)	Reason for career is interest	Described as passive†
Reason for major is dealing with people: males	Number extracurricular activities		Described as obedient†
Reason for major is competence: females†	Offices held in extra activities		Acceptance of white authority (factor)†
			Black heritage (factor)
			Militance (factor): females

$N = 204$ (freshmen = 143; seniors = 61)

†Indicates freshmen scoring higher.

Each variable is significant at .05 level for up to three analyses of variance.

Table 20. Impact of Georgia Tech on White Students.

Academic Adjustment	Adjustment to College	Career Development	Psychosocial Adjustment
Satisfied with academic performance	Feelings about the administration	Career involvement (factor)	Plans to marry after college
Best of college is class and learning activities	Informal contact with faculty	Sought career assistance	Hypochondriasis[†]
Academic effort (factor): females[†]	Involvement with faculty (factor)	Plans to attend graduate or professional school	Personal threat (factor)
Time spent studying: females[†]	Teachers are interested and encouraging: females	SES level of career choice	Personal stress (factor)
Time spent studying during exams: females[†]	Influence of college was self-development[†]		Described as outspoken
Importance of good grades (factor)[†]	Best of college is extracurricular activities		Described as leader
Importance of getting good grades[†]	Offices held in extracurricular activities		Described as enterprising
Good grades essential to career[†]			Extroversion (factor)
Good grades in major essential to career[†]			Described as nice: females[†]
			Described as irresponsible: females[†]
			Shyness (factor)[†]
			Fear of confrontation[†]
			Genital Stage[†]

$N = 134$ (freshmen = 97; seniors = 37)

[†]Indicates freshmen scoring higher.

Each variable is significant at .05 level for up to three analyses of variance.

Table 21. Impact of University of Houston on White Students.

Academic Adjustment	Adjustment to College	Career Development	Cognitive Growth	Psychosocial Adjustment
GPA for last semester	Worst aspect of college is instructors	Reason for major is good job market[†]	Thematic Analysis	Described as domestic person
Cumulative GPA	Best of college is new people	Sought career assistance		Number of female children desired
GPA in major for last semester	Admire member of faculty			Hypochondriasis[†]
Cumulative GPA in major	Extracurricular involvement (factor)			Personal stress (factor)
Honors status	Number of extracurricular activities			Described as obedient[†]
Satisfaction with major subject: females	Offices held in extracurricular activities			Described as dogmatic: females
Demanding course of instruction[†]				Described as lazy
				Fear of confrontation (factor)
				Shyness (factor)
				Fear of success[†]
				Need for affiliation
				Fear of power: females
				Phallic stage[†]

$N = 109$ (freshmen = 70; seniors = 30)

[†]Indicates freshmen scoring higher.

Each variable is significant at .05 level for up to three analyses of variance.

Table 22. Impact of "Northern University" on White Students.

Academic Adjustment	Adjustment to College	Career Development	Psychosocial Adjustment
Best of college is learning and class activities	Feelings about the college	Career involvement (factor)	Ideal age for marriage
Satisfaction with major (factor)	Informal contact with faculty	Sought career assistance	Length of illnesses
Academic effort: females (factor)	Best of college is socializing[†]	Plans to attend graduate or professional school	Personal stress (factor)
The importance of grades (factor)[†]	Extracurricular involvement (factor)	Ambivalent graduate school plans: females	Test anxiety (fear of failure)[†]
Estimate of general ability	Number extracurricular activities	Investigative vocational interest	Described as nice[†]
	Offices held in extra activities	Educational aspirations (scale)	Described as considerate[†]
		Highest degree planned is B.A.[†]	Described as incompetent[†]
		Highest degree planned is M.A.	Described as lazy[†]
		Plans to work after graduation[†]	Described as dogmatic[†]
		SES level of career choice	Described as liking social gatherings[†]
		Obstacle to career is ability[†]	Described as happy: females[†]
		Woman's role preference (scale)	
		Prefer to be working wife: females[†]	
		Prefer to be career wife	
		Importance of career: females	
		Positive effect of marriage on career	

N = 145 (freshmen = 81; seniors = 64)

[†]Indicates freshmen scoring higher.

Each variable is significant at .05 level for up to three analyses of variance.

References

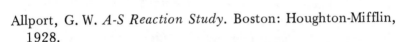

Allport, G. W. *A-S Reaction Study*. Boston: Houghton-Mifflin, 1928.

Allport, G. W., and Allport, F. H. *The A-S Reaction Study: A Scale for Measuring Ascendance Submission in Personality*. Boston: Houghton-Mifflin, 1928.

Anastasi, A. *Differential Psychology*. (3rd ed.) New York: Macmillan, 1958.

Anderson, E., and Hrabowski, F. "Graduate School Success of Black Students from White Colleges and Black Colleges." *Journal of Higher Education*, 1977, *48*, 294-303.

Astin, A. W. *Preventing Students from Dropping Out*. San Francisco: Jossey-Bass, 1977.

Atkinson, J. W. (Ed.). *Motives in Fantasy, Action and Society*. New York: Van Nostrand, 1958.

Atkinson, J. W., and Feather, N. (Eds.). *A Theory of Achievement Motivation*. New York: Wiley, 1966.

Atkinson, J. W., Heyns, R. W., and Veroff, J. "The Effect of Experimental Arousal of the Affiliation Motive and Thematic Apperception." *Journal of Abnormal and Social Psychology*, 1954, *49*, 405-410.

Atkinson, J. W., and Litwin, G. H. "Achievement Motive and

Test Anxiety Conceived as Motive to Approach Success and Motive to Avoid Failure." *Journal of Abnormal and Social Psychology,* 1960, *60,* 52–63.

Babbie, E. R. *The Practice of Social Research.* Belmont, Calif.: Wadsworth, 1979.

Baltes, P. B., Reese, H. W., and Lipsitt, L. P. "Life-Span Developmental Psychology." *Annual Review of Psychology,* 1980, 31, 65–110.

Baughman, E. E., and Dahlstrom, W. G. *Negro and White Children.* New York: Academic Press, 1968.

Bayer, A. E., and Boruch, R. F. "Black and White Freshmen Entering Four-Year Colleges." *Educational Record,* 1969, *50,* 371–386.

Bem, D., and Allen, A. "On Predicting Some of the People Some of the Time: The Search for Cross-Situational Consistencies in Behavior." *Psychological Review,* 1974, *81,* 506–520.

Bernard, J. *Marriage and Family Among Negroes.* Englewood Cliffs, N.J.: Prentice-Hall, 1965.

Billingsley, A. *Black Families in White America.* Englewood Cliffs, N.J.: Prentice-Hall, 1968.

Bloom, B. S. *Stability and Change in Human Characteristics.* New York: Wiley, 1964.

Bowles, F., and DeCosta, F. *Between Two Worlds.* New York: McGraw-Hill, 1971.

Boyatzis, R. E. "Affiliation Motivation." In D. C. McClelland and R. S. Steele (Eds.), *Human Motivation: A Book of Readings.* Morristown, N.J.: General Learning Press, 1973.

Boyd, W. M. *Desegregating America's Colleges.* New York: Praeger, 1974.

Branson, H. R. "Black Colleges of the North." In C. V. Willie and R. R. Edmonds (Eds.), *Black Colleges in America.* New York: Teachers College Press, 1978.

Browning, J., and Williams, J. "History and Goals of Black Institutions of Higher Learning." In C. V. Willie and R. R. Edmonds (Eds.), *Black Colleges in America.* New York: Teachers College Press, 1978.

Bynum, C. "The Motive to Avoid Love." *Radcliffe Quarterly,* 1974, *60,* 18–19.

Campbell, B. (Ed.). *Sexual Selection and the Descent of Man.* Chicago: Aldine, 1972.

Campbell, D. T., and Stanley, J. C. *Experimental and Quasi-Experimental Designs for Research.* Chicago: Rand McNally, 1963.

Carnegie Commission on Higher Education. *From Isolation to Mainstream: Problems of the Colleges Founded for Negroes.* New York: McGraw-Hill, 1971.

Centra, J., Linn, R., and Parry, M. "Academic Growth in Predominantly Negro and Predominantly White Colleges." *American Educational Research Journal,* 1970, 7, 83-98.

Chickering, A. W., and Associates. *The Modern American College: Responding to the New Realities of Diverse Students and a Changing Society.* San Francisco: Jossey-Bass, 1981.

Chodorow, N. *The Reproduction of Mothering.* Los Angeles: University of California Press, 1978.

Christmas, J. J. "Self-concept and Attitudes." In K. S. Miller and R. M. Dreger (Eds.), *Comparative Studies of Blacks and Whites in the United States.* New York: Seminar Press, 1973.

Clark, K., and Plotkin, L. *The Negro Student at Integrated Colleges.* New York: National Scholarship Service and Fund for Negro Students, 1963.

Clark, R. A., and McClelland, D. C. "A Factor Analytic Integration of Imaginative and Performance Measures of the Need for Achievement." *Journal of General Psychology,* 1956, 55, 73-83.

Cohen, J. *Statistical Power Analysis in the Behavioral Sciences.* New York: Academic Press, 1969.

Coles, R. *The Desegregation of Southern Schools: A Psychiatric Study.* New York: Anti-Defamation League, 1963.

Cook, S. D. "The Socio-ethical Role and Responsibility of the Black-College Graduate." In C. V. Willie and R. R. Edmonds (Eds.), *Black Colleges in America.* New York: Teachers College Press, 1978.

Cooper, R. "Black People and High Blood Pressure." *Urban Health,* 1975, 4 (6), 9.

Crowne, D. P., Stephens, M. W., and Kelly, R. "The Validity and Equivalence of Tests of Self-Acceptance." *Journal of Psychology,* 1961, 51, 101-112.

Darley, J. G. "A Preliminary Study of Relations Between Attitude, Adjustment and Vocational Interest Tests." *Journal of Educational Psychology*, 1938, *29*, 467–473.

Davis, J. A. *Elementary Survey Analysis.* Englewood Cliffs, N.J.: Prentice-Hall, 1971.

Davis, J. A., and Borders-Patterson, A. *Black Students in Predominantly White North Carolina Colleges and Universities.* Research Report 2. New York: College Entrance Examination Board, 1973.

Davis, K., and Swartz, J. "Increasing Black Students' Utilization of Mental Health Services." *American Journal of Orthopsychiatry*, 1972, *42*, 771–776.

Day, R. E. "Part 2, North Carolina." In United States Commission on Civil Rights, *Civil Rights U.S.A.–Public Schools, Southern States.* Washington, D.C.: U.S. Government Printing Office, 1962.

Dizard, J. D. "Black Identity, Social Class and Black Power." *Psychiatry*, 1970, *33*, 195–207.

Donley, R. E., and Winter, D. G. "Measuring the Motives of Public Officials at a Distance: An Exploratory Study of American Presidents." *Behavioral Science*, 1970, *15*, 227–236.

Douvan, E. "Capacity for Intimacy." In A. W. Chickering and Associates, *The Modern American College: Responding to the New Realities of Diverse Students and a Changing Society.* San Francisco: Jossey-Bass, 1981.

Entwisle, D. R. "To Dispel Fantasies About Fantasy-Based Measures of Achievement Motivation." *Psychological Bulletin*, 1972, *77*, 377–391.

Epps, E. G., and others. "Effect of Race of Comparison Referent and Motives on Negro Cognitive Performance." *Journal of Educational Psychology*, 1971, *62*, 201–208.

Erikson, E. "The Concept of Identity in Race Relations: Notes and Queries." In T. Parsons and K. B. Clark (Eds.), *The Negro American.* Boston: Beacon Press, 1965.

Erikson, E. *Identity: Youth and Crisis.* New York: Norton, 1968.

Feldman, K. A., and Newcomb, T. M. *The Impact of College on Students.* San Francisco: Jossey-Bass, 1969.

Fleming, J. *Approach and Avoidance Motivation in Interper-*

sonal Competition: A Study of Black Male and Female College Students. Unpublished doctoral dissertation, Harvard University, 1974.

Fleming, J. *Fear of Success and Biracial Competition Among Black Male and Female Students: A Pilot Study.* Unpublished manuscript, Radcliffe Institute, 1975a.

Fleming, J. *Significance of Fear of Success Imagery Among Black Male and Female Students.* Unpublished manuscript, Radcliffe Institute, 1975b.

Fleming, J. *Motivational Determinants of Biracial Competition in Black Male College Students.* Unpublished manuscript, Radcliffe Institute, 1975c.

Fleming, J. "Fear of Success, Achievement-Related Motives and Behavior in Black College Women." *Journal of Personality,* 1978, *46,* 694-716.

Fleming, J. *Impact of Predominantly White and Predominantly Black College Environments on Black Students.* Unpublished technical report, United Negro College Fund, September 1980.

Fleming, J. "Early Learning Environments and the Development of Mastery Motivation." Paper presented to the American Psychological Association, Washington, D.C., August 1982a.

Fleming, J. "Sex Differences in the Impact of College Environments on Black Students." In P. J. Perun (Ed.), *The Undergraduate Woman: Issues in Educational Equity.* Lexington, Mass.: Lexington Books, 1982b.

Fleming, J. "Black Women in Black and White College Environments: The Making of a Matriarch." *Journal of Social Issues,* 1983a, *39* (3), 41-54.

Fleming, J. "Sex Differences in the Educational and Occupational Goals of Black College Students: Continued Inquiry into the Black Matriarchy Theory." In M. S. Horner, C. Nadelson, and M. Notman (Eds.), *The Challenge of Change.* New York: Plenum, 1983b.

Fleming, J., Beldner, J., and Esposito, R. *On the Projective Measurement of Fear of Success.* Paper presented to the Eastern Psychological Association, Philadelphia, April 1979.

Fleming, J., and Watson, R. I. *Examination of the New Empiri-*

cally Derived Scoring System for the Motive to Avoid Success. Unpublished manuscript, Barnard College, 1979.

Frazier, C. F. *Black Bourgeoisie.* New York: Collier Books, 1962.

French, E. G., and Thomas, F. H. "The Relation of Achievement Motivation to Problem-Solving Effectiveness." *Journal of Abnormal and Social Psychology,* 1958, *56,* 46-48.

Gallagher, B. G. (Ed.). *College and the Black Student.* NAACP Tract for the Times. New York: The National Association for the Advancement of Colored People, 1971.

Gibbs, J. T. "Black Students/White University: Different Expectations." *Personnel and Guidance Journal,* 1973, *51,* 463-469.

Gibbs, J. T. "Patterns of Adaptation Among Black Students at a Predominantly White University." *American Journal of Orthopsychiatry,* 1974, *44,* 728-740.

Gibbs, J. T. "Use of Mental Health Services by Black Students at a Predominantly White University: A Three-Year Study." *American Journal of Orthopsychiatry,* 1975, *45,* 430-445.

Goldman, F. H. "Integration and the Negro College." In F. H. Goldman (Ed.), *Educational Imperative: The Negro in the Changing South.* Chicago: Center of Liberal Education for Adults, 1963.

Good, C. V., and Scates, D. E. *Methods of Research.* New York: Appleton-Century-Crofts, 1954.

Gough, H. G., and Heilbrun, A. B. *The Adjective Checklist Manual.* Palo Alto, Calif.: Consulting Psychologists Press, 1965.

Graham, D. T., and Stevenson, I. "Disease as Response to Life Stress." In H. I. Lief, V. F. Lief, and N. R. Lief (Eds.), *The Psychological Basis of Medical Practice.* New York: Harper & Row, 1963.

Green, R. L. "The Black Quest for Higher Education: An Admissions Dilemma." *Personnel and Guidance Journal,* 1969, *47,* 905-911.

Greene, D., and Winter, D. "Motives, Involvements and Leadership Among Black College Students." *Journal of Personality,* 1971, *39,* 319-332.

Guilford, J. P. *Psychometric Methods.* New York: McGraw-Hill, 1954.

Guilford, J. P., and Zimmerman, W. S. *The Guilford-Zimmerman Temperament Survey.* Beverly Hills, Calif.: Sheridan Psychological Services, 1956.

Gurin, P., and Epps, E. G. *Black Consciousness, Identity and Achievement.* New York: Wiley, 1975.

Hall, W. S. "Two Variables Associated with Differential Productive Cultural Involvement Among Lower-Class Negro and Caucasian Young Men." *Journal of Social Psychology,* 1971, *83,* 219-228.

Hamburger, M. *A Revised Occupational Scale for Rating Socioeconomic Status.* Unpublished manuscript, New York University, 1971.

Hansen, C. F. "The Scholastic Performances of Negro and White Pupils in the Integrated Public Schools of the District of Columbia." *Harvard Educational Review,* 1960, *30,* 216-236.

Hedegard, J., and Brown, D. "Encounters of Some Negro and White Freshmen with a Public Multi-university." *Journal of Social Issues,* 1969, *25,* 131-144.

Heidbreder, E. "The Attainment of Concepts: VI. Exploratory Experiments on Conceptualization at Perceptual Levels." *Journal of Psychology,* 1948, *26,* 193-216.

Holland, J. L. "A Personality Inventory Employing Occupational Titles." *Journal of Applied Psychology,* 1958, *42,* 336-342.

Holland, J. L. *The Self-Directed Search: A Guide to Educational and Vocational Planning.* Palo Alto, Calif.: Consulting Psychologists Press, 1970.

Holland, J. L. *Making Vocational Choices: A Theory of Careers.* Englewood Cliffs, N.J.: Prentice-Hall, 1973.

Holmes, T. H., and Rahe, R. H. "Life Crisis and Disease Onset-I. Qualitative and Quantitative Definition of Life Events Composing the Life Crisis." Unpublished manuscript, Navy Medical Neuropsychiatric Research Unit, San Diego, Calif., 1967.

Horner, M. S. *Sex Differences in Achievement Motivation and Performance in Competitive and Non-competitive Situations.* Unpublished doctoral dissertation, University of Michigan at Ann Arbor, 1968.

Horner, M. S. "Toward an Understanding of Achievement-Related Conflicts in Women." *Journal of Social Issues,* 1972, *28,* 157-176.

Horner, M. S. *Success Avoidant Motivation and Behavior: Its Developmental Correlates and Situational Determinants.* Washington, D.C.: U.S. Office of Education, 1973.

Horner, M. S. "The Measurement and Behavioral Implication of Fear of Success in Women." In J. W. Atkinson and J. A. Raynor (Eds.), *Motivation and Achievement.* New York: Winston-Wiley, 1974.

Horner, M., and Fleming, J. *Revised Scoring Manual for an Empirically Derived Scoring System for the Motive to Avoid Success.* Unpublished manuscript, Barnard College, 1977.

Horowitz, E. "The Development of Attitudes Toward the Negro." *Archives of Psychology,* 1936, *194* (entire issue).

Hughes, R., and Works, E. *The Self-Concepts of Black Students in a Predominantly Black School and in a Predominantly White School.* Unpublished manuscript, California State University, Fullerton, 1976.

Hummel-Rossi, B., and Weinberg, S. L. "Practical Guidelines in Applying Current Theories to the Measurement of Change." *Journal Supplement Abstract Service* (American Psychological Association), No. 916, 1973.

Institute for Higher Educational Opportunity. *The White Student Enrolled in the Traditionally Public Black College and University.* Atlanta, Ga.: Southern Regional Education Board, 1973.

Institute for the Study of Educational Policy. *Equal Educational Opportunity for Blacks in U.S. Higher Education: An Assessment.* Washington, D.C.: Howard University Press, 1976.

Jackson, J. J. "Black Women in a Racist Society." In C. V. Willie, B. M. Kramer, and B. S. Brown (Eds.), *Racism and Mental Health.* Pittsburgh: University of Pittsburgh Press, 1973.

Jaffe, A. J. *Negro Higher Education in the 1960s.* New York: Praeger, 1968.

Jencks, C., and Riesman, D. *The Academic Revolution.* New York: Doubleday, 1968.

Jones, A. *Uncle Tom's Campus.* New York: Praeger, 1973.

Jones, J. *Prejudice and Racism.* Reading, Mass.: Addison-Wesley, 1972.

Jones, J. C., and others. *Differences in Perceived Sources of Academic Difficulties: Blacks in Predominantly Black and Predominantly White Colleges.* Educational Resource Information Center (ERIC) Document Reproduction Service: Washington, D.C.: 1970. (ED 074 164)

Jones, M. "The Responsibility of the Black College to the Black Community: Then and Now." *Daedalus,* 1971, *100,* 732-744.

Jones, S. J., and Weathersby, G. B. "Financing the Black College." In C. V. Willie and R. R. Edmonds (Eds.), *Black Colleges in America.* New York: Teachers College Press, 1978.

Jordan, V. E., Jr. "Blacks in Higher Education: Some Reflections." *Daedalus,* 1975, *104,* 160-165.

Kahl, J. A. *The American Class Structure.* New York: Holt, Rinehart and Winston, 1957.

Katz, I. "Review of Evidence Relating to Effects of Desegregation on the Intellectual Performance of Negroes." *American Psychologist,* 1964, *19,* 381-399.

Katz, I. "Motivational Determinants of Racial Differences in Intellectual Achievement." *International Journal of Psychology,* 1967, *2,* 1-12.

Katz, I., and Benjamin, L. "Effects of White Authoritarianism in Biracial Work Groups." *Journal of Abnormal and Social Psychology,* 1960, *61,* 448-456.

Katz, I., and Cohen, M. "The Effects of Training Negroes upon Cooperative Problem Solving in Biracial Teams." *Journal of Abnormal and Social Psychology,* 1962, *64,* 319-325.

Katz, I., Epps, E., and Axelon, L. "Effects upon Negro Digit Symbol Performance of Anticipated Comparison with Other Negroes." *Journal of Abnormal and Social Psychology,* 1964, *69,* 77-83.

Katz, I., Goldston, J., and Benjamin, L. "Behavior and Productivity in Biracial Work Groups." *Human Relations,* 1958, *11,* 123-141.

Katz, I., and Greenbaum, C. "Effects of Anxiety Threat and Racial Environment on Task Performance of Negro College Students." *Journal of Abnormal and Social Psychology,* 1963, *66,* 562-567.

Katz, I., Henchy, T., and Allen, H. "Effects of Race of Tester,

Approval-Disapproval and Need on Negro Children's Learning." *Journal of Personality and Social Psychology,* 1968, *8,* 38-42.

Katz, I., Roberts, S. O., and Robinson, J. M. "Effects of Task Difficulty, Race of Administrator, and Instructions on Negro Digit-Symbol Performance of Negroes." *Journal of Personality and Social Psychology,* 1965, *2,* 53-59.

Katz, I., and others. "Factors Affecting Response to White Intellectual Standards at Two Negro Colleges." *Psychological Reports,* 1970, *27,* 995-1003.

Katz, I., and others. "Race of Evaluator, Race of Norm, and Expectancy as Determinants of Black Performance." *Journal of Experimental Social Psychology,* 1972, *8,* 1-15.

Keil, C. *Urban Blues.* Chicago: University of Chicago Press, 1970.

Kilson, M. "Blacks at Harvard: Solutions and Prospects." *Harvard Bulletin,* 1973a, *75* (8), 31-32, 41-42.

Kilson, M. "Black Students at Harvard: Crisis and Change." *Harvard Bulletin,* 1973b, *75* (10), 24-27.

Klinger, E. "Fantasy Need Achievement as a Motivational Construct." *Psychological Bulletin,* 1966, *66,* 291-308.

Knowles, L. W. "Part 1, Kentucky." In United States Commission on Civil Rights, *Civil Rights U.S.A.–Public Schools, Southern States.* Washington, D.C.: U.S. Government Printing Office, 1962.

Kysar, J. "Social Class and Adaptation of College Students." *Mental Hygiene,* 1966, *50,* 398-405.

Lachman, S. J. *Psychosomatic Disorders: A Behavioristic Interpretation.* New York: Wiley, 1972.

Langston, I. W., and Watkins, T. *SAT-ACT Equivalents.* Unpublished manuscript, Office of School and College Relations, University of Illinois, 1976.

LeMelle, T., and LeMelle, W. *The Black College: A Strategy for Relevancy.* New York: Praeger, 1969.

Levitan, S., Johnston, W., and Taggart, R. *Still a Dream: The Changing Status of Blacks Since 1960.* Cambridge, Mass.: Harvard University Press, 1975.

Liebert, R., Poulos, R., and Marmor, G. *Developmental Psychology.* Englewood Cliffs, N.J.: Prentice-Hall, 1974.

Litwin, G. H., and Stringer, R. A. *Motivation and Organizational Climate.* Cambridge, Mass.: Harvard University Press, 1968.

Loevinger, J. *Ego Development: Conceptions and Theories.* San Francisco: Jossey-Bass, 1976.

Lowell, E. L. "The Effect of Need for Achievement on Learning and Speed of Performance." *Journal of Psychology,* 1952, *33,* 31-40.

McClelland, D. C. *The Achieving Society.* New York: Wiley, 1961.

McClelland, D. C. *Assessing Human Motivation.* Morristown, N.J.: General Learning Press, 1971.

McClelland, D. C. *Power: The Inner Experience.* New York: Irvington, 1975.

McClelland, D. C., and Winter, D. C. *Motivating Economic Achievement.* New York: Free Press, 1969.

McClelland, D. C., and others. *The Achievement Motive.* New York: Appleton-Century-Crofts, 1953.

McClelland, D. C., and others. *The Drinking Man.* New York: Free Press, 1972.

Maccoby, E., and Jacklin, C. N. *Psychology of Sex Differences.* Stanford, Calif.: Stanford University Press, 1974.

McDaniel, R., and McKee, J. *An Evaluation of Higher Education's Response to Black Students.* Bloomington: Indiana University, 1971.

McGrath, E. J. *The Predominantly Negro Colleges and Universities in Transition.* New York: Teachers College Press, 1965.

Mandler, G., and Sarason, S. "A Study of Anxiety and Learning." *Journal of Abnormal and Social Psychology,* 1952, *47,* 166-173.

Mays, B. E. "The Black College in Higher Education." In C. V. Willie and R. R. Edmonds (Eds.), *Black Colleges in America.* New York: Teachers College Press, 1978.

Meyers, M. "For Civil Rights, No Compromise: Racism and All-Black Colleges." *Los Angeles Times,* Dec. 26, 1978.

Miller, C., Knapp, S. C., and Daniels, C. W. "MMPI Study of Negro Mental Hygiene Clinic Patients." *Journal of Abnormal Psychology,* 1968, *73,* 168-173.

Mischel, W. *Personality and Assessment.* New York: Wiley, 1968.

Monro, J. U. "Teaching and Learning English." In C. V. Willie and R. R. Edmonds (Eds.), *Black Colleges in America.* New York: Teachers College Press, 1978.

Monroe, S. "Guest in a Strange House: A Black at Harvard." *Education-Saturday Review,* February 1973, pp. 45–48. Also in M. Merbaum and G. Stricker (Eds.), *Search for Human Understanding.* New York: Holt, Rinehart and Winston, 1975.

Moos, R. H. *Evaluating Educational Environments: Procedures, Measures, Findings, and Policy Implications.* San Francisco: Jossey-Bass, 1979.

Morgan, D. C., and Murray, H. A. "A Method for Investigating Fantasies: The Thematic Apperception Test." *Archives of Neurology and Psychiatry,* 1935, *34,* 289–306.

Moynihan, D. P. *The Negro Family: A Case for National Action.* Washington, D.C.: U.S. Government Printing Office, 1965.

Murstein, B. I. *Theory and Research in Projective Techniques.* New York: Wiley, 1963.

Nuttal, R. L. "Some Correlates of High Need for Achievement Among Urban Northern Negroes." *Journal of Abnormal and Social Psychology,* 1964, *68,* 593–600.

Pace, C. R. "The Measurement of College Environments." In R. Tagiuri and G. H. Litwin (Eds.), *Organizational Climate: Explorations of a Concept.* Cambridge, Mass.: Division of Research, Harvard Business School, 1979a.

Pace, C. R. *Measuring Outcomes of College: Fifty Years of Findings and Recommendations for the Future.* San Francisco: Jossey-Bass, 1979b.

Panos, R. J., and Astin, A. W. "Attrition Among College Students." *American Educational Research Journal,* 1968, *5,* 57–72.

Perry, W. G. "Cognitive and Ethical Growth: The Making of Meaning." In A. W. Chickering and Associates, *The Modern American College: Responding to the New Realities of Diverse Students and a Changing Society.* San Francisco: Jossey-Bass, 1981.

Peterson, M. W., and others. *Black Students on White Campuses: The Impacts of Increased Black Enrollments.* Ann Arbor, Mich.: Institute for Survey Research, 1979.

Pifer, A. *The Higher Education of Blacks in the United States.* New York: Carnegie Corporation of New York: 1973.

Pleck, J. H. *The Myth of Masculinity.* Cambridge, Mass.: MIT Press, 1981.

Preston, M. G., and Bayton, J. A. "Differential Effect of a Social Variable upon Three Levels of Aspiration." *Journal of Experimental Psychology,* 1941, *29,* 351-369.

Radke, M., Sutherland, J., and Rosenberg, P. "Racial Attitudes of Children." *Sociometry,* 1950, *13,* 154-171.

Rahe, R. H., McKean, J. D., and Arthur, R. J. "A Longitudinal Study of Life-Change and Illness Patterns." *Journal of Psychosomatic Research,* 1967, *10,* 355-366.

Rahe, R. H., and others. "Social Stress and Illness Onset." *Journal of Psychosomatic Research,* 1964, *8,* 35-44.

Rainwater, L., and Yancy, W. *The Moynihan Report and the Politics of Controversy.* Cambridge, Mass.: MIT Press, 1968.

Ramseur, H. *Continuity and Change in Black Identity: A Study of Black Students at an Interracial College.* Unpublished doctoral dissertation, Harvard University, 1975.

Rathus, S. A. "An Experimental Investigation of Assertive Training in a Group Setting." *Journal of Behavior Therapy and Experimental Psychiatry,* 1972, *3,* 81-86.

Rathus, S. A. "A Thirty-Item Schedule for Assessing Assertive Behavior." *Behavior Therapy,* 1973, *4,* 398-406.

Rose, A. *The Negro in America.* Boston: Beacon Press, 1956.

Rose, R. M., Holaday, J. W., and Bernstein, I. S. "Plasma Testosterone, Dominance Rank and Aggressive Behavior in Male Rhesus Monkeys." *Nature,* 1971, *231* (5302), 366-368.

Rose, R. M., Gordon, T. P., and Bernstein, I. S. "Plasma Testosterone Levels in the Male Rhesus: Influences of Sexual and Social Stimuli." *Science,* 1972, *178,* 643-645.

Shinn, M. *Secondary School Coeducation and the Fears of Success and Failure.* Unpublished honors thesis, Harvard University, 1973.

Shipley, T. E., and Veroff, J. "A Projective Measure of Need for Affiliation." In J. W. Atkinson (Ed.), *Motives in Fantasy, Action and Society.* New York: Van Nostrand, 1958.

Simon, B. D. "Women's Fears of Success Increase at Radcliffe, McClelland Study Shows." *Harvard Crimson,* Oct. 23, 1975.

Simpson, G. E., and Yinger, J. M. *Racial and Cultural Minorities*. New York: Harper & Row, 1972.

Smith, C. P. (Ed.). *Achievement-Related Motives in Children*. New York: Russell Sage Foundation, 1969.

Sowell, T. *Black Education: Myths and Tragedies*. New York: McKay, 1972.

Spitzer, S. P., and others. "The Self Concept: Test Equivalence and Perceived Validity." *Sociological Quarterly*, 1966, *7*, 265-280.

Stallings, F. H. "A Study of the Immediate Effects of Integration on Scholastic Achievement in the Louisville Public Schools." *Journal of Negro Education*, 1959, *28*, 439-444.

Staples, R. "The Myth of the Black Matriarchy." *Black Scholar*, 1970, *1*, 9-16.

Stern, G. C. "Student Ecology and the College Environment." In College Entrance Examination Board, *Research in Higher Education*. Princeton, N.J.: College Entrance Examination Board, 1965.

Stewart, A. J. *Longitudinal Prediction from Personality to Life Outcomes Among College-Educated Women*. Unpublished doctoral dissertation, Harvard University, 1975.

Stewart, A. J. *Analysis of Argument: An Empirically Derived Measure of Intellectual Flexibility*. Boston: McBev, 1977a.

Stewart, A. J. *Scoring Manual for Stages of Psychological Adaptation to the Environment*. Unpublished manuscript, Boston University, 1977b.

Stewart, A. J., and Winter, D. G. "Self-Definition and Social Definition in Women." *Journal of Personality*, 1974, *42*, 238-259.

Sullivan, H. W. *The Interpersonal Theory of Psychiatry*. New York: Norton, 1953.

Tanner, J. C. "Integration in Action." *Wall Street Journal*, Jan. 20, 1964.

Thompson, D. C. *Private Black Colleges at the Crossroads*. Westport, Conn.: Greenwood Press, 1973.

Thompson, D. C. "Black College Faculty and Students: The Nature of Their Interaction." In C. V. Willie and R. R. Edmonds (Eds.), *Black Colleges in America*. New York: Teachers College Press, 1978.

Tidball, M. E. "Perspective on Academic Women and Affirmative Action." *Education Record,* 1973, *54,* 130-135.

Trivers, R. L. "Parental Investment and Sexual Selection." In B. Campbell (Ed.), *Sexual Selection and the Descent of Man.* Chicago: Aldine, 1972.

United States Commission on Civil Rights. *Second Annual Conference on Education, Gatlinburg, Tennessee.* Washington, D.C.: U.S. Government Printing Office, 1960.

Veroff, J. "Development and Validation of a Projective Measure of Power Motivation." In J. W. Atkinson (Ed.), *Motives in Fantasy, Action and Society.* New York: Van Nostrand, 1958.

Veroff, J. "Social Comparison and the Development of Achievement Motivation." In C. P. Smith (Ed.), *Achievement-Related Motives in Children.* New York: Russell Sage Foundation, 1969.

Veroff, J., and Peele, S. "Initial Effects of Desegregation on the Achievement Motivation of Negro Elementary School Children." *Journal of Social Issues,* 1969, *25,* 71-92.

Veroff, J., Wilcox, S., and Atkinson, S. W. "The Achievement Motive in High School and College-Age Women." *Journal of Abnormal and Social Psychology,* 1953, *48,* 108-119.

Warner, W., and others. *Social Class in America: A Manual of Procedure for the Measurement of Social Status.* Chicago: Science Research Associates, 1949.

Weathersby, R. P. "Ego Development." In A. W. Chickering and Associates, *The Modern American College: Responding to the New Realities of Diverse Students and a Changing Society.* San Francisco: Jossey-Bass, 1981.

Welsh, G., and Dahlstrom, W. (Eds.). *Basic Readings on the MMPI in Psychology and Medicine.* Minneapolis: University of Minnesota Press, 1956.

White, R. W. "Humanitarian Concern." In A. W. Chickering and Associates, *The Modern American College: Responding to the New Realities of Diverse Students and a Changing Society.* San Francisco: Jossey-Bass, 1981.

Willie, C. V., and Edmonds, R. R. (Eds.). *Black Colleges in America.* New York: Teachers College Press, 1978.

Willie, C. V., and McCord, A. (Eds.). *Black Students at White Colleges.* New York: Praeger, 1972.

Winchel, R., Fenner, D., and Shaver, P. "Impact of Coeducation on 'Fear of Success' Imagery Expressed by Male and Female High School Students." *Journal of Educational Psychology,* 1974, *66,* 726-730.

Winkler, K. J. "Minority Enrollments." *Chronicle of Higher Education,* 1974, *9* (18).

Winter, D. G. *The Power Motive.* Glencoe, Ill.: Free Press, 1973.

Winter, D. G., and McClelland, D. C. "Thematic Analysis: An Empirically Derived Measure of the Effects of Liberal Arts Education." *Journal of Educational Psychology,* 1978, *70,* 8-16.

Winter, D. G., McClelland, D. C., and Stewart, A. J. *A New Case for the Liberal Arts: Assessing Institutional Goals and Student Development.* San Francisco: Jossey-Bass, 1981.

Winter, D. G., and Stewart, A. J. "Power Motive Reliability as a Function of Retest Instructions." *Journal of Consulting and Clinical Psychology,* 1977, *45,* 436-440.

Wolpe, J. *The Practice of Behavior Therapy.* Elmsford, N.Y.: Pergamon, 1973.

Wolpe, J., and Lazarus, A. A. *Behavior Therapy Techniques.* Oxford, England: Pergamon, 1966.

Wyatt, E. "Part 3, Tennessee." In United States Commission on Civil Rights, *Civil Rights U.S.A.—Public Schools, Southern States.* Washington, D.C.: U.S. Government Printing Office, 1962.

Wylie, R. C. *The Self-Concept: A Review of Methodological Considerations and Measuring Instruments.* Vol. 1. Lincoln: University of Nebraska Press, 1974.

Yarrow, M. R. (Ed.). "Interpersonal Dynamics in a Desegregation Process." *Journal of Social Issues,* 1958, *14* (entire issue).

Zuckerman, M., and Wheeler, L. "To Dispel Fantasies About the Fantasy-Based Measures of Fear of Success." *Psychological Bulletin,* 1975, *82,* 932-946.

Index

```
   :◆:
```

269